Totems and Teachers

Totems and Teachers

**Perspectives on the
History of Anthropology**

Sydel Silverman, Editor

Columbia University Press
New York

Acknowledgment is made to the following for providing photographs:
American Museum of Natural History (Boas); Wenner-Gren
Foundation for Anthropological Research (Kroeber); Stanley
Diamond (Radin); Helena Wayne Malinowska (Malinowski);
Rhoda Metraux (Benedict); Michael Steward (Steward); Beth
Dillingham (White); University of Chicago Library (Redfield).

Clothbound editions of Columbia University Press books are
Smyth-sewn and printed on permanent and durable acid-free
paper.

Library of Congress Cataloging in Publication Data
Main entry under title:

Totems and teachers.

Bibliography: p.
Includes index.
1. Anthropology—History—Addresses, essays,
lectures. 2. Anthropologists—Addresses,
essays, lectures. I. Silverman, Sydel.
GN17.T69   301'.092'2   80-18457
ISBN 0-231-05086-0
ISBN 0-231-05087-9 (pbk.)
8 7 6 5 4 3

Columbia University Press
New York   Guildford, Surrey

For our students

Contents

Introduction

THAT THE DEVELOPMENT of theory is a social process, a product of life histories embedded in time and place, is a principle that most anthropologists take as axiomatic. Yet the rapid expansion of anthropology over the past thirty years, and the necessity of simplifying its ideas for teaching purposes, have produced a standardized treatment of the history of anthropological theory—as seriated "isms," concepts, and names of notables divorced from the social and personal contexts out of which they emerged. As anthropological theory becomes codified in this manner, and as each generation of anthropologists and students becomes further removed from the seminal figures of the field, an understanding of their work as part of a life, a career, a personality, and a social and cultural setting, becomes more and more elusive.

The process of theory making in anthropology has not received the scrutiny that has been given to fieldwork, which has been examined in a now long series of personal accounts aimed at demystification of "the field." But if we understand little of the theory-making process itself, to recover it in the figures of the past is a task bedeviled by traps. The reader of today sees order and consistency in a life's work but misses the contradiction and serendipity, sees "forerunners" of trends that come to light only in retrospect, overemphasizes influences that are credited in print and neglects others that are not. For some figures biographies get written, but rarely are these read or taught as an integral part of the theories themselves.

It was out of a discussion, early in 1976, of this growing separation of anthropological theory from its own human background that this volume originated. A few years before, in 1971, Raymond Firth had given a lecture on Bronislaw Malinowski to an audience of anthropologists at the New York Academy of Sciences. Firth presented the talk as a personal recollection, not intended as a serious theoretical treatment (and he declined to have it published in the Academy's annals). Yet the audience was electrified, and many remembered that lecture as the most useful means they had encountered for understanding Malinowski's anthropology. Firth's talk became the inspiration for a lecture series, "Reconsidering the Ancestors," that was held at the Graduate Center of the City University of New York between February and December of 1976.

Seven anthropologists were invited to discuss the life and work of a major figure whom they had studied under, worked with, or otherwise known. Since no one could be paid honoraria or travel expenses—the city and the university were then in the depths of fiscal crisis—friends and associates in the New York area were called on. The only guideline given was the purpose of the series: to convey a sense of how ideas grow out of personal biographies. Inevitably, however, each speaker also reassessed the contribution of his "ancestor" in the light of the present state of anthropology, and in the process each underlined his own views and some of the themes of this own work. The papers thus presented a picture of the development of anthropology at two levels: the formative figures of professional anthropology, and those of the next generation who have recast their predecessors' influence into the concerns of contemporary anthropology.

Each lecture was followed by a discussion. The audience always included other anthropologists who had known the "ancestor" and who as often as not held views quite different from those of the speaker. The living, and sometimes combative, quality of theoretical development came out vividly in these discussions, providing some corrective to tendencies toward excessive praise of an admired teacher or overemphasis on the themes selected to organize a lecture.

Attendance at and enthusiasm for the lectures exceeded all expectations. Ironically, the backdrop to this demonstration of the vigor of anthropology was an attempt on the part of the senior administration of the City University to eliminate the subject from most of the undergraduate curricula. On the day of the opening lecture, the university chancellor announced a plan for reorganizing the liberal arts, in which anthropology (along with geology, foreign languages, and several other subjects) was declared "nonessential." Anthropology was the only field to respond to this assessment with a unified opposition that enlisted the profession nationwide and across institutional lines of all kinds. On the day of the final lecture of the semester, the chancellor's plan was laid to rest.

This collection presents, obviously, only a partial and highly selective view of the history of anthropology. A number of eminent anthropologists, who would immediately spring to mind in any listing of "ancestral" figures, are not represented. The explanation for this is historical, not evaluative. The persons who appear in the book—as subjects, authors, and discussants—are linked primarily through the institutional structure of anthropology in New York City.

Institutional anthropology in New York City begins with the American Museum of Natural History. Soon after its founding in 1869, the museum created archeological and ethnological divisions to gather and care for collections, but it

was in 1894 under the impetus of president Morris K. Jesup
(organizer of the Jesup Expedition of 1897) that the anthropology department became established. Frederick Ward
Putnam of Harvard was brought in to head it. In 1895 Franz
Boas joined the museum as an assistant curator. After he
began teaching at Columbia the following year, Boas
developed a close association between the Columbia department and the museum, which was continued by Clark Wissler,
his student and successor as curator. The museum provided
the only available research funds and fieldwork opportunities
at the time, and almost all of Boas' first generation of
students were trained there. The museum was also the home
institution of the most famous of New York anthropologists,
Margaret Mead (whose appointment at Columbia was always
in an adjunct status). Among the present members of the
museum staff is a contributor to this volume, Robert Carneiro.

The Columbia department is the primary connection
among the anthropologists in this book. Several got their
Ph.D.s under Boas in the first decade of the century, including
Alfred Kroeber, Robert Lowie, Paul Radin, and Alexander
Goldenweiser. After World War I and until his retirement in
1936, Boas trained another group of students, among them
Ruth Benedict, Alexander Lesser, Margaret Mead, Ruth
Bunzel, and Gene Weltfish. With Boas' retirement, the one-
man dominance of the department gave way to a pattern of
polarities among the most influential faculty members. The
first of these polarities was that between Ruth Benedict and
Ralph Linton. Benedict, still an assistant professor without
tenure, was acting chairman at the time of Linton's appointment to Boas' professorship in 1937, and for the rest of their
association in the department they maintained a hostile competition. The appointment of Linton, a Harvard Ph.D., was a
break in the Boasian tradition at Columbia; president
Nicholas Murray Butler, determined that Boas not name his
successor, designated a university committee to recommend a
candidate, and students of Boas were excluded (see Linton and
Wagley 1971:47–48). Despite their disagreements, both
Benedict and Linton fostered the interest in personality-and-

culture that dominated the department during this period, Linton's most notable contribution being the establishment with Abram Kardiner of the seminars on anthropology and psychoanalysis.

In the years following World War II, the department saw a much larger and quite different cohort of students: predominantly male, veterans, with materialist predilections and theoretical as well as personal interests in politics. This period at Columbia is described in the paper by Robert Murphy. After Linton left for Yale in 1946 he was replaced by Julian Steward, who immediately became a focus for these interests, while Benedict continued to attract her own following. When Benedict died in 1948, Kroeber arrived for a four-year stay as visiting professor, leaving Columbia the same year as Steward. Among the students of this period was a group who met regularly to discuss their developing research, and who in 1950 dubbed themselves the Mundial Upheaval Society (M.U.S.). Three members of the group are represented in this volume— Stanley Diamond, Sidney Mintz, and Eric Wolf. Other members were Morton Fried, Elman Service, Rufus Mathewson (a student of Russian literature), and John Murra, who took his degree at the University of Chicago but was in the Columbia orbit through his work, along with Mintz and Wolf, on Steward's Puerto Rico project. A few years later than this group, Marvin Harris, Robert Murphy, and Marshall Sahlins received their degrees.

Leslie White taught at Columbia for a summer session in 1948 (with Stanley Diamond assigned to him as a research assistant), and there continued to be a good deal of interest in his theories among the Columbia students. In the 1950s White brought Service and then Sahlins to Michigan (followed later by Wolf), creating the so-called Columbia-Michigan axis.

Several other institutions in New York City, dating mainly from the years between the world wars, trace further links among the anthropologists who appear in this book. At the New School for Social Research, created in 1919, Goldenweiser's courses provided the first introduction to anthropology for Benedict and for White. (The New School's current professors of anthropology are Diamond and Michael Harner, a participant in some of the discussions.) The municipal college system (whose oldest component, City College, granted a B.A. to Paul Radin in 1902) expanded during this period from two to four senior colleges, and anthropology began to be taught in all of them. Brooklyn College, founded in 1930, appointed Alexander Lesser to the faculty in 1939, the year that Sidney Mintz entered as a freshman. When Queens College was established in 1937, the original faculty included Hortense Powdermaker, who had taken her degree under Malinowski. One of the early students at Queens was Eric Wolf, who eventually returned to the city system as a professor at Lehman College. The series organizer, Silverman (who is married to Wolf), has been on the Queens College faculty since completing her Ph.D. at Columbia in 1963.

Three institutions outside of New York City are prominent in this volume: the University of California at Berkeley, whose anthropology department Kroeber founded, Steward was trained in, and Murphy taught in; the London School of Economics, where Firth and Powdermaker were among Malinowski's first students; and the University of Chicago, where White studied long before he became an evolutionist, where Robert Redfield spent his life, and where Nathaniel Tarn was launched by Redfield onto fieldwork which he wrote up under Firth. That Redfield is in this book reconsidered by an anthropologist-turned-poet, now a professor of comparative literature at Rutgers University, reflects not only geography but also the social history of New York anthropology.

In preparing their papers for publication, some of the contributors have retained them essentially as they were originally given (Lesser, Wolf, Diamond, Tarn), while others have expanded their lectures (Mintz, Murphy, Carneiro). The editor has also selected portions of the discussions for inclusion in the book, with minor revision in the interest of clarity. In addition, Firth agreed to revise and enlarge his Malinowski lecture for publication as part of this collection.

Each paper takes a different approach to its subject. Editorial introductions have been provided to fill in biographical information in those instances where it is not included in the paper, and to indicate the generally acknowledged significance of each figure for anthropology. No claim is made, however, that this book offers balanced assessments. Some of the intellectual ancestors of contemporary anthropology are reconsidered here with varying mixtures of objectivity and passion.

Totems and Teachers

Franz Boas demonstrating Eskimo harpooning
at the American Museum of Natural History (c. 1900)

1
Franz Boas
Alexander Lesser

In 1883 Franz Boas, then a twenty-five-year-old geographer, left his native Germany on an expedition to Baffin Island in the Arctic, which was to turn him toward a life's work in anthropology. A little over twenty years had passed since the publication of Darwin's *Origin of Species* and the almost concurrent publication of several major works setting forth theories of the evolution of culture—works by Henry Maine, J. F. McLennan, and E. B. Tylor in Britain, J. J. Bachofen in Switzerland, and Lewis Henry Morgan in America. A later work of Morgan's had influenced Marx and Engels, and Engels' book based on Morgan was about to appear. These writers of ethnology were lawyers, classical scholars, or gentlemen travelers; anthropology was not yet a subject taught in universities. The year of Boas' Arctic trip, Tylor (who himself had no university education) received one of the first university appointments in anthropology—at Oxford, subsequently becoming Oxford's first professor of anthropology. In the United States at this time, a variety of people were pursuing scholarly interests in American Indians, which encompassed ethnological, archeological, and linguistic studies, and societies devoted to these interests existed in various cities. An institutional organization of anthropology was just beginning to develop, as some of the major natural history museums began to expand their function from that of housing material objects to include research and education in ethnology and archeology.

Franz Boas was born in 1858 in Minden, Westphalia, of German-Jewish parents. His father was a businessman. He went to school and Gymnasium in Minden, and then attended universities in Heidelberg, Bonn, and Kiel. After studying a variety of subjects, he was awarded a doctorate in geography at Kiel in 1881.

Boas planned the Arctic expedition of 1883–84 primarily as a geographical study. However, he had long nourished an interest in cultural history and primitive peoples, and he combined his geographical work with ethnological research among the Eskimo. In 1885, while writing his Eskimo monograph, Boas decided to make anthropology his primary field, and he accepted an appointment as an assistant at the Royal Ethnological Museum in Berlin, serving under Adolf Bastian. His work with the British Columbia collections at the museum led to an expedition in 1886, which was the beginning of his lifelong research on the Indians of the Northwest Coast.

At the end of this field trip, Boas made the decision to settle in the United States. His first American position was as an assistant editor of *Science*, where he worked primarily on geographical material. In 1888 he was offered an appointment in anthropology at Clark University. He remained there until 1892, when he became chief assistant in anthropology at the World's Columbia Exposition in Chicago and then curator of the new museum that later was called the Field Museum. He left the museum in 1894 and was without a regular position for eighteen months, when he came to the American Museum of Natural History for what was to be a ten-year association. Boas joined Columbia University in 1896 as a lecturer in physical anthropology. He became professor of anthropology there in 1899, a post which he held until his retirement in 1936. He died in 1942.

In the course of his career, Boas fostered the development of American anthropology as an academic discipline and as a profession. Establishing systematic graduate training, he produced two generations of anthropologists, and his students went on to build departments at other major institutions: Alfred Kroeber and Robert Lowie at Berkeley, Frank Speck at Pennsylvania, Fay-Cooper Cole and Edward Sapir at Chicago, Melville Herskovits at Northwestern, and many others. Boas contributed to the professionalization of museums, played a leading role in founding anthropological journals and professional societies (such as the American Anthropological Association in 1902), and organized and promoted a vast amount of research.

His own indefatigable scholarly work spanned ethnology, physical anthropology, linguistics, and (with only one published work but that one a breakthrough) archeology. Under his influence these were established as components of the four-field approach in the training of American anthropologists. A relentless critic of the incautious theorizing of his day, Boas established new canons of empirical research, emphasizing the importance of field investigation. His distinctions among race, language, and culture; his transformation of the culture concept from its prior use as a synonym for "civilization"; and his insistence upon understanding cultures in their own historical contexts, apart from the observer's ethnocentric standards of evaluation, became premises of modern anthropology. Through his work on a wide range of problems, and through his institutional achievements, Boas redefined the scope and methods of American anthropology.

IN RETROSPECT, Franz Boas was the builder and architect of modern anthropology.[1] This has come to be a general consensus, despite certain controversies. I propose to focus on four themes in his life and work:

1. The way in which Boas filled the role of architect of modern anthropology.

2. What Boas brought with him into anthropology that was the effective factor of factors in modernizing it.

3. How Boas, anthropologist and scientist, was a *citizen-scientist* all his life, whose ethics and ideals for the study of

The author's title for this paper is "Franz Boas and the Modernization of Anthropology."

man were far-reaching, humane, and still hold true in our own day.

4. How Boas, far from being antitheory, was himself *the* great theorist of modern anthropology, who established the core of anthropological theory on which the science is based.

Modern anthropology begins with Franz Boas. It begins in the scientific skepticism with which he examined the traditional orthodoxies of the study of man, exposing and rejecting the false and unproven, calling for a return to empirical observation, establishing the truth of elementary fundamentals, opening new pathways and creating new methods. It begins in Boas' ways of thinking about man and his history, in his use of rigorous scientific requirements for data and for proof, in his rejection of old myths, old stereotypes, old emotionally charged assumptions.

Boas' contribution to the transformation of anthropology was therefore not a simple, single event, a formal statement of principles, or a generalized theory at a certain point of time. Boas worked from problem to problem, consolidating the truth gained and asking the next question. The framework and principles of the modern subject matter are emergents from this ongoing process, in part the residue of truth left after traditional materials and ideas were reevaluated, in part the positive discovery of empirical principles by fresh and original observation.

Boas was aware of this critical character of his method from his early professional years. In 1907, responding at Columbia to a Festschrift which was given him on the twenty-fifth anniversary of his Ph.D., he described himself as "one whose work rests essentially in an unfeeling criticism of his own work and that of others."[2] He wrote a defense of the cephalic index (head form) and its traditional importance as a hereditary trait only a few years before his own research proved it was not strictly genetically determined but was affected significantly by environmental change (Boas 1899, 1911a). He condemned his early Kwakiutl and other Northwest Coast research as questionable, superseded by later work (Boas 1897,

1901). He came to "disparage his early work on the Kwakiutl language," pointing out its shortcomings (Boas 1930b:ix, cited in Codere 1966:xiv). He was continually self-critical. "Flawless perfection, then, must not be sought in Boas," as Lowie has put it (Lowie 1944:64).

But in the end he restructured anthropology and its branches, leading physical anthropology from taxonomical race classification into human biology, breaking through the limitations of traditional philology into the problems of modern linguistics and cognitive anthropology, establishing the modern anthropological meaning and study of human culture.

Along his way, as Boas worked at problems in all fields of anthropology, he came to discoveries and understandings which, through his writing and teaching, became the convictions and effected the consensus from which the modern science of anthropology was born. Many of his writings were summations of plateaus of understanding he had reached in one area of anthropology or another. *The Mind of Primitive Man* in 1911 was his first great general consolidation in book form, a seminal book in modern social thought for technical readers and the lay public alike. In it, Boas reorganized and integrated studies of 1894 to 1911 into closely argued theses which became baselines of anthropology thereafter and fundamental conceptions in social science and social philosophy.

The book provided general anthropology and its separable branches—physical anthropology, linguistics, ethnology—with a structural framework. Establishing the relative autonomy of cultural phenomena, it gave to the concept of culture its modern meaning and usage. Boas proved that cultures are diverse historical developments, each the outcome of a prior history in which many factors and events, cultural and noncultural, have played a part. He made the plurality of cultures fundamental to the study of man (see Stocking 1968:203). He showed how languages, both semantically and morphologically, are each a context of perception that affects human thought and action. Analogously, he showed how cultural environments, especially as contexts of traditional materials, shape and structure human behavior—actions and reactions—in each generation. In so doing he ended the traditional ambiguity in the term *culture* understood interchangeably as both humanistic and behavioral—an ambiguity perpetuated by endless quoting of Tylor's "culture *or* civilization"—and started the modern era of the concept of *cultures*, viewed as contexts of learned human behavior.

A much earlier paper shows that the same essential conception was in his mind more than twenty years before. In "The Aims of Ethnology" (written in 1888), Boas stated, "The data of ethnology prove that not only our language, but also our emotions are the result of the form of our social life and of the history of the people to whom we belong" (Boas 1940:636). The concept of social heritage was basic to Boas' thinking all his life.

Several of the theses of the book *The Mind of Primitive Man*, taken together, establish the relative autonomy of cultural phenomena, showing that there are *no independent variables* on which the cultural is dependent. First, establishing that race (physical type), language, and culture have relatively independent histories and are not interchangeable terms in classifying man, Boas showed that inner inborn traits ("race" or heredity) are not causal determinants of similarities or differences of cultures. Second, showing that geographical or natural environments are not neatly correlated with cultures as adaptations but always involve preexisting cultures, Boas proved that outer environmental conditions are not *the* causal determinants of similarities or differences of cultures. Finally, establishing that ideas of *orthogenetic* cultural evolution do not fit the facts of actual cultural sequences and history, Boas showed that no necessary predetermining process of change makes similarities or differences of cultures expressions of unfolding stages of development. These theses became principles of modern anthropology.

It is, I think, important to understand what it was in Boas' training and point of view that led him into the critical reconstruction of anthropology that he accomplished. This is especially important because of further implications for the understanding of Boas' thinking on theory and scientific method. It has been widely held that it was Boas' training in physics and mathematics that was responsible for his scientific reconstruction of the field of anthropology, which was largely preprofessional and somewhat amateurish at the time. Actually, I am convinced that it was an entirely different phase of his education and scientific experience that led to his future work, and I believe he tried to make that clear in his own statements.

Central to Boas' education in science and scientific thinking was the study of natural history, in which he indulged that "intense interest in nature" that he later recalled as characteristic of his youth (Boas 1938a:201–4). Boas attended the Froebel kindergarten in Minden founded and taught by his mother, which provided special nature studies. This experience was unusual for Boas' time, for kindergartens were rare then. Periods of recuperation after illness, spent in the countryside of Clus or at the seaside at Helgoland, acquainted him with the plant life of the woods and the wealth of animals and plants of the sea. He collected his own herbarium and for years "treasured"—his own word—the sea life specimens he gathered at Helgoland. He had a mineral collection and began to study mineralogy early in his Gymnasium years. In mid-Gymnasium he studied some zoology (including study on his own of the comparative bone structure of geese, ducks, and hares); astronomy and geology; more botany—physiology, plant anatomy, and the geographical distribution of plants. His interest in this last subject almost stifled other hobbies, but the study of cryptogams (plants such as ferns, moss, and algae, which reproduce by spores), begun in his own early herbarium collecting, became with a special teacher a subject which fascinated him ever after.

In his later Gymnasium years, drawn to all the natural sciences, he studied plant anatomy and physiology, used microscopes in plant study and in work on crystal forms and systems in mineralogy, and made his own map of the distribution of plants in the Minden region. In the universities, the special professors he sought included two biologists (one also a marine biologist), a botanist, and two mineralogists (one also a geologist). He found his studies of plant distributions among his most exciting work, and was elated when, by mid-Gymnasium years—for the most part through study on his own—he could follow fairly well "the evolution of the animal and plant world" and "its transient geographical distribution" (APS, 1).

Natural history with its empirical approach involved Boas in observation, description, comparison and classification, inductive generalization, and *an acceptance of the external world* which became a habit of thinking for Boas. In attempting to understand Boas and what he contributed to modern thought, his statements about his "intellectual interest" in physics and mathematics have been overemphasized, while other statements about his "intensive emotional interest in the phenomena of the world"—along with his long concentration on natural history studies—have been given too little attention. Boas' background before he became an anthropologist included physics and mathematics as well as geography as part of his intellectual training. But to understand what he made of anthropology it is far more important to know that he came to the study of man as a naturalist, as a student of natural history, and tried to understand man and peoples as part of the natural phenomena of the world.

Among anthropologists, Marian W. Smith is virtually alone in emphasizing this mode of understanding Boas. In a paper on Boas' approach to field method, Smith draws a sharp contrast between Boas' "natural history approach to the social sciences" and the "social philosophy approach of British social anthropology," and she shows that the contrast affected both the methods and content of fieldwork done by the two schools (Smith 1959:46).[3] The American approach includes all of culture, considers data inviolable, and seeks in data only generalizations or theories that can be reached inductively. The British school, in contrast, begins with assumptions and theories and uses field data and the field situation to test hypotheses that have been deductively derived.

Marian Smith's paper limits the scope of her interpretation, but one suspects from some of her comments that she would have gone on to a conception of Boas and his thinking similar to my own. For example, she says:

Boas, more than any other person, first brought the very mind of man into the natural world. . . . Conceptualization and philosophy no longer breathed a finer air. They could be studied by the same techniques and approaches, by the same attitudes as other human characteristics and consequently lost much of their aura of revealed truth. (Smith 1959:46)

Smith's paper had a singular impact on some anthropologists. For example, Kroeber, in his discussion of "Boas as a Man," had emphasized the mathematical and physical character of Boas' education, training, and lifelong modes of thought (Kroeber 1943:5-7). Even earlier, in 1935, in a famous exchange with Boas on history, Kroeber had written:

To begin with, it is of indubitable significance that Boas' educational training was in the physical laboratory sciences, in physics in fact. This led him into psychophysics and physical geography. His doctoral dissertation was on the color of sea water. This in turn led to a one-man, two-year geographical expedition to Baffinland, which brought with it intimate contacts with natives. The result was *The Central Eskimo* and a career of anthropology since. From physics Boas brought into anthropology a sense of definiteness of problem, of exact rigor of method, and of highly critical objectivity. These qualities have remained with him unimpaired, and his imparting them to anthropology remains his fundamental and unshakeable contribution to our discipline. (Kroeber 1935:539-40)

This attitude of Kroeber's is completely contrary to Boas' own explanation of his manner of thinking. In a paper called "The Study of Geography," in 1887, Boas specifically contrasts the methods of physics with the methods of history (Boas 1940:639-47). He uses "physics" and "history" as conceptual terms for two general types of approaches, the former seeking laws and subordinating particular events to abstract generalizations, the latter seeking the thorough understanding of phenomena—even individual events—and making laws or

generalizations merely instrumental to that end. Boas iden-
tifies himself with the historical approach, temperamentally, in interests, and in methods, and he is unsympathetic to
that of physics.

In contrast to his earlier statements, Kroeber wrote in his
1959 preface to *The Anthropology of Franz Boas*, the volume
which contains Marian Smith's paper, that "natural scientists
have never questioned the status of Boas and the importance
of his massive contribution," that Boas' anthropological
activity at first stemmed largely from both natural history and
humanist interests, and that Boas dealt so extensively with
non-European and nonclassical languages because they are a
part of the total world of nature. "Given the combination of
Boas' natural science adhesion and his predilection for human
materials, it was almost inevitable that he should concern
himself with culture, for culture, including its semiautonomous
province of language, is precisely the phenomenal regularities
of human behavior" (Kroeber 1959:vi). This is fundamentally
different from Kroeber's statements of a few years earlier.

Solon Kimball has made a special point of relating the
"natural history" approach to anthropology itself. In a paper
presented at an American Anthropological Association meeting
some years ago, he offered the thesis that anthropology had
developed historically from the approach of natural history,
while sociology had developed from the approach of physics
and the formal deductive sciences. Kimball has consistently
taken the position—especially in studies of the relation of
anthropology to methods and principles of modern education—that anthropology is rooted in the method of natural history (as exemplified by Darwin) and involves "inductive empiricism based upon methods of classification and interde-
pendencies of components" (Kimball, personal communication).

Empirical methods to Boas meant firsthand experience
where data were lacking. It meant an end to brilliantly
constructed speculations as a substitute for observation. In
ethnology, of course, this meant fieldwork, and Boas' own work
on the Eskimos is generally recognized as one early example

which stimulated the development of fieldwork as the basis of ethnology and cultural anthropology. In discussions of the historical development of ethnology, attention is often drawn (as by Evans-Pritchard) to the Torres Straits Expedition of the English, in which W. H. R. Rivers and A. C. Haddon participated. Yet much of the work of that expedition was peripheral to ethnology, as, for example, the effort of Rivers to settle psychological questions of the sensibilities of indigenous peoples. Somewhat overlooked in this historical view are the monumental field researches of the Jesup North Pacific Expedition, which was mounted under Boas' inspiration, direction, and editorship while he was at the American Museum of Natural History and at Columbia. This project, which was contemporary with the Torres Straits Expedition, resulted in seventeen massive volumes on Siberia and Northwest Coast North America by various people (with an eighteenth still to be published) and far outweighs Torres Straits in its significance for the development of modern ethnological research.

There is another side to Boas as a scientist—the fact that he was a *citizen*-scientist. His careers as citizen and scientist are interwoven. He accepted a moral obligation to spread scientific knowledge as widely as possible, and he himself applied anthropological findings to human problems in education, race relations, nationalism and internationalism, war and peace, and the struggle for democracy and intellectual freedom.

In his first general book, *The Mind of Primitive Man*, the first words of the 1911 first edition are: "Proud of his wonderful achievements, civilized man looks down upon the humbler members of mankind." The last words on the last page read:

I hope the discussions outlined in these pages have shown that the data of anthropology teach us a greater tolerance of forms of civilization different from our own, that we should learn to look on foreign races with greater sympathy and with a conviction that, as all races have contributed in the past to cultural progress in one way or another, so they will be capable of advancing the interests of mankind if we are only willing to give them a fair opportunity. (1911b:278)

Later, in *Anthropology and Modern Life* (1928), he applied anthropological knowledge to racism, nationalism, eugenics, crime, and education. Still later, in *Race and Democratic Society*, published posthumously by his son in 1945, some of his hundreds of contributions to widely read magazines and newspapers were brought together.

Boas' commitment to active citizenship and social, liberal ideals began in his childhood home, enriched by the liberalism and free thought of his father and mother. Both had given up all formal religious activity and affiliation, and as Boas later recalled, he and his sisters were "spared the struggle against religious dogma that besets the lives of so many young people." With "an intense interest in nature," Boas was able to approach the world around him with an open mind, without religious preconceptions or inhibitions (Boas 1938a:201–4).

Politically, Boas found "the ideals of the revolution of 1848 a living force in [his] home." Relatives and friends of the family had been in the 1848 struggle in Germany and had left for the United States after its failure, some after getting out of jail. Drawn to the liberalism of his time, Boas was deeply troubled about Bismarck's Germany and the limitations and restrictions it could place upon his scientific career (Boas 1938a:201–4).

At twenty-five, while on his expedition to Baffinland, he wrote in a diary of letters that he sent to his fiancée, "Science alone is not the greatest good" (June 27, 1883). "I believe one can be really happy only as a member of humanity as a whole, if one works with all one's energy together with the masses toward high goals" (December 13, 1883). "And what I want, for what I want to live and die, is equal rights for all, equal possibilities to learn and work for rich and poor alike. Don't you believe that to have done even the smallest bit for this is more than all science taken together?" (January 22, 1884). And he added, "I do not think I would be allowed to do this in

Germany" and "I do not wish for a German professorship because I would be restricted to my science and to teaching, for which I have no inclination. I should much prefer to live in America and to further these ideas."[4]

It was in 1887 that circumstances combined to make it possible for him to remain in the United States when he returned to New York after a Northwest Coast trip—to marry, to apply for American citizenship (which he obtained five years later), and to begin his American career with the same "American dream" he shared with so many other immigrants to the United States.

Boas' active citizenship did not end with his effort to make his scientific work relevant to human affairs. He was active in matters of principles and in specific situations involving injustice and violations of academic freedom. He resigned from his first teaching position—at Clark University—in a joint protest with other faculty members against continuing infringement of academic freedom by the president, G. Stanley Hall. In his view, a college or university consisted of its faculty and students; trustees and nonacademic administrators were not inherent in it.

A first major test of his principles came in 1914, with the outbreak of World War I. Boas, a pacifist, opposed the war from the beginning. He saw it as fundamentally an imperialist war. In a series of letters to newspapers, he urged that the United States and Woodrow Wilson take the lead in forming a coalition of neutral countries to bring about a cease-fire, and he argued against actions by President Wilson that he charged were leading the United States into the war. In 1917, after the United States declared war, he denounced the action and Wilson in the press.

Boas was not pro-German, as of course was charged. I will support this with a single letter, a letter he wrote to his son Ernst from the field in British Columbia, a few days after the outbreak of war. It is a personal letter, from father to son; it was handwritten and clearly was never intended to get the public hearing I am giving it now.

August 6, 1914

Dear Ernst:

... You can imagine that I can think of nothing else than the unfortunate war and the danger to which our aunts and grandmother are exposed. To me it seems like a terrible dream. I cannot visualize how reasonable people and nations which are "leaders of civilization" can conjure up such a terrible war. If Germany loses, such hatred will be created that it will stir up her nationalism for years to come; if she is victorious, such arrogance, that it will lead to the same consequence. If people would only realize what a source of hatred and misfortune the highly praised patriotism represents! That one cherishes one's own way of life is a natural thing. But does one need to nourish the thought that it is the best of all, that everything that is different is not good but useless, that it is right to despise the people of other nations? In our private lives we would not follow such an unethical rule. Why should it prevail in our national life? If one could only exclude this "patriotismus" from our schools and teach our children the good in our culture, and appreciation of the good in other cultures. Instead they artificially cultivate envy and rivalry. (APS, 3)

During the war, Boas took public leadership of an effort to counteract wartime hysteria against German culture. Officially, all things German were condemned. The German language ceased to be taught in American schools. Orchestras eliminated German music from their programs. Boas once made a particular request of a conductor to include a certain Beethoven opus in his next concert; the conductor replied that he felt as Boas did about the quality of that opus, but regretted that it was impossible for him to perform it. Boas took the position that as an anthropologist he could not accept the identification of the art and literature of a people with its political administration at a particular time. Heine, Schiller, Bach, and other German artists represented cultural achievements and values that had nothing to do with the Kaiser. It was this position that he took with his students. When Columbia's president Nicholas Murray Butler, ardently prowar and anti-German, instituted student spying on what professors did and said, Boas responded by writing a full statement of his views and distributing it in mimeograph to all who came to his classes or requested it.

Boas was not alone at Columbia in his pacifism and antiwar ideas. After the 1917 U.S. declaration of war, when a draft to mobilize an army was being readied, J. McKeen Cattell, a professor of psychology, sent copies of a letter he had written to every member of the U.S. House and Senate. The letter urged that a military draft act provide exemption for those who objected to military service outside the continental borders of the United States. The letter was written on Columbia University stationery. President Butler terminated Cattell on twenty-four hours notice, making forfeit his right to tenure and his accumulations toward retirement. Faculty support for Cattell was immediate. Boas and John Dewey were members of a Cattell Committee, which worked in his support for years. Two other faculty members, James Harvey Robinson and Charles Beard, resigned and joined in the establishment of the New School for Social Research. In the end, Cattell took his case against Columbia to court and won a complete victory, Columbia settling out of court to avoid publicity. It was so quiet an ending to the case that many did not know and do not know that Columbia had lost its first case on academic rights.

Perhaps the most critical controversy involving Boas and World War I came in 1919, after the war, when he published the following letter in *The Nation*.

Scientists as Spies

To the Editor of *The Nation*

Sir: In his war address to Congress, President Wilson dwelt at great length on the theory that only autocracies maintain spies, that these are not needed in democracies. At the time that the President made this statement, the government of the United States had in its employ spies of unknown number. I am not concerned here with the familiar discrepancies between the President's words and the actual facts, although we may perhaps have to accept his statement as meaning correctly that we live under an autocracy, that our democracy is a fiction. The point against which I wish to enter a vigorous protest is that a number of men who follow science as their profession, men whom I refuse to designate any longer as scientists, have prostituted science by using it as a cover for their activities as spies.

A soldier whose business is murder as a fine art, a diplomat whose calling is based on deception and secretiveness, a politician whose very life consists in compromises with his conscience, a business man whose aim is personal profit within the limits allowed by a lenient law—such may be excused if they set patriotic devotion above common everyday decency and perform services as spies. They merely accept the code of morality to which modern society still conforms. Not so the scientist. The very essence of his life is the service of truth. We all know scientists who in private life do not come up to the standard of truthfulness, but who nevertheless would not consciously falsify the results of their researches. It is bad enough if we have to put up with these, because they reveal a lack of strength of character that is liable to distort the results of their work. A person, however, who uses science as a cover for political spying, who demeans himself to pose before a foreign government as an investigator and asks for assistance in his alleged researches in order to carry on, under this cloak, his political machinations, prostitutes science in an unpardonable way and forfeits the right to be classed as a scientist.

By accident, incontrovertible proof has come to my hands that at least four men who carry on anthropological work, while employed as government agents, introduced themselves to foreign governments as representatives of scientific researches. They have not only shaken the belief in the truthfulness of science, but they have also done the greatest possible disservice to scientific inquiry. In consequence of their acts, every nation will look with distrust upon the visiting foreign investigator who wants to do honest work, suspecting sinister designs. Such action has raised a new barrier against the development of international friendly cooperation.

New York, October 16   Franz Boas

In the light of controversies over ethics within the American Anthropological Association in recent years, this letter seems a direct and simple plea for scientific integrity. Its anti-Wilson innuendos were not new. Boas had opposed World War I openly and had criticized Wilson's policies in letter after letter in the *New York Times*.

However, Boas' letter in *The Nation* was denounced by the Anthropological Society of Washington in a lengthy statement to the American Anthropological Association at its meeting in December, 1919. The Harvard-Cambridge anthropology group sided with the Washington society. The statement of the Washington group read as follows:

Resolutions of the Anthropological Society of Washington

The attention of the Anthropological Society of Washington having been called to an open letter published in *The Nation* of December 20th by Dr. Franz Boas under the title, "Scientists as Spies," and after said article was read and duly considered, the following resolution was adopted and ordered to be submitted to the American Anthropological Association at its meeting in Boston; to Section H of the American Association for the Advancement of Science meeting in St. Louis; and to the Archeological Institute of America meeting in Pittsburgh, with the request that suitable action be taken by these associations. Also that a copy of this resolution be sent to *The Nation* and *Science* with a request for its publication.

Resolved: That the article in question unjustly criticizes the President of the United States and attacks the fundamental principles of American democracy; that the reflections contained in the article fall on all American anthropologists who have been anywhere outside the limits of the United States during the last five years; that the information thus given is liable to have future serious effects on the work of all anthropologists outside the boundaries of the United States; and that the accusation, given such prominent publicity and issuing from such a source, will doubtless receive wide attention and is liable to prejudice foreign governments against all scientific men coming from this country to their respective territories, particularly if under government auspices; therefore *Be it resolved*, that in the opinion of the Council of the Anthropological Society of Washington, the publication of the article in question was unwarranted and will prove decidedly injurious to the interests of American scientists in general; that the author has shown himself inconsiderate to the best interests of his American colleagues who may be obliged to carry on research in foreign countries, and that his action therefore deserves our emphatic disapproval.

At the meeting, after a great deal of discussion, the following resolution was moved instead of the long statement from the Washington Anthropological Society.

Resolved: That the expression of opinion by Dr. Franz Boas contained in an open letter to the editor of *The Nation* on the date of October 16, 1919, and published in the issue of that weekly for December 20, 1919, is unjustified and does not represent the opinion of the American Anthropological Association. *Be it further resolved:* That a copy of this resolution be forwarded to the Executive Board of the National Research Council and such other scientific associations as may have taken action on this matter.

I have presented the text of Boas' letter and if anyone can find a word in it that says it represents anybody's views but his own, I would like to know it. It was a personal statement of his convictions, and it involved no one else. He did not name the persons he was referring to. Nevertheless, Boas was censured, by a vote of about two to one.

The Washington Anthropological Society distributed its original statement widely, in spite of the fact that it had not been passed by the AAA. A great deal of the rancor aroused was allegedly due to Boas' publication of a professional statement in a public, nonprofessional magazine. Yet Boas had sent it earlier to *Science*, which was then edited by J. McKeen Cattell, the same Cattell who had been kicked out of Columbia for his pacifist letter to Congress on Columbia stationery. Cattell replied:

I fear I must decide that it would not be advisable to print the letter entitled "Scientists as Spies" in *Science*. I of course concur in all that you say, but it seems to me desirable for *Science* to avoid, especially at the present time, all questions of a political character, even though they do relate to scientific matters.

Sincerely yours,
J. McKeen Cattell

I don't know how Boas felt about that letter, but he sent his statement right off to Henry Raymond Mussey, a friend who was editor of *The Nation*. Mussey immediately accepted it for publication and wrote to Boas:

> Thank you very much for your disturbing letter on "Scientists as Spies" sent us for publication. It is indeed a distressing thing that scientific men should stoop to such dishonorable practices, and I am very glad indeed to have the opportunity of giving publicity to your protest.

That is how Boas' letter happened to appear in *The Nation* rather than in *Science*.

There is a final note to this early controversy over professional ethics. The next month (on January 9, 1920), Cattell published in *Science* the full text of the communication from the Washington Anthropological Society, in the form that had been *rejected* by the AAA meeting.

I close this page of history by noting that one scientist wrote the Washington Anthropological Society to ask, in view of the statement it had circulated and had asked everybody to act upon, whether Boas' charges in the *Nation* letter were true. He noted that the Washington group had made no reference to that question at all.

Following his censure, Boas resigned as representative of the American Anthropological Association to the National Research Council, who accepted the resignation regretfully. Apart from this, I have no evidence that his participation in the AAA was ever terminated, even transiently. Annual reports of the Association in succeeding years show him still to be a member of various committees that he had been on previously.

Stocking has treated this incident in the context of "The Scientific Reaction Against Cultural Anthropology,

1917–1920," the title of a paper in his book *Race, Culture, and Evolution*. He focuses on the manner in which opposition to the development of Boas' cultural anthropology, fortified by jealousy of his achievements, caused the *Nation* letter to be used as an excuse for violent anti-Boas action. I think the letter also stands as an example of Boas in action on issues of scientific ethics.

Over the years, as Boas became known through his work and public statements as a strong liberal on academic and political issues and on race relations, he accepted board memberships on and allowed the use of his name by many public-service citizens' organizations and ad hoc committees. He also organized some of his own. His main means of action was to make public statements to the press or through letters to the press, or to form a committee which then took public or private action as the matter required. It was in this way that Boas initiated two large-scale national actions in relation to the rise of Hitler and Nazism. The first followed a Nazi denunciation of Jewish science. Boas responded with a public statement signed by over 8,000 American scientists, affirming that there was only one science, to which religion and race were irrelevant. Later, after Hitler came to power in 1933 and Boas' books (among others) were burned, Boas organized a group at Columbia called the Committee for Democracy and Intellectual Freedom. The idea spread rapidly to other universities, where chapters were formed, until the committee had more than 11,000 members.

Boas also joined other American scientists in organizing committees to help scientific refugees from Hitler's Germany and other countries overrun by the Nazis. The primary effort was to find refugee scientists positions in the United States or elsewhere in the free world. Boas was engaged in this activity at the moment he died in December 1942. Along with Lévi-Strauss, Boas had arranged a luncheon at Columbia in honor of Paul Rivet, refugee linguist from Vichy France. Boas suddenly collapsed, in Lévi-Strauss' arms, and died even as he was in the middle of a sentence about a new idea on race.

A major part of Boas' scientific work and its application concerned race and race relations, especially the problems of the American Negro. He was probably the first scientist to publish that Negro and White were fundamentally equal, as were all so-called races. He embodied this view in the title of one paper, "The Genetic Basis for Democracy." American Negro leaders, organizations, and universities were quick to recognize in Boas a source of strength. For W.E.B. DuBois, a founder of the NAACP and editor of its publication *Crisis*, Boas wrote a paper for the first issue of that magazine, on the Negro and the race problem in America (1910). He gave a commencement address at Atlanta University in 1906. He participated in the organization and work of the Association for the Study of Negro Life and History and its publication *The Journal of Negro History*, and later of the Council on African Affairs, of which Paul Robeson was chairman and Max Yergan director.

As an indication of what such Afro-American leaders thought of Boas, I have a message Max Yergan sent to Helene Boas after Boas died (APS, 4).

Mrs. Helene Yampolsky,
Grantwood, N.J.

On behalf of the Council on African Affairs, I express deepest regrets over the death of your father. He was a guide and inspiration to us in our deliberation and activities for the welfare of African peoples. The work of organizations like ours is possible because Franz Boas has lived.

I began this discussion by selecting four principal points for emphasis. I have touched on three: (1) that Boas was the architect of modern anthropology; (2) that the element in his training and experience that made him the modernizer of the study of man was the empirical way of thinking of natural history; and (3) that Boas was a *citizen*-scientist who applied the work of anthropology to problems of society, and was an activist on academic and political issues—in both ways serving as a model for anthropology as a humanitarian science.

I come now to my final theme, Boas as theorist. Far from being antitheory, Boas was himself, I would argue, *the* great theorist of modern anthropology, who established the core of anthropological theory on which the science is based.

Inescapably, discussions of Boas on theory must begin with his handling of the theory of evolution. Here are his words on that subject in 1888:

The development of ethnology is largely due to the general recognition of the principle of biological evolution. It is a common feature of all forms of evolutionary theory that every living being is considered as the result of an historical development. The fate of an individual does not influence himself alone, but also all succeeding generations. . . . This point of view introduced an historical perspective into the natural sciences and revolutionized their methods. The development of ethnology is largely due to the adoption of the evolutionary standpoint, because it impressed the conviction upon us that no event in the life of a people passes without leaving its effect upon later generations. The myths told by our ancestors and in which they believed have left their impress upon the ways of thinking of their descendants. (Boas 1940:633)

Clearly, in his early anthropological thinking Boas (1) accepted biological evolution as scientifically valid, (2) understood evolution in *historical* terms, not as orthogenetic, and (3) affirmed evolution as a *first principle* of ethnology and anthropology.

These statements must be emphasized in view of oft-repeated assertions that Boas antievolutionary. No statement could show more clearly that he not only accepted evolution but accepted it as *basic*. Yet he did reject the so-called evolutionary ideas of some anthropologists. What did he reject, as distinct from the evolution that he affirmed?

In *Primitive Art* he wrote,

Evolution, meaning the continuous change of thought and action, or historic continuity, cannot be accepted unreservedly. It is otherwise when it is conceived as meaning the universally valid continuous development of one cultural form out of a preceding type. (Boas 1927:80)

Essentially he was opposing orthogenesis, which is defined as follows by Webster's dictionary:

In biology, variations which in successive generations of an organism, follow some particular line, evolving some new type irrespective of natural selection or other external factor. Determinate variation or evolution. Sociologically, the theory that social evolution always follows the same direction and passes through the same stages in each culture despite differing external conditions.

Orthogenesis, by its very definition, is a contradiction of Darwin's theory of evolution. Darwin based evolutionary change on the principle of natural selection; among the vast number of variations occurring in each new generation, some were "selected" to survive and reproduce, others were not. Natural selection in turn must be understood as historical in character. Forms or species are subject to variation and change. So, too, is the environment in which they occur. The interaction between variations of form and the changing environment is an event of a particular time, not predetermined by either system. In modern biology, orthogenesis is not a fundamental evolutionary process. The point is made in Simpson's *Meaning of Evolution* (1950:22) and in various other treatments.

It was this distinction between orthogenesis and evolution in its historical, Darwinian sense that Boas had in mind, as has been noted by some. Washburn has written about this, referring to "evolution" as the term was used by Tylor, Spencer, Morgan, and their contemporary throwbacks. "There is no evolution in the traditional anthropological sense. What Boas referred to as evolution was orthogenesis, which receives no support from modern genetic theory. What the geneticist sees as evolution is far closer to what Boas called history than to what he called evolution" (Washburn 1963:522). In an article on Boas I wrote, "Boas' critique was directed not against the principle of evolution as historical development, which he accepted, but against the orthogenesis of dominant English and American theory of the time. He opposed history to orthogenesis" (Lesser 1968:101).

Boas himself made the distinction in clear terms in several places. In 1920, he wrote in "The Methods of Ethnology":

. . . the hypothesis [of evolution in traditional anthropology] implies the thought that our modern Western European civilization represents the highest cultural development toward which all other more primitive cultural types tend, and that therefore retrospectively we construct an *orthogenetic* development towards our modern civilization. (Boas 1940:282; italics mine)

In 1919, in a discussion at an American Ethnological Society meeting, Boas is reported by the Secretary, Robert H. Lowie, to have spoken as follows:

Professor Boas pointed out that in comparing the doctrines of unilinear evolutionists to those of biologists we are not quite fair to the biologists, since they do not postulate a single line of evolution without any divergences; what the cultural theorists of the earlier period did was to stress the *orthogenetic* character of cultural evolution.[5]

In 1938, discussing problems of the laws of historic development, Boas wrote:

When these data are assembled, the question arises whether they present an orderly picture or whether history proceeds haphazardly; in other words, whether an *orthogenetic* development of human forms may be discovered, and whether a regular sequence of stages of historical development may be recognized. (Boas 1938b:3; italics mine)

Several aspects of this view of evolution help explain Boas' view of theory and his work as a scientific theorist. First, he uses the fact of evolution as proof "that every living being is the result of an historical development." He understands evolution as history and as evidence of the historicity of living things. In effect, Boas' view is a major theory, both of culture and of man. It states that every culture is the result of a long history, and that every such history involves a great complexity of events, accidents of history, and interrelation of factors.

In relation to Boas' view of evolution as basic to anthropology, note that he is speaking empirically. The empiricism he brought from natural history studies called for generalizations or scientific theories that are *inductive*—that come out of the data and that serve to bind them together.

As Darwin's theory of evolution expressed in a generalization both the continuity and change of living forms—*descent with modification*—so a similar theory of the historical evolution of cultures served to express their continuity through time and their diversification and change—the idea of *continuity with change*.

Additionally, Boas established the modern *theory* of culture. Stocking has shown that it was Boas who established the modern use and meaning of the term. But more than that, in doing so he established the central theory of modern anthropology.

When Boas showed that cultures and their diversities could not be explained by differences in outer environment, natural environment, or geography; when he showed that cultural diversity could not be explained by differences in inner makeup of human groups (the racial argument); and finally, when he showed that cultural diversity was not a matter of stages of predetermined development or orthogenetic evolution, he made cultures and their histories the primary determinants of diversities or similarities at any time. Cultures became the basic factor in the understanding of cultural man. In anthropological thinking and explanation, the concept *cultural* replaced the concept *natural*. The culture concept did away at one blow with efforts to explain human nature biologically and physiologically (as with concepts of instinct or of inherent drives).

I would suggest, then, that two great theories in anthropology were contributed by Boas: the idea that in culture history, culture is the primary determinant, rather than some noncultural independent variable; and the theory of culture in its modern sense, as learned behavior. Both of these are inductive theories, based on the comparison and contrast of human cultures.

The immense influence of this anthropological discovery and development is indicated, for example, by John Dewey in his article, "Human Nature":

Anthropology, on the other hand, has made it clear that the varieties of cultural and institutional forms which have existed are not to be traced to anything which can be called unmodified human nature, but are the products of interaction with the social environment. They are functions, in the mathematical sense, of institutional organization and cultural traditions, as these operate to shape raw biological material into definitively human shape.

If we accept the extreme partisan stand, it may be regarded as now generally accepted that the immense diversities of culture which have existed and which still exist cannot possibly be derived directly from any stock of original powers and impulses, that the problem is one of explaining in its own terms the diversification of the cultural milieus which act upon original nature.

As this fact gains recognition, the problem of modifiability is being placed upon the same level as the persistence of custom or tradition. It is wholly a matter of empirical determination, not of *a priori* theorizing. (Dewey 1932:536)

Dewey adds further on:

The present controversies between those who assert the essential fixity of human nature and those who believe in a great measure of modifiability center chiefly around the future of war and the future of a competitive economic system motivated by private profit. It is justifiable to say without dogmatism that both anthropology and history give support to those who wish to change these institutions. It is demonstrable that many of the obstacles to change which have been attributed to human nature are in fact due to the inertia of institutions and to the voluntary desire of powerful classes to maintain the existing status (Dewey 1932:536).

In Boas' own view of theory (in the sense of scientific generalizations or laws), as he outlined it in his early paper "The Study of Geography" (1887), he made the historical character of human phenomena basic (Boas 1940:639–47). The goal in such a field of study is "the thorough understanding of phenomena"; in other places he speaks of "complex phenomena." Regularities or generalizations which are discoverable are viewed pragmatically, not as an end in themselves, but as an additional tool in analysis. This, I suggest, is not an antitheory or antigeneralization position, but a reversal of emphasis. He suggests that in the complex field of human cultural history, theory—read laws or generalizations—is not the end, but, where discoverable, one means among others to be used in scientific analysis and for the understanding of phenomena.

As a generalizer in his own right, Boas is the most generalizing anthropologist I have read. I once wrote a paper called "Research Procedure and Laws of Culture," in which I tried to show the nature of laws as working assumptions. I limited myself to selected illustrations from Boas, because he was supposed to be nontheoretical. I found most of the illustrations in the lengthy article he wrote years ago for the *Encyclopedia of the Social Sciences* on "Anthropology" (Boas 1930a). In that article, on every phase of the subject, he tries to generalize as much as possible what the import of the data is. The article is full of generalizations, some of which even take the specific form of attempts to state laws. I think it is important to realize that a generalization for him was arrived at inductively and was an attempt to sum up, to pull together, the meanings of the many facts so far known. In practice, it was always subject to further questions, further inquiries, further verification.

Boas moved onward from problem to problem throughout his active scientific life. He taught his students to attempt to do the same. He left anthropology an open field of inquiry, its methods rooted in empirical observation and experience, its goal an ever wider and deeper knowledge of man, its ideal—contributions toward a better world for all men.

Discussion

ERIC WOLF: Kroeber at one point—in fact, in the debate with Boas that you quoted from—accused Boas of not being really historical, of not being interested in history. Boas apparently defended himself—he was amazed that Kroeber would say that. What went into that controversy?

LESSER: From Kroeber's standpoint what went into it was his own concept of history. All Boas meant by history was the kind of history you read in any history book; he wasn't thinking of anything more than that. Kroeber also attacked Boas for publishing a whole book on primitive art and not discussing style. Boas replied that this was beyond his understanding, because there was a chapter called "Style" and also a long chapter on the style of the North Pacific Coast. He didn't know what Kroeber meant by saying he had never discussed style. In the same way, he didn't know what Kroeber meant by saying that he was not historical. Kroeber was willing to grant that *The Central Eskimo* was an historical study, to which Boas demurred, saying that apart from one or two comments it was a descriptive study, and there wasn't one word of reconstruction or a major historical statement in the entire book. Why Kroeber should call a descriptive ethnological study history, he didn't know.

As in his position on theory, on historical reconstruction Boas was very wary of anticipating the facts. He gave a talk once, "The History of the American Race," in which he told his audience—because it was primarily a lay audience—that he was going to let down his hair and speak about whatever he thought about the subject, and it wasn't based upon facts; it was based on his own speculations. He gave a brief talk on the origins and history of American Indians. This paper, because it was so lucid and simple, was immediately adopted by many people as a basic reference on the actual origins and history of American Indians, and it was quoted, almost line by line. So he stopped. He said to himself (as he later told me): If I can't say anything speculative and let people know I am thinking and dreaming about this now, and let it be taken as such, I'm not going to say anything. So he stopped making speculative reconstructions, except where he thought they would be understood as such. He never said they were necessarily accurate, and he used to change them every few years.

He didn't believe in historical reconstruction unless it was based upon sound methods, and for history of peoples without written history, sound methods to him meant that you began with archeology. On this point he was clear, that if you didn't have archeology you didn't have anything. He promoted archeology in the Jesup studies, and at the establishment of the Mexican International Institute he promoted and worked on archeology, uncovering the stratification of the Valley of Mexico and establishing the existence of the Archaic below the advanced strata. This was the first clear case of stratigraphic results in American archeology. He wasn't particularly interested in doing archeology, but he stimulated others to. A number of young archeologists got their Ph.D.s with Boas at Columbia, and he worked closely with archeologists, at the American Museum of Natural History and elsewhere. For instance, he went with J. Alden Mason to Puerto Rico one time, where Mason did some archeology.

I think that the whole problem is that Kroeber's meanings and concepts are vague and indecisive. Among the letters of Boas, there are some commenting on his students, and of Kroeber he said one time, "He never thinks anything through." If you are familiar with some of Kroeber's work you may decide what you think of that statement. In contrast to that, he said that Sapir was his great illustration to himself of an anthropologist. He tried all his life to get Sapir to Columbia and never succeeded.

GENE WELTFISH: Dr. Lesser, I think that in some ways you have made anthropologists sound much too logical as personalities. Their shenanigans have been enormous. For one thing, in the 1920s, when the Americanist Congress was held at the American Museum, we—the Boas school—were accused of being too theoretical and not knowing our facts, while the Harvard school really had the facts. So we rose up and spilled the facts. Then, in 1939, at the meeting of the Anthropological Association at which Sapir presided, the question of a resolution against the Nazi classification of the races came up. Sapir proposed the resolution. Thereafter the whole meeting split. On one side were most of the people; on the other side was a poor little group which included Boas, you, me, May Edel, and Gladys Reichard. We voted for this resolution. All the rest of the gang rose up and voted against it, on the grounds that the Germans were a friendly power. Thereafter Sapir, with his fine sense of humor, said, "This resolution was proposed by A. E. Hooton of Harvard." Everyone thought they were voting against a resolution proposed by Boas. So the shenanigans of anthropologists over time should be made clear. It isn't really logical.

LESSER: I thank you for that statement, but I was not talking about the shenanigans of anthropologists, but about Boas. I don't think he was guilty of many shenanigans. One of the reasons, I think, has been correctly discussed by Stocking in his historical analysis of the reaction against cultural anthropology. He credits the attacks on Boas not only to a disagreement with his concept of culture as basic, but also to the fact that many of these individuals were deeply envious of Boas and his achievements; and also to the fact that he persisted in his concepts and ideas and didn't withdraw them and eclectically accept the opposite because somebody insisted upon it. I think Stocking has a point there. In other words, it took a long time for non-Boasian anthropologists to accept the modern concept of culture, to give up the emphasis upon instinct and look at learning and culture instead. These things, and the fact that there were no inferior races, came hard. Even in 1919 there were a lot of anthropologists who were still using the idea of inferior races and publishing old-fashioned physical anthropology.

Roland Dixon's book *The Racial History of Man* was for twenty-five years on the shelves of most colleges and universities, as if it were a basic study of the history of races and their spread. It was based upon a simple error, which is shown in the discussion of his method at the beginning of the book; namely, that if you have a normal curve distribution, with extremes and a middle, then the extremes are pure types and the middle is hybrid. He used this idea in his analyses of statistical results from all over the world on three measurements—nose, head, and height of head. On this basis there is a four-hundred-page book of analysis of the racial history of man—not one word of which is science. Dixon, who was a professor at Harvard, never retracted a line. There was a whole series of typological thinkers in physical anthropology at Harvard who refused to recognize the problems of biometrics.

This went on while Boas was teaching the exact opposite. He reviewed these things, he had his say about them, but he couldn't stop people from having their right to free speech. In the long run he won; that's the important point. The reaction against him is another story.

Biographical Note

Alexander Lesser was born in 1902 and grew up in New York City. He went to Columbia College (1919–23), majoring in philosophy under John Dewey. A course with Boas aroused his interest in anthropology, and led to evening courses with Alexander Golden-weiser at the New School for Social Research. After college Lesser spent three years in business, then decided to go on with graduate work in social philosophy. He thought, however, that this required an empirical base in social science, and he turned to Boas' anthropology, which seemed to him the most scientific of the social sciences at Columbia. He completed his Ph.D. in 1929 with a dissertation on Siouan kinship, one of a series of kinship studies in which he attempted to show that general laws exist in social phenomena.

During the 1930s Lesser did extensive field research among the Plains Indians, principally on social organization, religion, and linguistics. His *Pawnee Ghost Dance Hand Game* (1933), a groundbreaking study of the Indian rejection of assimilation, was also an innovative statement of the necessary interdependence of synchronic and diachronic analysis. In 1935 he served as field leader for the Laboratory of Anthropology (Santa Fe) Field Training Expedition among the Kiowa Indians. Organized collaboratively, it resulted in a series of studies that reflected Lesser's emphasis on economic factors in the contact situation.

Lesser presented his views on history and functionalism at an anthropological meeting in 1935, provoking the heated objection of A. R. Radcliffe-Brown. In 1939 he again caused a sensation at a meeting with a paper on evolution, a subject still taboo at the time. Lesser argued that evolution in the Darwinian sense was compatible with culture history, which led Lowie, Malinowski, and others to declare that they had never been "antievolution."

After holding a series of temporary teaching positions at Columbia and elsewhere (including a course taught jointly with Boas at New York University in 1934), Lesser joined the Brooklyn College faculty in 1939. From 1947 to 1955 he served as executive director of the Association on American Indian Affairs, promoting legal action to protect Indian rights and to oppose assimilationist government policies. Returning to academia, he taught at Brandeis University and in 1960 went to Hofstra University as chairman of the department of anthropology and sociology. Since 1974 he has been a professor emeritus at Hofstra.

Lesser's views on social regularities, the role of history in cultural analysis, the dynamics of Indian-European contact, and the concept of "social fields" to replace notions of primitive societies as isolates—all have proven to be ideas ahead of their time.

Alfred Kroeber as president of the Anthropology Today
symposium in 1952

Alfred L. Kroeber
Eric R. Wolf

In 1901, Boas' department at Columbia awarded its first Ph.D.,
to Alfred Kroeber. That same year Kroeber was appointed as an
instructor in the anthropology department that had just been
created at the University of California, although Boas thought he
was not ready to work independently. Kroeber would pursue a
career of prodigious scholarship, and training of other scholars,
for sixty years. He attained an eminence in American anthropology second only to that of Boas, becoming after Boas' death
the senior figure in the field.

Kroeber's approach was firmly rooted in that of his teacher,
although there were significant differences between them. He
took Boas' historicity, which Boas had introduced as a corrective to theories based on preconceived schemes of cultural
development, and made it the central feature of his anthropology.
He inherited from Boas the concept of culture as an autonomous
realm, which could not be explained in terms of race or
geography or "mentality," and extended it into an explicit statement of cultural determinism (which, however, he later re-
canted). Like Boas, he described culture-environment relation-

ships while denying environment any explanatory power, but went farther than Boas in stressing cultural creativity. Unlike Boas, his view of history excluded any role of the individual and any interest in personality.

Kroeber's substantive specialty was American Indian (especially Californian) ethnology and languages, but his writings were encyclopedic in scope, ranging over the subfields of anthropology and over the cultures of all parts of the world and all periods. He was one of the first anthropologists to undertake analysis of complex "high" civilizations, endeavoring to show that aesthetic and intellectual achievements followed principles of cultural history. Kroeber's syntheses stand as embodiments of the "grand view" in anthropology.

TO REASSESS Kroeber's work—to reconsider what it was that he said and what he meant—is a difficult undertaking, for he has left more than 700 publications, many extremely weighty and very few that are simply occasional remarks. They range all the way from studies of Romance glottochronology to studies of California Indian basket designs and Zuni clans, discussions of the novel in Europe and Asia, and studies on changes in women's dress over a period of one hundred years. In order to truly master this body of material, one would have to be Kroeber and start at the beginning and live as long as he did.

For anthropologists of my generation, Kroeber was the living embodiment of American anthropology. His books and his words accompanied us through graduate school, and he appeared in our professional lives again and again. I knew him only after his retirement, when he gave a course at Columbia, a course entirely dedicated to the Yurok. But his influence at Columbia was strong through his students, especially Julian Steward, whose understandings of anthropology should, I think, be seen as a reaction to Kroeber—in a sense an outcome of a dialectic between Kroeber and himself. When I met Kroeber personally, I found him personable and delightful, a benign, Apollonian, Olympian figure. But at that time he must have been more mellow than he had been earlier in life, because there were many people who lived in terror of him. I saw him last in 1960, shortly before his death, at a conference he had organized on the "Horizons of Anthropology" at Burg Wartenstein in Austria. He had brought together the oddest assortment of people I have ever had the pleasure of meeting. It included Lévi-Strauss, Fürer-Haimendorf, Wilhelm Milke (who will go down in history as the man who included a measurement of the curvature of the earth in his calculations of diffusion rates), and Dell Hymes, among others. I asked him why he had invited us all, and he said that he did so because we were all mavericks. It is as a maverick, then, that I address myself to the task of assessing this ancestor. I am helped in this by several biographies or biographical statements that have come out on Kroeber, especially that by his second wife, Theodora (T. Kroeber 1970), by Steward's short appreciation of him (1973), but especially by Dell Hymes' obituary in *Language* (1961).

Kroeber was born in Hoboken, New Jersey, in 1876; he died in Paris in 1960, on his was back home from that "Horizons" conference. His parents were German-Americans. His father had come to the United States at the age of ten. His mother was born in New York, where Kroeber grew up. The parents were Protestants. The language of the home in Kroeber's youth was German; Kroeber said that he spoke English with an accent when he went off to school. Kroeber himself characterized the comfortable world in which he lived—his father imported European clocks—as "Deutsch-amerikanisch." It was a liberal bourgeois world in which German Jews and gentiles still shared the illusions of the bourgeois Enlightenment, a respect for learning, and the literary-philosophical heritage of Kant, Goethe, and the German idealists.

Kroeber and his friends were also raised in the German tradition of natural historical interests—a tradition that insisted on the preparation of herbaria, on the collection and mounting of butterflies and beetles, and that sent boys and girls to Bronx Park to explore for minerals and fossils. Kroeber retained throughout his life an interest in and gift for the observation of insect and animal existence. Theodora Kroeber tells of him spending most of a day on the shore of northern Peru, sitting on a rock a few yards offshore, observing an octopus and slowly stroking its tentacles with a reed over a long period of time, as if to reassure the wary beast that he meant no harm. One of his unfinished book-length manuscripts is called "Hard and Small"—a whole book on insectivores—where he waxed especially enthusiastic about the aquatic shrew. He similarly retained an active interest in literature. He translated Heine into English and Housman into German, spent hours comparing different versions of Keats, and wrote a comparative study of the novel in Europe and Asia.

Kroeber entered Columbia College at the age of sixteen and got his B.A. in English in 1896. He went on to write on the Romantic drama for the M.A. in 1897. But in 1896, he had by chance taken a course with Boas, who had just arrived at Columbia. It was concerned with the analysis of American Indian languages, and Kroeber felt enormously stimulated by it. "Boas's method," he would write later, "was very similar to that of the zoologist who starts a student with an etherized frog or worm and a dissecting table" (T. Kroeber 1970:47). He then embarked upon the study of anthropology, with psychology as a minor. In 1901, after two summers among the Arapaho, he wrote his doctoral thesis on decorative symbolism of the Arapaho, receiving the first Ph.D. in anthropology awarded by Columbia. A field trip for the Academy of Sciences in San Francisco took him to California in 1900, and the following year he became the first member of the Department of Anthropology at Berkeley. He was associated with Berkeley until his retirement in 1946. He continued to write and to lecture, holding visiting appointments at various universities, until his death fourteen years later.

Except for one period of disruption, he was an extraordinarily well-attuned man. This period deserves some explication. In 1913, his first wife died of tuberculosis. Shortly afterwards, Kroeber himself became seriously ill with what we

now know to have been Ménière's syndrome—an affliction of
the inner ear—but which was then thought to be due to a case
of nerves. The disease left him permanently deaf in the left
ear.[1] In 1916 he experienced the death of a friend, the last
Yana Indian, Ishi, whom Kroeber had befriended after he was
found exhausted and lost outside a California town. I think
this death had a considerable impact upon Kroeber. Then in
1917, Kroeber had completed the massive *Handbook of the
Indians of California* (which was not published, however, until
1925); with this body of work done he didn't quite know where
to go next. Finally, the long shadow of war starting for the
United States in 1917 must have dimmed that naive liberal
faith of the German-Americans in their new land. Whatever
the reasons, Kroeber went into psychoanalysis in 1917. He
became a practicing analyst in 1918, continuing this practice
until 1922. This period of uncertainty, to which Kroeber would
later refer as his "hegira," ended in 1926, with his second marriage to Theodora Kracaw, a gifted storyteller and writer. He
never returned to an interest in psychoanalysis after 1922.

Kroeber wrote a great deal and contributed to all the
subfields of anthropology. I will refer to only a few items from
his prodigious bibliography. The *Handbook of the Indians of
California* was followed by *Anthropology* (1923), which for a
long time was the only textbook on the subject available to
American students. It was a textbook for students who went
into anthropology in the '20s and '30s, was still the basic text
at Queens College when I went there in 1940, and was one of
the ten books required of all students in the first year at
Columbia during the late '40s. In 1931 Kroeber completed
Cultural and Natural Areas of Native North America, which
was not published until 1939 (an example of the long history of
publication lag). The dates for *Cultural and Natural Areas* are
significant, because they show that the element surveys of the
'30s—the collection and mapping of thousands of traits in
hundreds of tribes—came *after* Kroeber completed the book
that presents an integrated picture of the North American
cultural map. A key sentence that explains the idea behind the

element surveys appears in *Areas*:

It should be possible to determine an approximately objective measure of cultural intensity by measuring culture content—by counting distinguishable elements, for instance. This is a task which no one is ready to perform for the continent, but theoretically it is feasible and it might be worthwhile. (1939:222)

After finishing *Cultural and Natural Areas*, he began *Configurations of Culture Growth*, which was started in 1931, completed in 1938, and set in type only in 1944. The revised version of *Anthropology* appeared in 1948, with chapters 7 to 14 on patterns and configurations the essential new additions. Several books of essays followed, including *The Nature of Culture* (1952) and his lectures on *Style and Civilizations* (1957).

Kroeber came to anthropology through linguistics, and he maintained an abiding interest in the study of language throughout his career. It is his view of the study of language and linguistics that affords us the most productive point of entry into this vast corpus of his theoretical writings. It can be argued, without danger of distortion, that his understanding of linguistic data and findings provided a cognitive map for much of his anthropology. He was clearly aware that language was only a part of culture, but he thought that its study—as a part of culture—held lessons for the study of other aspects of culture as well.

This approach is best exemplified by his remarks at a Viking Fund talk in 1947, which is included in *The Nature of Culture* as item 12, "The Causes of Culture." We have here the programmatic statement of some of his theoretical understandings. It is true, as Ralph Beals has noted (1968:457), "that many of his theoretical formulations are embedded more or less incidentally in a profusion of phenomenological data." It is also true that his varied interests led him in many different directions, some of which he would pursue for a while, and then abandon, at times to the disappointment of students whose dissertations he initiated and then never returned to. Yet I think that his basic theoretical thrust was remarkably of one piece, was set very early, and was highly consistent. In this paper written in 1947, Kroeber says:

Now there are actual, established fields of organized study which deal almost exclusively with quasi-cultural forms, and which therefore serve as useful touchstones for the qualities that may be expected to distinguish sciences of the narrow as compared with the broad construction of culture. Of such studies, linguistics is the best known, most reputable, and neatest and most advanced in method. Relatively to other studies of man, linguistics is characterized by several traits: (1) Its data and findings are essentially impersonal, anonymous. (2) Its orientation is spontaneously historical, and potentially historical even for languages whose past has been lost. (3) The emphasis is on pattern, or structural interrelation, and away from so-called "functional" interpretation involving need satisfaction, drives, stimulus-response, and other explanations which "decompose" the phenomena dealt with into something ulterior. (4) Explanation is not in terms of genuine scientific cause, that is, efficient causes in the Aristotelian sense, but of "formal causes," that is, of other forms as being antecedent, similar, contrasting, or related. (5) Indeed, "explanation" in terms of producing cause is largely replaced by "understanding" in terms of historic contexts, relevance, and value significance. (1952:107)

Kroeber here states the major points of his anthropological approach. I would like to take these points up one by one, because they apply to a vast range of things that he was interested in. The first among the characteristics of linguistics that he sets forth is "impersonality," the stress on language structure and not on how language is spoken; as De Saussure might have said, on *langue* and not on *parole*. Transposed to aspects of culture other than language, this criterion emerges as the principle of the superorganic. The term is, of course, Herbert Spencer's; Kroeber borrowed it knowingly and made use of it in his paper, "The Superorganic," first published in the *American Anthropologist* in 1917.

That essay is multifaceted; it covers a very wide agenda. One of its aims was to protest "the blind and bland shuttling back and forth between an equivocal race and an equivocal civilization" (1952:22), in other words to counteract the confusion between race and culture. Closely related to this was a second intent—and this needs to be underlined—to speak out against the danger of applying Darwinian or post-Darwinian principles of the evolution of life to the evolution of culture. Kroeber admits the reality of cultural evolution: "there is obvious, even to the least learned, a growth or evolution of civilization." It is true, he argues, that culture "exists only in and through living members of the species" and is "outwardly so similar to the evolution of plants and animals" in this regard; but one must guard against "sweeping applications of the principles of organic development to the facts of cultural growth" (1952:23). To paraphrase him further: the growth of new species of animals takes place through changes in their organic constitutions. Human cultures, however, change through invention and diffusion, without concomitant organic alterations. No amount of reference to biology and heredity will explicate cultural cumulation and variation.

Then Kroeber takes one additional step. Galton, Pearson, and others have argued that heredity operates in the domain of the mind as well as that of the body, but their supposed corollary "that therefore heredity is the mainspring of civilization, is an entirely different proposition, without necessary connection and without established connection with the former conclusion" (1952:40). Civilization is "not mental action but a stream of products of mental exercise. . . . Mentality relates to the individual. The social or cultural, on the other hand, is in its essence non-individual" (1952:40). Darwin and Mendel dealt with populations made up of individuals, "but a thousand individuals do not make a society" (1952:41), and cultural products and knowledge cannot be explained by reference to the individual whose name is associated historically with their invention or diffusion. Even individual geniuses are but "indicators of coherent pattern growths of cultural value."

When we cease to look upon invention or discovery as some mysterious faculty of individual minds which are randomly dropped in space and time by fate; when we center our attention on the plainer relation of one such advancing step to the others; when, in short, interest shifts from individually biographic elements and attaches wholeheartedly to the social or civilizational, evidence on this point will be infinite in quantity, and the presence of majestic forces or sequences pervading civilization will be irresistibly evident. (1952:45)

This, written in 1917, is essentially the program for *Configurations of Culture Growth*, begun in 1931, the book Kroeber regarded as his best and most original contribution. It best demonstrates how he translated the linguistic criterion of impersonality into the anthropological concept of the superorganic.

Take the second characteristic. Linguistics is "spontaneously historical." It is important to recognize that here Kroeber has reference to historical linguistics and not structural linguistics as we now know it. The implication is that cultural forms, like linguistic forms, are connected genetically in time and contextually in space, and if we are to understand cultural phenomena we must always visualize them in their context of time and space. Again, in *The Nature of Culture* there is an essay in which he makes the point that historical understanding tries to maintain the context of time and space, whereas those people interested in general processes, that is, scientists, try to abstract from particular connections in time and space to more abstract analytic propositions. He accuses Boas of being interested much more in process than in history.

The dealing with time sequences is likely to be the first answer. But this trait seems only an incident. The essential characteristic of the historic approach appears to be the endeavor to achieve a conceptual integration of phenomena while preserving the quality of the phenomena. This quality the strictly scientific approach does not attempt to preserve. On the contrary, it destroys phenomena as phenomena in utilizing them for its own conceptualizations of a different order. Time and space certainly enter into the considerations and results of science proper; but its findings or end-results are timeless and spaceless formulations, in the sense that they are independent of specific or particular time and place. The findings of the historical approach, on the other hand, are necessarily always given in terms of specified time and space-phenomenal time and space, we might say, in contrast to the abstract measure of time and space in science. A dateless and placeless finding in human history, natural history, paleontology, geology, or astronomy would make no sense. If a dateless and placeless block of phenomena is discovered, the first problem of any historical discipline is recognized to be the findings of its date and place. Conversely, where a phenomenal lacuna appears in the date-place frame, the filling of this lacuna with the relevant phenomena is felt to be a need and problem. The historical approach is therefore always reconstructive in its nature—reconstructive as to the phenomena themselves and as to their dates and places. (1952:70)

This, then, is the source of his intellectual quarrel with Boas, a matter that has been the subject of some misunderstanding. Just as the task of historical linguistics is the reconstruction of the probable linkages between linguistic forms in time and space, so the task of culture history, Kroeber says, is the probabilistic reconstruction of connections between cultural forms both temporally and spatially. Sometimes, probable connections could be discovered through application of the age-area principle, even where other temporal perspectives were missing. Here Boas departed from the argument and refused to have anything to do with it, and Kroeber accused him of being interested in "process," like sociologists and functionalists, and lacking an interest in history. Kroeber held the task of reconstruction to be valid and primary. Only thus would laws of change be discovered, and they would be—to underline another phrasing of Kroeber's—not laws of causality, but laws of formal variation, as in the sound shifts of historical linguistics.

Kroeber's studies of changes in women's fashion reveal his search for laws of formal variation, not of causality. These studies are numerous and have always been perplexing, because he seemingly disregards questions about the fashion designers, the audiences that buy the fashions, how the clothes are produced, and the like. These are studies of formal changes and variations in particular dimensions of female skirt length and skirt width over time; he is interested in defining the sound shifts, if you like, the cyclical shifts back and forth within a particular pattern that is made up of a series of elements. These studies of fashion seem to me to be some of the exercises most diagnostic of his particular interpretation.

Kroeber's first criterion marking linguistics—and by implication the kind of cultural study he favored—was impersonality; the second was history. The third criterion was "the emphasis . . . on pattern, on structural interrelation, and away from so-called 'functional' interpretation," which Kroeber stigmatizes as essentially psychological and biological in character. The term *pattern* conjures up Ruth Benedict's patterns of culture, but Kroeber had something rather different in mind. Benedict's patterns were essentially psychological; his were not. He says he is not interested in the psychological domain; he is not interested in the socialization of personalities into a culture.

In the Benedict approach a pattern is a psychic constellation molding the typical personality of a society by imparting a certain warp to that society's culture. The basic patterns referred to [in Kroeber's essay] are the more pervasive and permanent forms assumed by a specific mass of cultural content, and they tend to spread from one society to others. In short, basic patterns are nexuses of culture traits which have assumed a definite and coherent structure, which function successfully, and which acquire major historic weight and persistence. (1952:92)

Elsewhere he uses the imagery of culture as a stream. In looking at the overall stream of culture, and the jostling of the culture elements or traits that make up that stream, one can notice eddies or whirlpools in time and space. These are particular cultures, exhibiting eddy-like or whirlpool-like patterns of greater or lesser duration. There are also other patterns—flows or waves, he says—that crosscut these eddies and whirlpools. They are what he called "systemic patterns," in his 1948 *Anthropology*. Examples of such systemic patterns are the alphabet, the calendar, the universal religions, and plow agriculture. Once again, writing in 1951, he drew a parallel from historical linguistics, likening these patterns to groups of

historically related languages such as the Indo-European ones or the Semito-Hamitic. These share a pervasive pattern of structure. This may be considered a grand system, to which the smaller correspondent would be any particular language with its tendency to maintain much of its particular plan of structure through successive periods of alteration. (1952:94).

I think the image of language was never very far below his consciousness. He compared style to grammar on numerous occasions. One such is in *Style and Civilizations*.

That the members of our civilization and of others are very little aware of total style need not discourage us much. Every human language has such a patterned style—we call it its grammar—of which the speakers are unaware while speaking, but which can be discovered by analysis and can be formulated. The coherence of a grammar is never total or ideal, but is always considerable; it certainly much exceeds a catalogue of random items. Cultures are larger, more varied and complicated sets of phenomena than languages as well as more substantive and less autonomous. But the two are interrelated—in fact, language is obviously a part of culture, and probably its precondition. So the structure of cultures, like that of languages, also seems potentially describable in terms of an overall patterning. (1957:106)

Although he doesn't say it, I would then add: —in terms of a grammar.

Thus, there is an interest in the recognition, delimitation, and characterization of "patterns," small and large, temporary and enduring, localized and widespread, in occurrences of phenomena and their co-occurrences, but not in causality. This is the fourth criterion. "Explanation is not in terms of genuine scientific causes, . . . but of 'formal causes,' that is, of other forms as being antecedent, similar, contrasting, or related" (1952:107). His *Configurations of Culture Growth* deals with the appearance and disappearance of clusters of inventions. In his conclusions to the book, he notes that some have held that there might be a correlation of such clustering with wealth or population, but he postpones discussion. "No serious long-range and comparative studies appear, however, to have been undertaken on this problem, and it seems wise to defer opinion until they shall have been made" (1944:839). *Cultural and Natural Areas of Native North America* (1939) is full of suggested correlations between aspects of the environment and aspects of culture. This work, in fact, led him to studies of native populations and their clustering. But the purpose of the study was not the analytic study of processess. Kroeber reiterates that "while it is true that cultures are rooted in nature, and can therefore never be completely understood except with reference to that piece of nature in which they occur, they are no more produced by that nature than a plant is produced or caused by the soil in which it is rooted. The immediate cause of cultural phenomena are other cultural phenomena" (1939:1).

It is not adequate, he felt, to explain the process of cultural production by reference to general analytic processes. Once again he accuses Boas of being interested in process, to the detriment of history—"the purpose of history is genetic." Culture must not be explained in terms of analytic reference back to psychology or biology. It must also not be referred back to "behavior." For example, kin terms—contrary to Morgan and Rivers—are only indirectly and and not directly shaped by social life. They "reflect unconscious logic and conceptual patterning" (1952:172). Kroeber criticized "the injection into anthropology of the concept of behavior, first developed as a corrective in the internal emancipation or purification of psychology" (1952:8). He always hated the idea that anthropology might someday come to be ranked among the behavioral sciences, and he detested sociology as ameliorative dogooding that mixed sloppy values with science. In the end, however, he made his peace with Talcott Parsons by dividing up the world between sociology and anthropology, much as the kings of Spain and Portugal divided up the world between the Spanish empire and the Portugese empire in the Treaty of Tordesillas of 1494.

This distrust of sociology and behavioral references seems to me to be strongly influenced by his particular liberal German bourgeois background, which distrusted politics to the utmost and stayed away from involvement in it. In this milieu, people believed in peace among men, universal understanding, the increase of enlightenment, the happy coexistence of German gentiles and Jews in the midst of ever-increasing prosperity. They believed in progress: the world would grow more civilized, and people would come to understand one another. Politics, however, was dirty business. Kroeber lived in the environment of the New York Ethical Culture Society that was, and still is, an embodiment of those values. I suspect that much of Kroeber's view of the world came filtered through this set of values.[2]

Thus, Kroeber was grimly determined not to mix science and politics. He played a leading part in the organization of language programs for the U.S. Army in World War II (the ASTP, or Army Specialized Training Program), but he saw this as nonpolitical. He took part in the Indian Claims cases of the 1950s, but the involvement made him deeply uneasy. He unleashed a veritable bolt of lightning against Dorothy Gregg and Elgin Williams, who launched a kind of premature New Leftist attack on anthropology, criticizing it as the "the dismal science of functionalism" (1948). Kroeber lashed into them as advocating "an authoritarian panacea" and stated his belief that "the method of science is to begin with questions not with answers, least of all with value judgements," and "Science is dispassionate inquiry" (1949:320).[3] He was enraged when Morris Swadesh—with whom he entertained close collegial relations—protested his ouster from City College for radical activities and tried to address a session of an international congress then meeting in New York City. Kroeber opposed the reorganization of the American Anthropological Association into a larger professional organization, wanting to keep it a collection of scholars without applied or public interests. One can find throughout his writings a strong sense of distaste for anything that had to do with politics, with involvement in nonscience, and I think also with sociology—all those enterprises that had to do, he thought, with trying to improve the world.

The fifth criterion in Kroeber's list is "value significance." In linguistics, Kroeber says approvingly, "'explanation' in terms of producing cause is largely replaced by 'understanding' in terms of historic contexts, relevance, and value significance" (1952:107). Kroeber came to think of culture as having two ingredients (so he calls them), one of which he calls *reality culture*, the other *value culture*. Oddly, Kroeber rarely defined values; he preferred instead to list exemplifications of the concept in terms of concepts put forth by others, such as ethos, eidos, patterns, and postulates. Yet there are passages in his posthumous *Roster of Civilizations and Culture* (1962) which come closer to a definition of his own than I have been able to find elsewhere. He wrote, apparently in 1957, that *value culture* was to be so called

on the ground of having value, or being an end in itself, and not merely means to practical ends. It includes all purely aesthetic and intellectual activity; but without being rigorously delimited to such activity. It certainly includes an element in every religion, though religion usually also contains organization and institutionalization; and it includes some part of morals, though morality is directed also to personal conduct and action. What is called "creativity" coincides pretty closely with a concern for value culture as just defined. (1962:9–10)

Values are thus culturally produced ends in themselves. Culturally produced, they are superorganic. They may not be explained with reference to physiology, biochemistry, or psychology. Such an explanation, he said on an earlier occasion, disregards the essential specific properties of values. These are retainable only as long as the phenomena of value continue to be "inspected" on the cultural level (1952:138). The inspector of values must make no value judgments of his own. He must focus his interest on "values as they exist in human societies at given times and places . . . as they make their appearance in the history of our species; in short, . . . values as natural phenomena occuring in nature—much like the characteristic forms, qualities, and abilities of animals are defined in comparative zoology" (1952:137).

What, then, is the role of the anthropologist who wishes to understand culture as a stream of forms sui generis, without reference to human biology, psychology, ecology, or sociability—the anthropologist who turns away from science with its apparatus of cause and effect, and seeks instead to discover the laws of motion of constellations of forms without an appeal to movers; who wishes to note the gamut of human values without reference to human creators but as ingredients located in the arrays of cultural forms? His task is to classify the cultural eddies and whirlpools, to delimit and contrast such patterns as are discernible in the stream of culture; classification, above all. Kroeber said on many occasions that classification *is* what the anthropologist is supposed to do.

I feel that the study of both culture and language is in crying need, in its own right, of far more systematic classification of their multifarious phenomena. Perhaps we have a surplus of bright ideas and a shortage of consistent ordering and comparison of our data. (1960a:17)

And elsewhere:

Anthropologists . . . do not yet clearly recognize the fundamental value of the humble but indispensable task of classifying—that is, structuring—our body of knowledge, as biologists did begin to recognize it two hundred years ago. (1960b:14)

Again:

Culture area classifications were somewhat comparable to the pre-Darwinian taxonomies of the plant and animal kingdoms; and like them they contained an implicit developmental theory. . . . I regard such a formulation as one of the things that the world of learning has the right to expect from anthropology. (1962:15–16)

To order and classify, Kroeber relied heavily on counting, that is, on statistics. I will cite only a few examples out of many. In 1919, in order to discover the relationships between 67 dialects of 21 California linguistic stocks, he sorted 225 cognates into tables, thus inventing an early form of lexicostatistics. In 1916, he carried out a seriation of surface sherds of sites near Zuni, unaware of the fact that A. Kidder had already introduced this method a year earlier (an instance of parallel invention). In 1919, he began his plotting of variations in women's fashions—an interest carried forward with Jane Richardson in a quantitative analysis in 1940—in order to show that a constellation of forms obeyed an inherent rhythm of variation and stability. In the years between 1934 and 1938 the culture element survey of native western North America went forward, in which 13 field investigators collected data from 254 tribes or bands. In the 1950s he wholeheartedly embraced glottochronology, applying the method to Romance and Athabascan languages. In 1960 he added "Comparative Notes on the Yurok Culture" to W. W. Elmendorf's *The Structure of Twana Culture*, showing that the two cultures differed in only 4 elements out of about 2,000 but that these 4 elements were decisive in imparting to Yurok culture its distinctive patterned difference from the other (Elmendorf and Kroeber 1960).

I undertook to write about Kroeber to try to understand this body of work which accompanied many of us through so much of our lifetimes. In pondering the corpus of his work, I found there were themes in it that continue to have resonance for us. I would summarize them as follows:

1. The emphasis on societies and cultures as open sets or systems, existing in mutual interchanges with each other.
2. The emphasis on cultural form and the possible implications of cultural forms, a problem that still remains with us though often muted in the search for function.

3. The interest in style or pattern cohesion, a phenomenon that still defies explanation in its own terms in anthropology.
4. The suggestion that some aspects of culture may be generated without specific utility or cause, which provides a salutary antidote to the sour utilitarianism of adaptationists.

Yet what is most striking now is that totally absent from Kroeber's work is any sense of relevance of the concept of adaptation.[4] This was, above all, the contribution to American anthropology of Julian Steward, and it was something that Kroeber never understood, cared about, or paid any attention to. There were any number of occasions when Steward tried to explain to Kroeber what he was about, and Kroeber would continue to talk about theories of pottery on the Peruvian coast or about the importance of knowing the connectedness of cultural elements in time and context. Steward's concern with cultural causality and his attempt to plot parallels in culture types and sequences of culture types were simply of no interest to him.

What did Kroeber think he was doing? He thought of his anthropology as a variant of natural history. He returned to this definition many times, but nowhere more clearly than in 1955 when he said:

The phenomena are given as directly as possible and in their contextual relation of occurrence. This context is preserved: if explanations are made, they are marginal, as it were, and do not fundamentally disturb the context. This is the method of what in the earth and life sciences is widely known as natural history. The use of this very term natural history for a branch of knowing that deals with phenomena far more by description than by narration is indication that the difference between these two techniques of narration and description is incidental to the more fundamental quality of organized presentation of knowledge with all possible preservation of the data in themselves and in their relations of occurrence. *In short, it is phenomenal presentation.* (1963:110–11)

Taking this view as a definition of his own efforts and as a portrayal of his discipline allows us to unravel some of the theoretical threads that run through the body of the man's work.

As a natural historian he is in the tradition of Alexander von Humboldt, who called himself a cosmographer (a geographer, we would say nowadays) and defined the task of cosmography as follows: (1) to seek "a knowledge of the chain of connections, by which all natural forces are linked together, and made mutually dependent upon each other"; and (2) "to analyze the individual paths of natural phenomena without succumbing beneath the weight of the whole" (von Humboldt, quoted in Kluckhohn and Prufer 1959:12). Classification and taxonomy were the tasks through which these connections would emerge, by noting similarity or difference of form, but following out a logic of forms. Here we may recall that Kroeber often referred to his interest in cultural taxonomy and classification as being Linnean and pre-Darwinian—noting the multitude of organisms (cultural phenomena) in their total array and variation, but without any theory of natural selection (or cultural selection).

But Kroeber at the same time aimed at being a natural historian of the superorganic. In his article on the superorganic he speaks of the emergence of culture as a saltation, a jump, a change from quantity into quality, but occurring in *nature*. "Nature is not set aside." This is fundamental, for it distinguishes him from culture historians like Wilhelm Windelband and especially Heinrich Rickert (1863–1936), with whom he carried on a running debate in numerous publications. Rickert, a neo-Kantian, held that science was applicable to the study of matter, but that the phenomena of value (mind) could not be reduced to matter and required a method of their own: the famous "understanding" or Verstehen of phenomena in their space and time continuity (a concept that also crops up in Max Weber). Kroeber's solution to the problem posed by these German idealists is surprising. Rickert's contraposition of science as adequate to the study of matter, and history as adequate to the study of culture, is false, Kroeber says, because there are genuinely historical components to the sciences of astronomy, geology, and biology. Moreover, if the superorganic occurs in nature, if nature is not set aside, then values— quintessential ingredients of culture—must be "natural phenomena occurring in nature—much like the characteristic forms, qualities, and abilities of animals as defined by comparative zoology" (1952:137). While in organic species values are inherent in their genetic equipment, in culture they are superorganic: inherent in cultural patterns. But in the search for cultural connections, for the connection of elements and patterns in time and space, Kroeber was a cosmographer like Humboldt, a seeker after the chain of connections by which all natural forces are linked together; one could paraphrase this, for Kroeber, as the chain of connections by which all cultural forms are linked together. This is the concept of The Great Chain of Being which Arthur Lovejoy has so lovingly analyzed. It is the pre-Darwinian idea that all things manifest in nature are connected in some way ultimately in the mind of God.

Finally, Kroeber thought of himself as a *natural* historian of culture, and he argued at length against those like Hegel, Toynbee, Danilewski, Spengler, Sorokin, and many others who would endow history with a teleological meaning. Yet beneath the scrupulous historian of culture there lurks ultimately a natural philosopher, a Naturphilosoph of the German Romantic tradition. There may be no causality in Kroeber, but there is a principle—a prime mover—that appears in disguise wherever a pattern climax enters its ascendant phase and reaches towards its culmination. It is the prime mover of "cultural productivity" or "creativity," the active concern with value culture. There is one reference in Kroeber's *Nature of Culture* that shows that he was himself aware of an inconsistency in his demand for impersonality and noncausality.

My own theory of "deterministic" pattern realization and exhaustion contains a concealed factor of striving and will, in the individuals through whom the realization is achieved. A creative urge and spark must be accorded them, and potentialities of the same to all men. (1952:9)

He goes on to say that if he has once compared culture to a coral reef, reflection should have caused him to note that the reef consists of living polyps. "The free will of the polyp may be minute, and his individuation somewhat limited, but his activity is definite." Behold, beneath the array of culture moving like a coral reef or iceberg—another metaphor of Kroeber's—there is *creativity*. It is, however, not the creativity of determinate men, in determinate relationships with and against one another, but an abstract flicker of creativity present in all organisms. When he was once asked why molluscs had produced no Newtons or Alexander the Greats, he answered half in jest but half seriously, that maybe they had but perhaps no one had noticed. Thus in the movement of the coral reef, the mollusc biota, and human culture, creativity is the abstract prime mover.

With this, we have returned to the fold of German idealist philosophy from which the cosmography of Alexander von Humboldt took its departure. What is this creativity but Hegel's Geist, becoming manifest in world history, or Schelling's universal Spirit ever bent on individualizing, particularizing itself? At the bottom of the iceberg stands—God; and it is perhaps in this sense that Kroeber once said—it was at the conference just before his death—that anthropology was his religion. Where, after all, does the Great Chain of Being of pre-Darwinian naturalism derive its unity, if it is not from the mind of God?

Discussion

STANLEY DIAMOND: You stimulated me to think of the period at Columbia when Kroeber was there. With reference to the culture-language analogy, it's also true that Kroeber was strong on the distinction between race, language, and culture which Boas had formulated, and also very strong on the fact that grammar did not express meaning. I wonder how you would handle that.

WOLF: I think that Kroeber had no interest in meaning. His linguistic analogy is somewhat similar to Lévi-Strauss', that is, an interest in the externality of form—that people eat with chopsticks, that sitting on chairs involves a certain arrangement of the furniture, that the European novel is written in a certain style and pace and pattern, and the like. Questions of meaning are, as far as I know, rarely discussed. What comes to mind is a discussion of Yurok narrative and poetry, which is a splendid wording of the quality of the Yurok style of delivery. It talks about how the Yurok recite and talk, but it never touches on what they're talking about. It describes the outward manifestation of the style, but doesn't get to meaning. Values in themselves are also highly disembodied things; concern with the body, concern with afterlife, asceticism—these are abstract labels for meaning. But I think that meaning is not there.

DIAMOND: I meant that Kroeber insisted that grammar was merely formal and in that sense did not express meaning, which was the general view of the Boas "school." The second thing: with reference to Kroeber's belief in progress, he listed a number of factors as criteria of progress—the quantitative accumulation of cultural traits; the diminution of the focus on the body (and he was prone to reduce ritual performances among primitive peoples to physiological performances, a curiously reductionist formulation despite—or perhaps because of—his superorganic); his insistence that there had been an improvement in such things as the treatment of prisoners of war; and so on. These criteria went parallel with Boas', and they antedated Redfield, who apparently lifted them from Kroeber in his *Primitive World and Its Transformations*. Kroeber also made an interesting formulation in his textbook, either prior to Redfield or at about the same time, on the folk-sophisticate polarity, which I always thought was better, if less elaborate, then Redfield's.

WOLF: I do think that he had a belief in progress, and he expressed it that way. I find that somewhat inconsistent with the view of culture as a coral reef or iceberg; it doesn't quite fit. There are various points where he waxes biological or psychological without any kind of mea culpa. I found that discussion of what is "primitive"—having to do with the focus on the body—terribly revealing. Kroeber's views in this matter are perhaps a reflex of the subculture from which he stems: that anything to do with blood and body fluids must be primitive. This view is also strangely at odds with his reified picture of culture as an iceberg. Suddenly, we shift from culture to biology. Yet to get away from biology, you need progress, which means doing away with all these body fluids.

I agree that his formulation of the sophisticated element in contrast to the folk is useful, but contrary to Redfield he was never interested in the carriers of culture. Redfield worried about who the people were who were communicating with one another—the sweet-voiced singer on the temple steps who transmits a particular myth to other people who listen, the difference between sacred figures and lay preachers, the audiences and publics. Kroeber had no interest in who was talking to whom, and there is nothing in his polarity of folk/sophisticate about communication interchange relationships, which Redfield did have an interest in.

DIAMOND: But Kroeber does mention the greater density of communication.

WOLF: Yes, he talks of *more* culture content and *more* people. But there is nothing of the communication process, the transfer of meaning and information, or the relationship between sender and receiver. There are, in fact, no people. His program in *The Configurations of Culture Growth* is to note these cumulations of cultural growth or their disruption, never asking who the people are, the elites or the specialists or the people who produced the culture content. His Florence is a set of blips on a curve—there are so many people painting in particular styles who happen to be living in Florence, for reasons unexplained. There is no concern with the Italian city-state, for example, or with the kind of organization of the libido that made these things possible, or with any other of the possible ways of going about an explanation. He's not interested in that. It all remains very abstract, very Olympian—frightening, ultimately.

DIAMOND: I agree. But I was referring to Kroeber's expression of the greater density of communication in *primitive* societies. He recognized that, even if he failed to understand or empathize with it. It is a paradoxical footnote to his overriding progressivism.

MICHAEL HARNER: I think Kroeber would have enjoyed your presentation. There are two points I want to make. First, I think that Kroeber, being located in northern California, was faced—to a degree that no other major university anthropologist was—with the responsibility of salvage anthropology. This may have reinforced his natural history bent. He had the great responsibility to utilize his own talents and those of his students in salvaging for posterity what was left of the Californian and western North American Indian cultures—and of course there was near unanimity about the value and priority of such activity at that time among anthropologists working in the western United States.

Another point: Kroeber had a tremendous capacity for recall. He could remember the comment of a particular informant, and say "On the twelfth of August in 1923, Mary So-and-so told me such-and-such." I often wondered whether this remarkable ability for recall and retention of data might have been related to his tendency not to go the route of causally oriented reductionistic analysis.

WOLF: Your second comment makes sense to me. I didn't say much about his various Indian friends, from whom he learned a great deal and recorded a great deal. At the same time, I'm not so sure about the salvage ethnography, because there were a lot of salvage ethnographers—in a way, we were all salvage ethnographers. Yet many people working with North American

Indians had the sense that ethnography was a record of *people*, not just abstract museum traits but people who had once lived, had problems, used their culture, and behaved in certain ways. While it is intellectually permissible to abstract at any given point, I think that you have to remain aware that you are abstracting, and at some point the abstraction has to come back to the point of origin if it is to be fruitful. In Kroeber, this tendency to take the culture element out of the behavioral matrix, or the societal matrix, or the adaptational matrix—the real life of people—was quite complete. He was insistent on it.

SALLY McLENDON: Kroeber found in California an astounding number of distinct social groups—a far greater number than the chapter headings in the *Handbook of California Indians* suggest—in the midst of rapid culture change and devastation by depopulation. California seems to have been, in fact, one of the areas of greatest ethnographic and linguistic diversity in native North America, and Kroeber must have found a research situation best approximated in recent times by the New Guinea highlands in the early '50s. Harner is right about the pressure of salvage anthropology in shaping Kroeber's California research, and yet Kroeber and his interests seem to have largely shaped the nature of salvage anthropology in California. California offered a research situation which could have occupied dozens of anthropologists productively during several years of intensive research. However, Kroeber chose to attempt to handle this research opportunity almost single-handedly, except for the assistance of his own early students, S. A. Barrett, T. T. Waterman, and Goddard and Dixon, who were already involved in California ethnography, and later his colleague at the museum, E. W. Gifford, who had joined the museum as an ornithologist. Able professional peers like Sapir were not encouraged or supported, and less well-trained but experienced fieldworkers like C. H. Merriam and J. P. Harrington felt themselves to be positively excluded.

Many of the ethnographic sketches in the *Handbook of California Indians* were written on the basis of two or three weeks of fieldwork. Such short periods of fieldwork meant that little participant-observation was possible, and in fact the fieldwork seems to have been intended primarily to sample a certain range of ethnographic and linguistic phenomena in California. Once surveyed, however, there was surprisingly little subsequent in-depth research on individual cultures, social groups, or languages. Rather, the focus seems to have been on increasingly detailed surveys, culminating with the Culture Element Distribution studies in the '30s. One wonders how much Kroeber's interest in pattern and generalization was triggered by his attempt to deal singlehandedly with the ethnographic and linguistic diversity of California and by his own propensities for fieldwork, as well as how much our present conception of California ethnography and ethnology was excessively shaped by Kroeber's research strategy.

GENE WELTFISH: I think we shouldn't gloss over lightly the culture element studies. For almost ten years an enormous amount of work was done, and a great many people invested their whole careers in it. Then one terrible day at a meeting of the Anthropological Association, Kroeber stood up and announced that it wouldn't work, that he had hoped that by accumulating all the traits he would be able to get at which cultures were related, but not one single insight had come to him. You can't imagine what—after ten years and an enormous amount of material—happened at that meeting.

WOLF: I think this is very characteristic of Kroeber. He put a lot of people onto work on problems, and when after years they came up with something and showed it to him, Kroeber had lost interest in it.

ROBERT CARNEIRO: I think there is some connection between Dr. Weltfish's observation and Kroeber's attitude toward evolution. He stood between the two poles of history and evolution. He did not want to do history, in the particular and narrow sense. What he wanted to do he called "descriptive integration"—a step or two away from history—in which you begin to isolate patterns from their particularistic matrix. At the same time, he was loath to go much beyond this, and he was very unhappy with Leslie White's cultural evolutionism.

He was afraid, I think, of finding really broad patterns, general trends that went beyond the data as he saw them. This is reflected in the conclusion of *Configurations of Culture Growth*. He expressed there a disappointment that after all the years he had invested in this work, there wasn't more in the way of obvious trends and general direction. There was cyclicity—things peaked and then went down again—but what he had hoped to find wasn't there. I think this can be explained partially by the fact that the very things in which he chose to look for order and pattern were things that would show only a limited amount, that would show cyclicity but not the broad directional changes that one sees in, say, economics, technology, or political organization.

WOLF: I think you are absolutely correct. All the problems that Steward and the Whiteans began to think about Kroeber simply had no interest in, and was probably afraid of. This kind of interest in narrow patterns, their variability, and their formal implications is by no means dead. I recently received a letter from a colleague expounding on the history of the form of chairs in China. If Kroeber were alive he would say that that's the kind of anthropology he understands, and the fact that the Chinese have had a revolution he would probably not find very interesting.

PAUL TOLSTOY: I wonder whether you are not criticizing Kroeber for something that he didn't do. One of the things that he did not do, of course, was to look for causes. But would you not allow his reticence in that regard as a legitimate stage in the search for knowledge? Perhaps he did not feel at that time that the kind of information was available or the kind of conceptual tools were available that made a search for causes appropriate.

WOLF: It's true that you ought not to criticize somebody for what he doesn't set out to do. At the same time, in such work as *Configurations of Culture Growth*, there is no pointing out a program that other people—economic historians, art historians, sociologists of the Renaissance—could pick up or in some way make use of his material. The work is not organized so as to invite comment from people like Joseph Needham working on Chinese science or Marvin Becker working on the social organization of Florentine artists. It is totally self-contained and, as such, has a kind of elegance. It gives form to an incredible quantity of material. But there is no invitation to others to connect it with anything outside, and the world in 1930 was not devoid of people who might have addressed themselves to the problem. He liked ordering phenomena, and I suppose I think that ordering phenomena is not really sufficient.

WARREN DeBOER: Do you have any comments on the circumstances by which Kroeber spawned Julian Steward?

WOLF: I don't know the facts that would provide an adequate answer to your question. Steward himself often talked about the North Berkeley gang to which he belonged, which included Jaime De Angulo, now known to most people by his delightful little book called *Indian Tales*. Those were Prohibition days, and they used to make gin in the bathtub. Lowie would occasionally come around, but Kroeber would not. Kroeber warned them about the iniquities of their conduct, professional and otherwise. That's one kind of light on their relationship. Another one is that Steward worked on that elements survey—in which he had to go out and collect thousands of elements. He hated it but he did it, and Kroeber forced him to do it. Steward was always falling sick, sometimes with the imaginary illness that he developed at just the right point. He tells of being sent out to the Hopi to collect endless elements while he was running a 104 fever. Kroeber said, "You get out there and you collect them"—more or less in those terms. I think their relationship was essentially that of tyrant to student. It was very productive. This was a person who had written, after all, *Cultural and Natural Areas of Native North America*, and he pointed Steward in that direction. Steward's interest was in trying to see how those relationships actually worked out in the case of the Paiute and Shoshoni band, and it must have fueled Steward's energy quotient considerably. I suspect a lot of it was addressed to Kroeber, who then never read it.

TOLSTOY: Wouldn't you call that an invitation?

WOLF: Yes, of a kind. I don't know what would have happened to Steward without Kroeber. Steward always maintained a very respectful attitude towards Kroeber. The one thing that comes out in the introduction he wrote to Kroeber's writings, which are fundamentally at odds with everything that Steward himself stood for, is a highly respectful attitude. There is a wish to recognize Kroeber for who he was. Kroeber, for his part, saw in Steward a promising but not very interesting student. At the meeting where Steward presented his paper on "Cultural Causality and Law," Kroeber reacted to it by not paying attention. That is a form of invitation, but of opposites.

DIAMOND: Kroeber's antagonism and opposition to White has been brought up here, but I have never really seen that except in a trivial methodological sense, not in terms of outcomes. That is to say, Kroeber is a superorganicist, an idealist ultimately, and White is a mechanical materialist; but they have in common that they lack dialectics, and at critical points you can exchange one method for the other and even one set of findings for the other. So that Kroeber is surprisingly reductive all of a sudden; and then you find White doing the same kind of thing, despite his emphasis upon the symbol and upon what he calls culturology. There are parallels of an inverted kind with Kroeber, but what they lacked was dialectics.

WOLF: I think that Carneiro put his finger on the essential difference; White was interested in explanation—in terms of economic, political, demographic, and other factors—mechanical though they may be on occasion. For instance, White's review of *Configuration of Culture Growth* says essentially: here we've got this book with all these curves and all these geniuses popping into existence at various points, and the book *never* really poses the question of why this should be so, and never refers to the economics of the time, never refers to the politics of the time. So that they could have had a good argument going. I do think that neither of them is dialectical; in fact, both are extraordinarily positivistic. Kroeber is, to my mind, natural-scientific positivism in anthropology driven to the end.

DIAMOND: My candidate for that award is White.

MERVYN MEGGITT: You made a point parenthetically that I think is revealing: the references to those aquatic metaphors—the river, the whirlpools, the eddies, the drops of water that can't be distinguished in the stream. Here we see in Kroeber what is essentially a vacuous hydrography. When you referred in passing to Lévi-Strauss, it seemed to me that there was a fairly good fit: Kroeber with his novels that write themselves, Lévi-Strauss with his myths that think themselves. It's true that Lévi-Strauss attempts to avoid vacuousness with a kind of Cartesian bearing of structures in the pineal gland. Nevertheless, I think that the analogy here is more than an analogy. I believe you are seeing here homologous products of a similar kind of cultural background.

WOLF: I have a feeling that the business about streams has a historical connection, and your comment then applies to that whole historical school. The German nature philosophers are continuously streaming and eddying. The ultimate referent is probably Mother Nature with her milk and effluvia, but they would hardly admit this.

Biographical Note

Eric R. Wolf was born in Vienna in 1923. As the child of an Austrian father and Russian mother, as a Jew in the decaying Habsburg state, and living from the age of ten in the contested Sudetenland in Czechoslovakia (where his father was the manager of a textile factory), cross-cultural comparisons and ethnic conflicts were endemic in his experience. Sent to England in 1938, his first discovery of social science came two years later in an alien's detention camp, where another internee, Norbert Elias, gave some lectures on sociology. Later that year Wolf came to the United States. He spent two years at Queens College, where he learned through an accidental choice of a course that the discipline he had already read in had a name. The war then intervened, and he joined the U.S. Army's Tenth Mountain Division, serving in northern Italy.

After the war, Wolf returned to Queens College, where he studied with Hortense Powdermaker, Joseph Bram, and Kimball Young. Upon his graduation in 1946, he used his G.I. Bill benefits to enroll in the anthropology department at Columbia. His main teachers were Benedict and Steward, the books of Karl Wittfogel and V. Gordon Childe, and several of his fellow students. Steward's Puerto Rico project gave him the opportunity for his first fieldwork (1948–49), and for the beginning of his long involvement in the study of peasants. After receiving his Ph.D. in 1951, Wolf went to the Bajío region of Mexico to study nation formation; his association there with Pedro Armillas and Angel Palerm brought him into contact with new trends in archeology.

From 1952 to 1955 Wolf was a research associate of Julian Steward's at the University of Illinois. His academic appointments thereafter took him to the University of Virginia (1955–58), Yale (1958–59), and Chicago (1959–61). In 1960 he returned to interests formed early in his life—peasants of the Alps and problems of ethnicity—and carried out a study of two ethnically contrastive villages in the South Tyrol. Returning from the field, he accepted an appointment at the University of Michigan (a telegram to Italy offered him "penure"). He remained at Michigan until 1971, when he joined the City University of New York as a Distinguished Professor.

Wolf's work, which has played an important role in the development of the anthropology of complex societies, combines concerns with history, political economy, and social relations viewed as embedded in larger political and cultural contexts. He is currently writing on the effects of European expansion on the peoples who make up the anthropologist's ethnographic record.

Paul Radin in 1958

Paul Radin 3
Stanley Diamond

The term "Boasians" conceals the substantial differences that existed among Boas' students and the divergences that many of them took from Boas' own views. Paul Radin, who received his doctorate under Boas in 1911, is a case in point. Putting into practice Boas' prescription to record aboriginal cultures through intensive work with informants in the native language, he produced one of the most exhaustive investigations of a tribe ever achieved; but his concentration on a single tribe differed from the ways most of his contemporaries carried out the Boasian program. Devoted, like Boas, to careful documentation of cultural facts, he was at the same time highly critical of the statistical methods and distributional studies of culture traits that Boas developed. Like Boas and Kroeber he defined his task as history, but he disagreed with both of them on what that meant. Above all, he stands out among anthropologists of his time for his concern with the individual. Like Boas and Sapir, but more than either, he saw a central task of ethnology as that of understanding the relations of individuals—"specific men and women"—to their cultures. He became the first anthropologist to publish an informant's autobiography (popularized as *Crashing Thunder*).

Radin's main interests were in the religion, mythology, and world view of primitives. In line with his belief that to do history required "intensive and continuous study of a particular tribe," his ethnographic work was devoted primarily to the study of a single culture, the Winnebago Indians, but he derived from this work a broad, philosophical view of the nature of primitive culture in general.

UNDERSTANDING PAUL RADIN, his position in the intellectual life of our time, and his role as an anthropologist in particular, requires more than the usual effort at social biography.[1] He was one of the last artisans of modern scholarship, at the threshold of the computer age. He was an immigrant, but more than an immigrant, for he linked two continents. His life expressed two civilizations, European and American, and one aboriginal culture in depth, the Winnebago. He was himself a Jew of the Enlightenment. He was born in Lodz, in Russian Poland, in 1883. He was brought to the United States in infancy, and he died in New York City in February 1959. But he never severed his European roots, and he could never abandon himself to the New World completely, except, ironically, for his association of nearly half a century with the Winnebago Indians of Wisconsin. The Old World solidarity of his family of origin, like that of so many immigrants, had shattered under the impact of the American experience, and neither his siblings, who predeceased him, nor their children, could have given or can give us now a coherent recounting of his life. He had no children, though he was married twice, the second time in his late forties. Even formal resumés of his career are sparse. They are usually inaccurate, because Radin rarely bothered to put himself on record in international directories of famous men. Since he moved from establishment to establishment, state to state, country to country, and job to job, there was very little institutional continuity to trace. Only his work reflects the inner unity of his life.[2]

The host of friends he left behind, from Sweden to Mexico, knew him only in phases and primarily as a teacher, yet his gift for spontaneous intimacy made each friend feel that he shared a particular secret about Paul which was best left unspoken, and that may have been true. But the notoriety that this Chinese vagabond of a scholar was bound to generate turned him into a figure both widely known and mysterious, even impenetrable in certain ways; that is to say, a legend. If, as Valéry pointed out, no one has ever gotten to the bottom of a word, no one ever sounded the depths of Paul, because Paul was preeminently a man of words in the most involved sense of that term. He was deceptively transparent; he was a kind of a poet in that respect. Almost without exception, his friends and acquaintances, whether celebrated or not, viewed him with the special affection reserved for the pure in heart or for a child or scamp or free spirit, or for the innocent and not-so-innocent trickster. Paul Radin was an authentically distinguished person. He was no mere schoolman, scribe, or high priest of some establishment of learning, and he was more than the sum of the influences that helped to shape him.

The personal and social background against which he constructed his life was complex. He was the offspring of a German-Russian Jewish family that had become secularized in the mode of the *Haskalah*, the Jewish strand in the Western European Enlightenment which had diffused from a German center to the restive youth of ghetto and pale, carrying with it the anticlerical, antifeudal, experimental and rationalist faith of the French Encyclopedists. The transformation of Orthodox Judaism, which had among its objectives the replacement of Yiddish—the voice of the ghetto—by Hebrew as a literary and secular tongue, and the adoption of modern European languages along with the modification of Judaism, was reflected in the fact that Radin's father was a rabbi of the Reform movement, a Hebrew scholar, and a linguist. Herman Radin, who was Paul's oldest brother, became a New York physician, and

Max Radin, next in line, was a distinguished legal scholar. These secular professions, which refocused the traditional Jewish concern with ritual learning but did not abandon learning as a ritual, were ideologically correlated with a humane and skeptical liberalism. But such skepticism and rationalism were largely reactive, a protest against the cramping social-intellectual orthodoxy of the patriarchal and theocratic past. Yet the passion for scholarship, the commitment to human realization in the world, and in Paul's case, the fascinated concern with religion and ethics, maintained a distinctively Jewish cast. Moreover, Radin's intellectual cosmopolitanism, his radicalism, his conception of learning as a moral enterprise, and his capacity to live almost exclusively the life of the mind, thereby depending upon a legion of friends for a variety of services, represent further elements that characterize the Jewish scholar *en passage* from the traditional milieu to the modern industrial and urban world.

Radin received an elite education at the College of the City of New York, entering as a subfreshman and pursuing a five-year course. He graduated in 1902, at the age of nineteen, and then began a "flirtation with zoology," as he called it, at Columbia. After completing a thesis on the embryology of sharks, he became restive with the limitations of natural science and was attracted in his second year at Columbia by James Harvey Robinson, who was a skeptical and rationalist historian. But it wasn't until 1907 in Munich, where he had gone to study the zoology of fish and substituted work in physical anthropology under Ranke, the noted anthropologist, that Radin began to consider anthropology as a career. The following year he made the decision final. Studies at the University of Berlin under Karl von den Steinen, Eduard Seler, and Paul Ehrenreich (whose acceptance of Andrew Lang's theory of primitive monotheism influenced Radin's later work) helped draw Paul in the direction of anthropology.

Radin had an early excursion into material culture, working for a month or so at the museum in Prague and writing his first paper on the technique of net-working among the South American Indians, but the interest was temperamentally alien to him and quickly abandoned. He returned to Columbia under the tutelage of Robinson, and he took a minor in history while majoring in anthropology under Boas, receiving his Ph.D. in 1911. Unlike his contemporaries, then, Radin was not initially drawn to anthropology by Boas but first pursued his subject in Europe; and before he became an ethnologist, he was trained in historiography and had reflected upon the problems of history. Despite the fact that Radin never labored in the Boasian vineyards, going forth early and alone into the world (as Lewis Mumford recalled) and without the master's blessing, it was probably the combined effect of Robinson's skeptical humanism and Boas' empirical insistence upon the indivisible potential of primitive and civilized mentalities that originally led Radin to question all notions of primitive inferiority.

He soon settled into a permanent preoccupation with the *Weltanschauung* of primitive peoples. His first field trip to the Winnebago was undertaken in 1908. Subsequent monographs and articles on almost every aspect of their lives were to develop into one of the monuments of American anthropology. This work includes ten substantial books, among them a general account of Winnebago culture (1923), the informant's autobiography *Crashing Thunder* (1920), and several studies of mythology.

But Radin was also a student of contemporary Western civilization and had been even before he became a professional anthropologist. As Cora DuBois relates, James Harvey Robinson grilled him relentlessly in 1910 during his doctoral orals at Columbia on medieval education and the order of argument in Saint Augustine. Anthropologists were expected to be grounded in their own culture before being considered fit for the study of another. But this grounding was in Radin's view the basis for an understanding of his own alienation from the prevailing values, without which "the task of understanding the primitive could not be accomplished." His alienation, wedded to his self-knowledge and his knowledge of his culture of origin, freed him from any presuppositions governed by ad hoc acceptance of Western values, or equally important, by merely blind and personal disaffection from them. He emerges then as a kind of self-liberated intellect, a shaman who cured himself. He was his own patient throughout his life in that respect, an anthropologist who recognized that he must be engaged in a lifelong dialogue with his own culture. This assumption was more fully appreciated by European than American intellectuals, whether anthropologists or not, who were perhaps less skilled than the Americans in the art of critical accommodation to society. Indeed, Radin is celebrated in Europe as an intellectual *and* an anthropologist. He lectured at Cambridge under Rivers from 1920 to 1925, later at the four major Swedish universities, and at the Eranos Conference at Ascona in 1949. In 1952 he was recalled to Cambridge, and he lectured subsequently at Oxford, Manchester, and finally at Jung's institute in Zurich.

Radin, who remained a cheerful exile in his own society to the end, found a way of life of studying primitive peoples that precluded opportunistic or unreflective commitment to the major institutions of his own time and place. He migrated from coast to coast—as between the United States and Europe—during his half-century as a professional anthropologist. But he was never at a loss for a job. Among other places, he taught at Berkeley, Fisk University, the University of Chicago, Kenyon College, and finally Brandeis. In the words of Julian Steward, "his charm . . . got him about every job in Anthropology in the country." During the early Depression years, when many of his colleagues and students were unemployed, he managed to find support for anthropology from government agencies hitherto unconcerned with such efforts. He undertook an exhaustive survey of ethnic minorities, the first of its kind, in the San Franciso Bay area for the W.P.A. in 1935. Bibliophile, bibliographer (and quondam book thief), he compiled a catalogue of over 1,000 pages on Mexican literary and historical materials at the Sutro Library in 1939. Moreover, a variety of foundations over the years pressed modest but sustaining funds into Radin's hands, permitting him a continuum of work. Radin had as lively a talent for attracting personal angels as he did for alienating bureaucrats. Mary Mellon of the Bollingen Foundation, Leonard Althwaite of the Rockefeller Foundation, and Paul Fejos of the Wenner-Gren Foundation were among those who extended material and moral support during critical periods.

Radin was not without administrative pretentions. He organized and served as secretary of the Southwestern Ethnological Society and spent a year in a government agency, at the Bureau of American Ethnology. Toward the end of his life, he served as arbiter of grants in anthropology for the Bollingen Foundation. His accomplished friends, as usual, were beneficiaries.

Radin's ability to create associations beyond the limits of the anthropological profession was an index of his cultivation. Anthropology was never really a career for Radin. It was never a specialized discipline; it was a way of life. If he had no permanent home anywhere, he was at home everywhere. His personal and professional lives were of one piece; that is to say, he had style. Friends and antagonists alike never questioned the integrity of his pursuit. Like a hunter after game, he followed the human spirit in its manifold shapes throughout history and across cultures, bent upon discovering the conditions for its most vigorous existence, unappalled by whatever he found, always alert to the universal implications of a particular cultural form. He had no patience with sectarian jargon or other contrivances that had the effect of turning the study of man into an academic mystery, and he never deflected his concern from the great recurring troubling themes in human history. Typically, in concluding *Method and Theory of Ethnology*, he called for renewed effort in determining basic human nature. "That the culture pattern hides this knowledge from us forever," he wrote, "is a counsel of despair" (1933a:267). Radin believed in "the existence of universal dimensions of human psychology which exist outside the framework of history." It was grasping these, he believed, that would then make it possible to distinguish the primitive from the civilized with more sophistication. This was related to

Feuerbach's—and to a degree Marx's—notion of a species-being or human essence, the normative sense of a human potential; that is what he was getting to.

Although, as his professional history shows, he had a sure instinct for survival, Radin never came to terms with modern techniques. He never learned how to use a typewriter, and he laboriously wrote out his voluminous notes and manuscripts in so medieval and minute a hand that a magnifying glass was sometime necessary to decipher the script. A contemporary transformation of an eighteenth-century Hasidic rabbi, Radin commanded his environment by the power of his expression, by the variety and immediacy of his insights, by his verve and spiritual generosity. The more practical arrangement of things for his own convenience he left to others. As an intimate from his Berkeley period wrote, he was the least mechanically talented man imaginable. I often wondered how he survived in bachelorhood without a roommate or some other attendant. He could not or would not learn to drive a car, and therefore spent hours in streetcars. He could not use a screwdriver or hammer for minor household repairs, and he scarcely knew how to turn on a gas range. Thus, he would rail against leaking faucets in his apartment and other newfangled cultural elements that he could not manage or subdue.

For all of his ceaseless traffic with colleagues and students, with whom he would spontaneously set up his Hasidic court, most memorably outside the classroom, Radin remained—as Mark Van Doren has noted—an essentially lonely person. One is tempted to speculate in this connection on the role of an adored and catered-to youngest son in a transitional Jewish family, and on the isolation that threatens those who have learned to depend upon others for the practical conduct of their lives. Paul did not mind being disliked, but he subtly insisted upon love in return for the gift of his being to the world—and he was usually loved, for as a natural teacher he found himself only in giving himself.

He was a creator and formulator of meaning. Whatever the personal background of his predisposition, he was a thinker, a "poet-thinker," a "thinker-artist," a "priest-thinker," designations that he himself used to describe one of his two contrasting historical temperamental types—first in *Primitive Man as Philosopher* (1927), then in *Primitive Religion* (1937) and in subsequent works. He was decidedly not a man of action, not a layman. He could live only in a cerebral blaze of reality. The degree to which his own commitment to the intellectual life drove him to see and perhaps to exaggerate the culture- and class-determined dichotomy between action and thought that others had also expressed (if not in precisely the same terms) as a universal temperamental division, remained a difficult question. (I refer to William James, Robert Lowie, Jung, and others, who had made this distinction before Radin had.) At least Radin's background in learning sensitized him to analogous processes elsewhere. Late in life, Radin adopted the position that these two contrasting temperaments can and usually do, in reality, complexly coexist in the same person. Therefore, in retrospect, he seems to have invented ideal types, despite his antipathy to such abstract efforts. Although a student of Greek civilization capable of pursuing research in the classical language, Radin was not attracted to the notion of the Aristotelian mean, either as a description of human temperament or as a guide to behavior.

Yet the intensity of his intellectual commitment never moved him to glorify the position of intellectuals, particularly since the rise of civilization. I have never met a man who was more suspicious of intellectuals and who was himself more of an intellectual. He regarded them as dependent upon the official academy, which was in turn linked to the ruling establishment; along with Boas in this respect, he therefore viewed them as bound by convention and, for the most part, incapable of pursuing interests other than their own—they knew which side their bread was buttered on. He was constantly aware of the linked exploitative and creative roles of intellectuals of the kind he called "priest-thinkers." He regarded them as the inventors of religious systems, thereby reflecting their own profound need to create a coherent universe of meaning, while catering to the intermittent needs of their "layman followers." He imagined that the priest-thinkers, or shamans, or medicine men, were the original formulators of the primitive monotheistic synthesis—a later social convention in Judeo-Christian-Islamic civilization, but actually as a "pure" faith as common, or uncommon, among primitive peoples as among ourselves. If the drives of the priest-thinkers were "neurotic" and their hunger "economic," this did not for Radin inevitably throw the significance of their insights into question. It is important to understand that; Radin was not a reductive thinker. But the exploitative reality and potential of civilized intellectuals troubled him all his life.

However personal and obscure the origins of this feeling may have been, it gave him good reason to deny identification with any bureaucracy except on his own idiosyncratic terms. It was hard to believe that he ever made a formal reply to a formal memorandum. His informality with students and hostility to administration, his penchant for teaching in experimental environments, such as Black Mountain College and Fisk University (where he collected still unpublished life histories of former slaves and accounts of Black conversion experiences), his flexible arrangements at Kenyon College, and his fruitful and footloose periods of residence and work in Europe attest to his ambivalence about the social role of the intellectual. He was in the Socratic tradition himself, or tried to be. That is, the public aspects of the pursuit of knowledge meant for him extended exchanges in the marketplace, not isolation within the Platonic academy.

This sensitive and refined urban intellectual was at home in the cognitive worlds of primitive peoples, which seemed more real to him in basic respects than our rationalizing civilization. He quotes with approval the words of an old Eskimo to Knut Rasmussen:

Our narratives deal with the experiences of man, and these experiences are not always pleasant or pretty, but it is not proper to change our stories to make them more acceptable to our ears, that is if we wish to tell the truth. Words must be the echoes of what has happened, and cannot be made to conform to the mood and the taste of the listener.

Or, in Radin's own words, "If one thing can be said to hold true for primitive civilizations everywhere, it is the ruthless realism and objectivity with which man has been analyzed there." But Radin did not believe, any more than Rousseau (whose work was not a direct influence on him) in a "return to the primitive." Neither one entertained the notion of an idealized or noble savage (Diderot's notion, not Rousseau's). Quite the contrary, Radin's aim was to reveal the whole gamut of human possibilities, expressed in the daily lives of primitive peoples, as the foundation for a more critical evaluation of civilization. The primitive experience was in Radin's view an essential part of our historical consciousness, and it was also an index to the universal psychic character and needs of the species.

In *Primitive Man as Philosopher* (1927), he dismissed theories about the automatism of primitive life as being merely projective of an increasingly routinized modern condition. One concludes from the totality of Radin's work that he found primitive mentality to differ in degree but not in kind from its civilized counterpart. He believed that despite the variety of cultural forms involved, primitive peoples respond to the major challenges of life in sophisticated, profound, and—to a civilized person endowed with self-knowledge—understandable ways. That is, if we are human, he felt that they were quintessentially human. Therefore, Radin rejected all theoreticians who stigmatized or seemed to stigmatize primitives as being incapable of abstraction (technically defined), as reflexive participants in an inchoate entity, as linguistically inadequate, or as lacking individuality. Above all, Radin never merely analyzed the lives of people called primitives; by some alchemy of insight he transmuted himself, time and again, into their spokesman. In his lifelong work on the trickster, for example, he emphasized the cosmic richness of the imagery, the ambivalence of the human impulse toward creation and destruction symbolized in the dual image of the deity, and the Sisyphyean struggle, expressed in trickster mythology, to create and consequently to rescue meaning from the chaos of sensory impressions, biological needs and appetites, enigmas of personal, social, and cosmic origins, and from death.

Radin's elaboration of the dual conception of the deity, and therefore of humanity and of the cosmos, had descended from Andrew Lang and had been anticipated in the work of Paul Ehrenreich, Franz Boas, Alfred Kroeber, and Roland B. Dixon. Indeed, both the Americanists and the German Historical School had been preoccupied with that issue. However, Radin, who was explicitly opposed to Catholic apologetics, was to explore the nature of god (or the nature of the views of god) among primitive peoples more fully than any other American ethnologist. These are universal human issues, but Radin saw them as central to the social and ritual life of primitive peoples. It is this question of the relative weight given to certain themes among primitive peoples, in comparison with ourselves, that led Radin to believe that although basic human nature is indivisible, it is more visible among primitive peoples. In dealing with African folktales, for example, Radin interpreted a Ba'ila story about a woman who went in search of god, which is parallel in theme to the Book of Job but more realistic in its climax. In the end the old woman dies because she is morally unaware, that is, she refuses to accept her existential burdens as part of the common lot of humanity.

Primitive life was then for Radin closer in its structure and ideology to the roots of comedy and tragedy—that is, what we would dichotomize and name as comedy and tragedy. It was precisely this conception of aboriginal society as the arena of a universal human drama, based on the quest for meaning and identity, and expressed in primitive rituals, that made his work and friendship—more than that of his contemporaries—memorable to a diverse group of writers, artists, and philosophers. Among them were Mark Van Doren, who wrote the foreword to *The Road of Life and Death* (1945), Lewis Mumford, C. G. Jung (who profited from Radin's knowledge of myths and folktales and who intrigued Radin because of his respect for primitive experience, but with whose theoretical conclusions Radin finally disagreed), Alan Tate, John Crowe Ransom, John Dewey (who in his foreword to *Primitive Man as*

Philosopher held that Radin's conception of a temperamental rather than scholastic origin of classic themes in philosophy was of revolutionary importance for the history of ideas), Huntington Cairns, Mabel Dodge Luhan, and others. Radin's anonymous translation of Hans Vaihinger's *Philosophy of As If*, and his translation of record of Alfred Adler's *The Practice and Theory of Individual Psychology* in 1925, among other distinguished works, further commended him to a larger circle than that of professional anthropology.

In the broader intellectual current of his time, Radin's work had a dual significance. He made the study of primitive perception intrinsically meaningful and intellectually worthwhile. Therefore, in Van Doren's words, "if we are without pride, we may learn something we had not previously known about the meaning of life on earth" (1945:xiv). Moreover, Radin helped clarify for us the sources of our discontent with our own culture, for he conceived, it has been said, the Western world as a conquest civilization. It appeared to him frequently that the values of social science itself were only reflections of the dominant social and economic currents peculiar to the civilization in which they existed. To the extent that this was the case, he felt that studies of primitive life continually face the risk of reflecting ourselves and the established framework of Western thought more than the dimensions of primitive society.

Radin was both a marginal man and profoundly radical, but his radicalism lay in the general historical meaning of his work, not in elaborated, or even specific political formulations or tactics. That meaning derives from his general conception of primitive society. This is clearly delineated in *The World of Primitive Man* (1953), which is among the more effective full-length syntheses that have thus far been attempted. There he writes, "If one were asked to state briefly and succinctly the outstanding positive features"—and he emphasized *positive features*—"of aboriginal civilizations [by which he meant cultures], I for one would have no hesitation in answering that there are three;" he then specifies respect for the person, a remarkable degree of social and political integration, and the existence of an irreducible minimum of socioeconomic survival which all human beings are under ordinary conditions guaranteed and which transcend all other conflicts and group interests. He then goes on to synthesize primitive economic and social structure, philosophy, religion, and psychology. The result is no less than an implicit, inductive, historical, and normative theory of human nature, or species-being.

Radin would have been shy of so sweeping an evaluation of his work, since he was theoretically grounded in the careful explication of specific cultures and persons. Nonetheless, his perspective on the primitive has an obvious forerunner in the Morgan-Marx notion of primitive communism. There is also a link to Robert Redfield and to the folk-urban polarity theorists. But Radin's work is richer, more substantive, and more historically realistic. Redfield, for example, describes primitive society in general terms; he does not succeed in establishing a functional model synthesizing the range of behavior in which actual persons engage. Another of the significant differences from Redfield is worth remarking. Redfield imagined, along with Kroeber, that moral consciousness has expanded with civilization. This is the confusion of the *is* with the *ought*. Radin, on the other hand, was at great pains to establish a remarkably subtle spectrum of moral insight as a primitive characteristic, generic, in fact, to the structures of primitive societies. In such areas he was skeptical of the idea of progress (although he understood the general dynamics of the evolution of civilization well enough and had outlined this in a very long and as yet unpublished manuscript). This attitude, together with his scrupulousness as a scholar, also accounts for his refusal to politicize his work programmatically. However, as a spokesman for native and minority peoples, he wrote widely for popular journals, and he also dissected the racial myth, in a book by that name (1934) and in a number of articles.

His radicalism, then, was rooted in his respect for the aboriginal human potentiality, which he insisted was already formed even among the most primitive of those societies that he held to be the proper subject of ethnology. He concludes

The World of Primitive Man by stating, "Perhaps it is fitting that primitive man, here in the guise of an Eskimo hunter, should teach us this: nature is great, but man is greater still" (1953:360).

Despite the fact that Radin refused to anchor himself to the anthropological establishment, his larger impact on the life of his time is a function of his dedication and accomplishment as an anthropologist. He never stopped writing, and although his range did not match that of Boas, who played the orthodox rabbi of the *shul* to Radin's rebellious Hasid, his work was more integrated than that of Boas and more extensive than that of any of his contemporaries, with the exception of Kroeber. But Radin achieved more depth in his range than did the latter. A glance at Radin's publications, some 200, reveals—in addition to the interests for which he is best known—formal linguistic, archeological, and social-structural material (all a primary function of his concern with the Winnebago), and unique and exhaustive bibliographical collections.

Radin's concern with the Winnebago forms the main thread of his life's work. From the time of his initial contact with them, he turned himself into an instrument of historical reportage. For Radin, this was a skilled, highly technical vocation. He always remained skeptical of the more romantic claims of participant observation, which—substituting a cheaply won rapport for the hard work of mastering the native idiom—too often resulted in what he called a pretentious impressionism. He wrote, "These defects could possibly be obviated if the investigator became a member of the tribe. This is generally out of the question." It would mean spending a good portion of one's life in a primitive community, and that no well-qualified ethnologist that he knew of was prepared to do, even were funds available for the purpose. (Frank Cushing was a man of whom he spoke with affection, because Cushing in fact became a Zuni priest and never wrote as much as he could have about these people. He chose a silence that spoke louder than words, as Radin contended.)

For Radin the question was never one of going native, but of understanding the native in oneself, while maintaining one's personal and social identity.[3] Learning well from Boas despite their temperamental antinomy, Radin had concluded earlier that only prologed association with specific primitive persons, intimate work with native informants in their own language, and faithful transcription and analysis of the native texts could produce reliable ethnographic and theoretical results. Thus he was always suspicious, as he states in *The Method and Theory of Ethnology* (1933a), of what he judged to be easily won insights into the most intimate patterns of native behavior, in the absence of familiarity with the language, long-term fieldwork, and grounding in the lives of specific individuals—as distinct from the generalized person fleshed out from an ethnological skeleton whom the ethnologist then endows with uniqueness. He was opposed, in short, to the merely abstract, methodological individual, the typical member of the particular culture that is deduced from the information that the anthropologist gathers.

For Radin, history was experience, and history could be more fully reflected, more complete, among primitive peoples in primitive cultures than among class-divided, occupationally compartmentalized, state-organized societies such as ours, wherein experience is dissociated and fragmented. In primitive societies, he believed, people were more likely to emerge in their natural variety, so to speak. This is one of the reasons that he emphasized basic temperamental distinctions in a nonpejorative way. He didn't think that such distinctions, or the whole variety of distinctions of which we are genetically capable, could emerge in modern society as we know it—modern capitalist or capitalist patterned class-divided society—because of the reduction of persons to social roles. He also believed, along with Boas, that only the native person could reflect his culture, and that—and here he was unique—only the ensemble of these individual reflections could be defined as history. To understand what he meant by that, one has to appreciate that the primitive person is in a situation in which his own society is largely transparent to him (as Marx might have said), whereas in our situation, our "complex," alienating society is *not* transparent to us but stands over and above us as an impenetrable reification. To Radin the experience of multifunctioning human beings in a primitive society was tantamount to the history of that society. History, in short, was not mere chronology, or an abstracted sequence of technological events, or some other aspect of the social whole, but the totality of human experience in the given culture, a totality which was ever present and which could be grasped by each fully engaged participant, although from personally distinctive, if complementary, perspectives. The role of the ethnologist was therefore that of a midwife, and all European interpretations of indigenous cultures were false if they were not inherent in the narratives of native individuals.

The relentless honesty of this view, whether one agrees or not, can hardly be denied, for what Radin meant was that anthropology acting as other than midwife presents a European conception of the past and does so for Europe's sake. The purpose might be comparative, for example, illuminating some aspect of modern civilization, but too often the function—if not the conscious purpose—of anthropology has been the rationalization of the imperial mission in one way or another; of this Radin was convinced, although he did not often use rhetorical language. For the problem, Radin wrote, resolves itself into finding the native. To this search he devoted a lifetime, and by 1920 he had published the autobiography of a Winnebago Indian, thus pioneering the discovery of the primitive as a *person* in American ethnology. Radin did ask questions of the data; he asked abstract questions and came up with answers. He did not depend only upon what informants said about their particular societies. However, the purpose of the kinds of questions he asked was almost always a critique of our civilization—that was his fundamental enterprise.

Radin's command of the Winnebago language and his respect for their unwritten literature have had few parallels in the history of ethnographic investigation. As Dell Hymes has noted, "Boas had no peer in American anthropology and in philological work except his students, Sapir and Radin" (1965:334). Hymes says that for Radin linguistics was a means to the ends of ethnography and aesthetic appreciation; as to the latter, it is possible to appraise him as a literary historian and exegete on oral literature in the grand tradition. Apart from voluminous Winnebago texts—many of which remain unpublished—and other raw materials in the archives of the American Philosophical Society, Radin authored a series of Wappo (1924), Huave (1929a), and Mixe (1933b) texts; a grammar of Wappo (1929b); notes on Tlappanecan (1933c); and a sketch of Zapotec (1930). He had been a joint Harvard-Columbia fellow at the International School of American Archeology and Ethnology in Mexico in 1912–13. He was also concerned with historical linguistics, publishing a classification of the languages of Mexico (1944) and carrying through a decade-long analysis of Patwin, 1930 to 1940. Most importantly, in one of his early papers called *The Genetic Relationship of the North American Languages* (1919), he argued for their essential continental unity. Sapir, ironically enough, at that time criticized this opinion, pointing out certain technical errors; yet many years later Sapir's distinguished student Morris Swadesh, in a revolutionary effort, developed conceptions that were parallel to those of Radin's 1919 paper. It deserves note that Radin's concern with the languages of primitive peoples was based, as was his inquiry into their cultures, on a thorough knowledge of his own civilization. He was at ease in German, French, Spanish, Latin, and Greek.

By the time Radin matriculated at Columbia, Alfred Kroeber and Clark Wissler had graduated. His older colleagues included Robert Lowie and Edward Sapir. His agemates were Frank Speck, Alexander Goldenweiser, and Ruth Benedict. Lowie and Sapir remained his closest friends in the profession. Lowie's and Radin's families had been intimate in the youth of both men, and Radin had spent four years (1913 to 1917) with Sapir in the geological survey of Canada, studying the Ojibwa (1913). But his deep respect for Lowie and Sapir and for Boas, whom he regarded as one of the seminal personalities of the century, did not restrain him from a cogent attack on the Boas circle along its entire circumference. In *Method and Theory of Ethnology* in 1933 (which apart from Lowie's conventional *His-*

tory of Ethnological Theory, published four years later, was the only systematic excursus into ethnological theory written by an American until more than a generation later), Radin assimilated ethnology to history and rejected the presuppositions of most of the Boasians. Partly as a result of his early training with Robinson and Ranke, he chastised Boas' quantitative and distributional approach to culture data as the fundamental error of the American school, an error which in Radin's view leads to overgeneralized, external, and patchwork histories of traits, in abstractly deduced time perspectives, rather than to specific histories of societies as experienced and created by their members. As Father Wilhelm Schmidt claimed, despite the demurrers of the Americanists, the general *methods* of the Boas group—as distinct from its premises and its conclusions—were not so different from that of the German Historical School. Radin always felt rather wistfully that there was a contradiction between this overall character of the Americanists and Boas' insistence on prolonged fieldwork and textual efforts in particular societies. After all, Boas as a grand—if necessarily, and thankfully, inconsistent—mentor, had stated as early as 1888 "that ethnology deals with the history of primitive societies."

Radin's reciprocated antipathy to Kroeber is symbolic of his alienation from the major trends of his time. The Kroeber-Radin polarity was evident in the total career of each scholar. Kroeber entered the institutional world early at the University of California. He was perhaps the single most powerful administrator in the history of anthropology. He labored to build a school and worked with teams of graduate students. He was a compiler and classifier of endless facts and quotes, and a power on the job market. He was a man of formal probity and bearing, a sort of Confucius to Radin's Lao Tsu, and the two personalities struck sparks against each other. Intellectually, Kroeber's notion of the superorganic and his consequent lack of interest in the person in history, his sweeping efforts to classify whole civilizations by configurations of traits and qualities, and the eclectic mix of the intuitive and the quantitative in his methods were opposed to Radin's approach to

anthropology. Moreover, Kroeber's insistence—in agreement
with Boas, despite other disagreements—that ethnology was a
natural science whose subject matter was composed of
discrete, isolable, and objectively determinable elements
which could be traced and categorized on their own terms, did
violence to Radin's focus on the person as the index and
measure of culture. Kroeber's approach violated his perception
that to probe deeply enough into particular forms was to reveal
universal meanings. Kroeber's view also abused Radin's sense
of history as the human agent, as the agency for revealing the
nature of humanity (including those aspects that he believed
existed outside the framework of history) and the necessary
conditions for human fulfillment. In short, Radin believed that
in the deepest ethnological sense (not in the ethical sense),
Kroeber's work lacked historical integrity. That summarized
his critique of American ethnology in general.

As an original, Radin fostered no formal genealogy of
students. He affected the lives of countless friends and
colleagues, but he never intruded on personalities. When in the
last years of his life contributions were invited to his
Festschrift, *Culture in History* (Diamond 1960), fifty-two
papers were submitted and published. The authors ranged
form Leslie White—who, astonishingly, wrote a very sympathetic paper on the (of course, inevitably irrelevant) world
view of the Keresan pueblo—to ten European scholars. Paul
died several months before the appearance of the book. Fortunately, he was aware that it was being prepared, and characteristically, he tried to take an active part in its preparation.
His final academic position was as professor of anthropology
and then, at the age of seventy-five, chairman of the graduate
department at Brandeis University, to which we called him
from four years of residence and work at Lugano. At Brandeis,
he was to join, besides myself, Robert Manners and Alexander
Lesser (who was appointed about the same time). Coming to
Brandeis, a relative stranger to the new, emerging American
scene, Paul felt and was led to feel that he had found a
permanent home, but that more recent version of the bureau-
cratization of American learning was even less compatible

than earlier ones, and proved more than he could bear. His heart had faltered for many years, and he finally died, full of plans and laughter, several days after a seizure that overtook him during a professional lecture in New York City. It was my misfortune that I was engaged in fieldwork in Nigeria at the time of his death.

There are those of us who believe that the passage of time will establish him as possessed of one of the finest sensibilities among that small band of distinguished intellectuals who defined the classic period of American anthropology.

Discussion

ALEXANDER LESSER: If I followed you, at one point you said that Radin was committed to textual studies and the analysis of peoples by way of their own languages, and at another point you said that he was critical of that approach and of the long time required to accomplish it. On the one hand, you emphasized that he *was* committed to it; on the other hand, you emphasized that he was *against* it. For myself, I find that typical of Radin, the taking of positions both ways.

DIAMOND: I don't think it is inconsistent in the pejorative sense. He spent fifty years working with the Winnebago. Almost everything that he did, all of his theoretical work, all of his conclusions, came from specific ethnographic work. He was among the first, perhaps *the* first in American ethnology, to publish a substantial autobiography of a native American. His textual work arose from weeks, months, years with informants. He could not become a Winnebago; but he worked with informants in the Winnebago language over long periods of time, and he spoke Winnebago fluently. He would translate the material and publish it. That was as close as one could humanly get to the necessity, as he viewed it, of representing the people's own history of their own society.

LESSER: When I visited the Winnebago in 1928, which wasn't too long after his work with them, the culture was in the kind of breakdown that was happening among many American Indian groups. Those of Radin's informants that I saw, I saw in the city and not anywhere else. I would say, then, that even at the time he visited them, he was engaged in what used to be called "getting back to the native condition," rather than seeing something that was going on at the time. It seems to me very doubtful that there was a viable Winnebago culture at the time he was there, any more than there were viable cultures for most other American ethnologists.

DIAMOND: That is correct. Yet most other important American ethnologists, Lowie, Kroeber, and Boas among others, also wrote and generalized about *primitive* cultures, trying to reflect the "native condition." They did this without dissimulation of the actual historical circumstances of their fieldwork. The point is that all so-called ethnological descriptions are constitutions of reality, constructions—there is no such thing as an ultimately accurate, final description of the positivistic "truth" of any society.

LESSER: But what Radin found was a nonviable survival of Winnebago—the effects of contact with non-Winnebagos. How he would get from that to some in-depth feeling of primitive life, I am not sure. Yet you make that the crux of his intellectual understanding. From my own experiences of working with some items of his, I know that he was pretty sloppy about what he put down about the Winnebago, for instance about kinship. That may not disturb you. You have created a beautiful picture of all the best things that could be said about Radin. But I don't know any evidence, for instance, that he ever discussed the idea of anthropology as a phase of the conquering West, which is a newly current view. It's a pretty good understanding that we've reached recently, that a great deal of anthropology has to be seen in the light of the imperialist era and the control of all peoples of the world.

DIAMOND: This isn't the place to evaluate Radin's work on

Winnebago kinship. But I don't think the idea about anthropology and imperialism is new. It has been latent for about 250 years, in my judgment, from our very origins in Montaigne through Rousseau, Marx and others. And Radin was more aware of these matters than any scholar of his time, including Boas. His whole definition of history runs counter to any Western bias. Only a radical anti-imperialist mind could have conceived *The World of Primitive Man.* At the same time, Radin has got to be seen against the background of his time—and in the light of his choice of language and subject. One might even say that his antipositivistic struggle with Boas, Kroeber, etc. was an aspect of his profound emancipatory consciousness.

In any event, I can hardly fault Radin for not using the precise emancipatory language of my generation. After all, who did in his generation or the one that succeeded it? But his convictions are clear in his work.

LESSER: Latent and current are two different things.

DIAMOND: What you say about the baseline of primitive existence is, of course, true; but it is far more complex than that. You can't go out positivistically and find a case which represents all of the various characteristics that we impute to primitive society. That is a result of the kinds of questions we ask, and a result of our subsequent syntheses. When I say Radin was steeped in Winnebago culture and in the Winnebago language, I do not mean to imply that he was *confined* to the Winnebago, no more than Boas was to the Kwakiutl. He also did work on African cultures, particularly through their literature, their poetry, their mythology, that is, their oral traditions (transmuting, I suppose, his Winnebago experience in this respect). Oral traditions reflect the experiences of people, and working with them was one of the wasy in which Radin began to develop a synthetic model, or quintessential notion, of what primitive society was about. We have been doing this in anthropology for a long time, in the absence of any positivistically arrived-at ethnographic present. This is one of the challenges—and at the same time one of the handicaps—of the profession, and is also, as I have indicated, a general historiographical problem.

We are all in quest of the same thing; each anthropologist using his or her own set of questions to discover something about the nature of man on earth, with reference to his or her own condition. The most significant results can be shown to converge, or reinforce each other. But there is no such thing as a perfectly objective portrait of a primitive society. Radin did not presume an ethnological present that was simultaneously an ethnological past; he was fully aware of the paradox. But he thought that by looking at these societies and getting a sense of a radically different way of life, he was casting light upon his own. The distinctions which he uncovered were significant and subtle and they justify the primitive-civilized dichotomy. That was all he ever pretended to do. It was, I think, enough.

LESSER: The question you have raised about getting at the primitive is not only sound, but is so sound that I would say that what anthropology was and *is* trying to do when it does that—and what Radin was trying to do—is impossible. If anthropology rests on the achievement of the impossible, it rests on nothing. There is no such thing, as you say, as the purely primitive, as the pristine primitive. But Radin did what other anthropologists did, which is not correct: to somehow derive what the primitive was all about from his imagination, from his literary and poetic feeling, rather than from any data that he could bring to bear.

DIAMOND: I think that you misconstrue that nature of "data." The myths, legends, oral traditions of primitive peoples represent data; and he spent a lifetime collecting that kind of information. But anthropology doesn't rest there. A merely abstract social science is an impossible enterprise. It is and must be a dialectical enterprise; it involves both what we formulate and what we do in relation to what we formulate, which in turn shapes our formulations. The most conscious, most highly developed dialectic is, in my judgment, revolutionary; its cutting edge is politics.

Now there is a powerful political undercurrent in Radin's work. Radin is always bearing in mind the existence of societies which had exploitative class and state apparatuses; that is the comparative basis of his work on primitive society. He was fully aware of the problems of our own society and he wrote quite a bit about them, particularly with reference to racism.

LESSER: One more thing about Radin. He spoke regularly, repetitively, about the necessity of working from textual materials and understanding the native language. But his *Primitive Man as Philosopher* from beginning to end is based upon translations that he accepted from other people, of languages he knew nothing about. The book opens with translations of Eskimo poems, and he accepts the translated versions as a basis for interpreting the thought of the Eskimo. This is the exact thing that had been done before linguistic anthropology. I don't say that his imagination and his grasp of the potential of primitive thinking was unsound; I do say that he never proved his view.

DIAMOND: I don't know what you would demand of the man. He knew as many languages as anybody I ever met. About the Eskimo: he depended upon sources that were ethnographically "reliable;" he depended upon Knut Rasmussen, for example. It's true he didn't know any African languages, either, and he had to depend upon translations, both in working with informants and in using the ethnographic literature. But who hasn't—in parallel circumstances? And "prove his view" is an empty, positivistic phrase, given the complexity of the anthropological enterprise.

LESSER: But in the case I am talking about, the translation was made by someone, an American poet, who had no real control over the Eskimo language, He went through that book with a group of us at Columbia before it was published, and he discussed it in detail in some lectures. I am saying that to use the words in a translation as the basic proof that certain conceptions and ideas were held by the people is contrary to what he himself said was the only sound approach.

DIAMOND: Again, Radin never thought in terms such as "basic proof." I think I made the point that Radin was not a thoroughly consistent man. I wouldn't like to meet a thoroughly consistent man. I think that the degree of inconsistency in anthropology is due to the nature of the material with which we work; its ambiguity is extreme. Moreover, inconsistency is in the very nature of language to begin with, and it is part of the inherent dialectic of thinking. Fortunately, people like Radin (or like Boas and Marx) were capable of expressing significant ideas and seminal notions in the face of these generic inconsistencies with which we must all deal.

There is a larger point, however. A translation of poetry, or of poetic language, is *always* an invention. That is a well known literary cliché. But—as Vico, Boas, and many others have pointed out—the languages of primitive peoples themselves are poetic, connotative, highly concrete, and metaphorical. As the contemporary ethnopoets believe, a practising poet among ourselves, or our poetic faculties as ordinary human beings, are most likely to bring us closest to their meanings. Even Evans-Pritchard said something like that with reference to the understanding of primitive religion—that the grasp of it requires the poetic faculty.

MERVYN MEGGITT: When I read Radin's *Method and Theory* as an undergraduate—when I was far too naive to appreciate how much there was in it—I was delighted by what appeared to be a kind of iconoclasm. But over the years I was more and more taken by the analogies between the approaches of Radin and Roheim, in the attempt to establish a dialectic between an investigator and a people. Radin, long working with Winnebago materials; Roheim, a relatively short period of time spent among aborigines but until the day he died wrestling with the data from Central Australia, within a specific kind of neo-Freudian framework. Both show a pitting of the overcivilized Western European mind—as I think they would see it—trying to come to grips with the mythology, ritual, world view of one particular society. Roheim, like Radin, never believed for a moment that the people in question were pristine. But I think that he and Radin were doing the same sort of thing, and we benefit from it.

DIAMOND: In a certain broad sense, although Radin would not have agreed with many of Roheim's psychoanalytic formulations.

ERIC WOLF: I wonder if you could say something about this temperamental figure of the shaman who constitutes meaning in Radin's universe.

DIAMOND: What he called the *speculum mentis*. I think there were two seminal figures in Radin's mind. One of them was the trickster, the other was the shaman. The trickster, he believed, was the authentic *speculum mentis*, a universal figure. Radin was fascinated by human ambiguity, and social ambivalence. He felt that they were repressed in contemporary society for various reasons (and therefore could not be confronted and transcended); bureaucratic structures obviously do not encourage the expression of ambiguity, or the tremendous creative energy that is involved with it. But Radin saw in the trickster myth (and he spent years and years going through all kinds of materials) a different mode of expression of ambiguity—its confrontation, its cultural history, so to speak, its transcendence. Much of his work on religion has to be understood in those terms. The trickster, of course, is giver and destroyer, creator and negator. He is the burlesque of the sacred; at the same time he *is* sacred. The world is the result of the trickster's energies, almost by accident; at the same time, the trickster can obliterate. He is the messenger of the gods, and he *is* God. Here we have the notion of the tragicomic duality of human life in the universe, a duality which Radin believed was personified and acted out over and over again in primitive society, both in religious projections and in rituals. This confrontation and transcendence is a primary source of art, and has bearing on our own time, I think, for we divide tragedy and comedy. It is only among certain fortunately situated persons (like Shakespeare) that there sometimes occurs a dramatic fusion which can be called tragicomic. In the rituals of earlier periods in the West, this fusion is sometimes evident. In the medieval cathedrals, all kinds of people and events converged—prostitutes, merchants selling their wares, religious ritual and the *opposite* of religious ritual. Among the Greeks, during the Dionysic festivals, there was the tragic trilogy and then the satyr play, which was a total reversal of the theme that had gone before—the comic reversal of the tragic. But these "fusions" must be understood as historically relative, for compared to what happens in primitive society, they remain dichotomized.

In primitive societies, Radin thought, the tragic and the comic formed an indissoluble entity. There are many examples. Among the Wintun during the winter festival, the most sacred of their initiation rites, a clown backs up in front of the initiate and does exactly the reverse of what the initiate must do; the struggle for personal-social identity is expressed in the ritual, but there is simultaneously a denial of identity. The point is that human beings construct the identity; and also can destroy the identity; we are capable of both; and we are obligated to understand this and somehow transcend it. This perception also elided with the dual image of the deity itself in Radin's work. This particular fusion is a classic—if repressed—theme in the Judeo-Christian tradition; it appears in the Book of Job, except that Job does not finally defend his own occasional insight. In the end, God *knows*, and God is unequivocal; the universe is an ethical structure, and we must hew to the line. In the primitive perspective, nothing could be more alien than the conclusion of the Book of Job.

As far as the figure of the shaman is concerned, Radin worried about that. He understood very clearly that the rise of church and state were related, so that the shaman turns into a priest as a certain point of socioeconomic development, and the exploitative potential of that combination has been one of the marks of high civilization. He wrote about that in a yet unpublished manuscript on the rise of civilization. In primitive society the shaman is not yet a determinate establishment figure but is, among other things, an aspect of Everyman. Radin told the story of the Winnebago who, while watching a shamanistic performance, turned to the ethnographer and said, "Well, it's good that some of us are that way some of the time, but it would be disastrous if all of us were that way all of the time." His notion—not terribly original I suppose—was that the shaman represents the unenacted portion of our consciousness; and that the shaman represents in his person the humanity of any given culture balanced on the knife-edge between meaning and chaos, between mere biology and symbolic existence.

This view is related to his notion of the trickster. The trickster incarnates mere biological energy, which is capable of generating symbolic performances, but the symbolic construction is always in danger of collapsing back into the inchoate energy. The shaman is the more positive, more evolved figure of symbolic creation, which is part of the substratum of the mentality of all human beings; that is, it represents the cultural potential. But precisely because of that, when, with the appearance of class divisions, the state, etc., that consciousness is broken off from its moorings in the people at large (when it is no longer an aspect of the shaman in each one, so to speak, which is the cultural creating capacity), then the resultant monopoly and displacement of symbolic usage can be transformed and can be used against people. The priest emerges in a determinate, alienating, exploitative structure, which includes such affairs as the paying of tribute. The society at large—not as a reification, but as the concrete interaction of human beings—is no longer sacred. Radin was well aware of that transition.

MEGGITT: For Roheim, the shaman is the precarious ego and the trickster is the unpredictable id.

DIAMOND: For Radin, the shaman would be the symboling self, or rather, selves.

PAUL RABINOW: You painted Radin's picture as a traditional intellectual, a secularized Jew at the end of his tradition who attempted to bring together the contradictions in it through thinking about them, much as your description of the trickster also takes places on a mythological level. And you implied that we can't return to that as a model of the intellectual. In what way did you mean that?

DIAMOND: I don't think we *can* return to that as a model. I think that Radin, like most of us, was the result of a dialectic between his own temperament and the historical and socioeconomic circumstances in which he was reared. Radin was full of important, almost paradigmatic, contradictions. Despite his emphasis on the concrete, he was an extremely abstract thinker; he was, occasionally, even abstract in his insistence upon being absolutely concrete at every point. He was also an extremely bookish man, probably more than was necessary; he was something of a *yeshiva bocher*. He turned learning into a ritual. He believed that the intellectual professions were the highest occupations that a man or woman could engage in, despite his suspicion of the basic structure and reification of intellectual life in our civilization. He was not pragmatically engaged with the real problems of his own society (or even of his own daily life), though he wrote about them and was fully aware of them. There are a number of reasons for that. First of all, he was fearful. This is not unknown in the academy. But there is another dimension in Radin: although he came from a family that achieved economic security and became distinguished, he was an Eastern European Jew, basically, and he always had an immigrant mentality. That is, he was afraid of the ultimate authorities in our society. He was afraid of the police, for example. He was bewildered by our technology, as I have tried to point out. He was afraid to miss a train; he didn't know how to make his own arrangements. One should not confuse those characteristics with intellectual work per se. But they indicate Paul's fear of being and doing anything other than intellectually. All his energies—and he had great energy—were poured into a single mold. One can understand this culturally, but I don't think it would serve us as a model for the use of the mind in the immediate and relentless present. I loved Paul Radin. But I was aware, sometimes painfully, of the results of the narrow socialization and cultural deprivation to which he was subject, but which he managed to surmount in many astonishingly creative ways. If he hadn't had the kind of intellectual opportunities that were offered him, and if he hadn't used those opportunities to "cure" himself, he could easily have become an extraordinarily deformed human being. In short, he was in many ways a victim.

Biographical Note

Stanley Diamond, born in New York City in 1922, grew up in the ethnic potpourri of Greenwich Village. By the time he graduated from the De Witt Clinton High School, he had become a political activist and a radical. He went on to New York University, majoring in English and philosophy. A course with E. Adamson Hoebel introduced him to anthropology, but its descriptions of types of arrowheads and of the "war to the death" between Neanderthal and Cro-Magnon men aroused his curiosity rather than his enthusiasm. When his B.A. was awarded him in 1942, Diamond was in North Africa as an American Field Service volunteer attached to the British Eighth Army. While in this service, he came into contact with African tribesmen who had been sold into the South African army by their chiefs. His experience with the British army was an education in the hierarchy of colonialism, and helped turn him toward the decision to become an anthropologist.

After the war, Diamond was accepted into the anthropology department at Columbia, delaying his admission for a year while he worked in a variety of jobs. At Columbia, he took courses with Julian Steward and Gene Weltfish, among others, and studied with the M.U.S. seminar (*see* general introduction), where he first presented the seminal research on the Dahomey proto-state that became his dissertation. After receiving his Ph.D. in 1951, he spent two years in Israel doing fieldwork in a kibbutz and in an Arab village. Subsequently, Diamond worked among the Anaguta of Nigeria (1958–60), among the Allegheny Seneca Indians (1962), and in Biafra during the Nigerian Civil War. He has also conducted research on the cultural background of mental illness and education in the United States, studying the families of schizophrenics (1960–63), and directing a project on the culture of schools (1965–67).

Diamond has taught at the University of California at Los Angeles (1953–54), Brandeis University (1956–60), Maxwell Graduate School of Syracuse University (1963–66), and Columbia University (1966–67). In 1966 he joined the New School for Social Research, where he organized and chaired the graduate anthropology program. He has also served as a distinguished visiting professor at Bard College and at the Free University of Berlin. In 1975 Diamond founded the international journal *Dialectical Anthropology*, of which he is editor.

The major themes of Diamond's work are the character of primitive societies as prestate paradigms and the processes of state and nation formation. An intellectual heir of Marx, Rousseau, and Montaigne, his predominant concern has been with the anthropological critique of Western civilization. According to a reviewer of his *In Search of the Primitive*, by "sensitively focusing on the human consequences of being born into a primitive society, Diamond simultaneously explores the human implications of civilizational existence."

Souvenir du "Paris", du 26 Octobre au 2 Novembre 1938
Le Commandant
E. del Jaramillo

Bronislaw Malinowski on his way to the United States in 1938

Bronislaw Malinowski
Raymond Firth

4

At the time that Radin was studying under Boas, Bronislaw Malinowski was reading about primitive cultures in Cracow, Poland. In 1910 Malinowski moved to England and began post-graduate work in ethnology at the London School of Economics. Academic anthropology had begun in England in the 1880s with E. B. Tylor's appointment at Oxford. At Cambridge it had been introduced by A. C. Haddon, a professor of zoology there who had organized the Torres Strait expedition of 1898. Haddon had also initiated a course in ethnology at the L.S.E. in 1904. The year that Malinowski arrived, the course was turned over to C. G. Seligman, a physician who had volunteered for the Torres Strait expedition, had been drawn into ethnology, and then had carried out fieldwork in New Guinea, among the Veddas of Ceylon, and in the Sudan.

Malinowski was born in Cracow in 1884. His father was an eminent linguist who also did some work on Polish ethnography and folklore. Malinowski attended the university in Cracow, where he took a doctorate in physics and mathematics in 1908, but ill health forced him to give up his research in the physical sciences. This allowed him to follow up a favorite side interest, reading Frazer's *The Golden Bough* and other works on primitive religion, as well as accounts of the Australian aboriginal family. The latter interest led to a "sociological study," published in 1913, in which he first used the concept of "function."

At the L.S.E., Malinowski worked under E. Westermarck and the sociologist L. T. Hobhouse as well as Seligman, his principal teacher. In 1914 Malinowski carried out his first expedition, to the Mailu off the coast of New Guinea, making a brief visit to the Trobriand Islands as well. It was en route to New Guinea that he first met A. R. Brown (later Radcliffe-Brown). His report on the Mailu earned him a doctorate from the L.S.E. in 1916.

Undertaking a second Melanesian field trip in 1915, Malinowski returned to the Trobriand Islands; he went there again in 1917, spending a total of about two years in fieldwork in the Trobriands. The Trobriand Islanders became the subject of an extensive series of monographs on economics, family life, magic and religion, and law, as well as the vehicle for Malinowski's analysis of culture as a universal phenomenon.

Malinowski taught courses at the L.S.E. in 1913 and again in the early 1920s. When he was offered a permanent appointment there in 1923, he proposed that it be called a Readership in Social Anthropology, to indicate the sociological emphasis of the department as distinct from the cultural anthropology being developed at University College, a sister institution within the University of London. (Social Anthropology, he also pointed out, had been the title used by Tylor at Oxford and later by Frazer at Liverpool.) During his years at the L.S.E., until 1938, Malinowski became a highly influential teacher, including among those who studied with him E. E. Evans-Pritchard, Raymond Firth, Meyer Fortes, Phyllis Kaberry, Edmund Leach, Lucy Mair, Ashley Montagu, S. F. Nadel, Talcott Parsons, Hortense Powdermaker, Audrey Richards, Isaac Schapera, Godfrey Wilson, and others.

Malinowski made three trips to the United States between 1926 and 1936. He returned in 1938 on what was intended as a year's sabbatical, but on being advised not to go back to wartime England, he accepted a visiting professorship at Yale. He remained at Yale until his death—three months before his permanent appointment there would have become effective. During the Yale years, he made two short field trips to Mexico, where he began a project on marketing among the Zapotec Indians of Oaxaca in collaboration with Julio de la Fuente. Malinowski died in 1942, the same year as Boas' death.

Reacting against both the speculative reconstructions of the evolutionists and diffusionists, on the one hand, and what he saw as the Boasian treatment of culture traits extracted from their contexts, on the other, Malinowski originated a functionalist approach to the study of culture. He saw culture as an integrated system of institutions derived from human needs, and he saw the goal of anthropology as that of constructing a "science of culture." His program for fieldwork—emphasizing long residence in the field, use of the native language, and participant observation—became basic features of anthropological method. Both his theory and his method were critical to the development of what came to be identified as the distinctive "anthropological approach"—the intensive, holistic study of functioning societies.

THERE IS still a paradox in the public image of Malinowski—a kind of disjunction between the very personal, critical estimates that have been given of him and the pervasive scientific influence that he seems to have left behind. A kind of wonderment seizes commentators as they review discrepant facets of Malinowski's life in the anthropological community and his contribution to its intellectual development. Two recent examples, one French, one British, can illustrate this. Michel Panoff, who has devoted a whole book to Malinowski (1972), begins with the observation that it has always been well understood among professional ethnographers that Malinowski was a very mediocre theoretician, then goes on to say that he was unequaled as a field worker, and credits him with some formidable anticipations of later French anthropological thought. Adam Kuper, poised between conflicting opinions of Malinowski's personality, complained that it is difficult to find a single objective portrait of him; and after granting him a grasp of the complexity of social reality "which amounted, almost, to a theory," does not hesitate to accuse him of theoretical naïveté, crude utilitarianism, and blindness to the notion of a social system (Kuper 1973:31, 36, 49).

In Malinowski's lifetime there were contrasting views about him, but the paradox was less of a puzzle. Things that he did or said could fascinate or shock, what he wrote could evoke enthusiasm or rejection, but his acts and utterances could more easily be seen and heard in context, and interpreted as the outcome of a single, complex, highly intelligent, highly articulate, vigorous, sensitive mind. Now, when it is more than thirty years after he has died, no professional anthropologist under the middle fifties in age is likely to have known him, and curiosity about the character of this unusual man who is rightly termed one of the founders of social anthropology is understandable. Since I worked closely with him for some years in the most productive period of his life, and retained ties of friendship (albeit at varying distance) with him until his death, it may be illuminating to some people for me to try and match what I remember of his personality with what I and others have thought of his theories.[1] There will be no revelations, and I do not claim the portrait as objective. But I have tried to make it dispassionate, with a perspective that may be helpful to others in forming their own opinions.

It is a simplification, but not a great one, to see a triple paradox in the public image of Malinowski for people who did not know him. He suffered continually from bad health, and a tragic illness of his wife absorbed much of his attention, yet he managed to write so much. He has been generally applauded for the magnificent quality of his fieldwork and decried for his theories, yet he managed to inspire so many people. And while his fieldwork was long regarded as his prime achievement, depending upon his rapport with the Trobrianders, his sympathy and understanding, by his own account in his diaries he turns out to have been bad-tempered, contemptuous in some of his attitudes towards the people—the idol, as Geertz put it, certainly had feet of clay.

The first and last of these paradoxes can to some extent be put together. He had an undoubted history of ill health. Much of his early education took place at home because he was regarded as what in contemporary English terms would be called "delicate." In his twenties, after completing his doctorate in philosophy in Cracow, he was directed to change his academic field on medical advice. And between his Trobriand expeditions and his settling in England he had or was threatened by tuberculosis. Yet he had great intellectual energy, and a constant, almost obsessional interest in maintaining his physical vitality. One of his friends has said that only someone as strong as a horse could have swallowed all the medicines he did without killing himself—but that may be an unwarranted gloss. Certainly he believed in exercise, in sunshine and clear air—which did not stop him from working in rooms with closed windows, and, in his early seminars at the London School of Economics, with a roaring fire in the grate. But he also "lived on his nerves," in the colloquial phrase, with a physical and psychological sensitivity which burst out at times: against people; in shouting; in profanity; in a kind of cruelty springing from a mixture of exhaustion and egocentrism; and which broke down periodically into migraine which incapacitated him for twenty-four hours or so.

Given this cyclical pattern—a driving force of intellectual interest, with some amalgam of personal vanity and ambition which he never denied; also some components of physical weakness, always threatening, sometimes breaking out; given too the ordinary frustrations and trials of fieldwork compounded by his emotional turmoil over the separate attachments to two women revealed in his diaries—and his occasional outbursts against Trobrianders become explicable even where they are regrettable.[2] His output of scientific books and articles was accomplished by high focus, enlisting the aid of family, servants, research assistants, and friends, and subjecting himself to a discipline of work which left much time for intellectual conversation but not too much for other pursuits. Walking he liked, but he played no games, did not garden, had no skills with his fingers and no hobbies that I can remember.

My own relationship with Malinowski covered nearly twenty years, from my first meeting with him when I was a graduate student in 1924 until his death in 1942. Before ever I knew he was in London I had been fascinated by *Argonauts of the Western Pacific* (1922), which I came across by chance in a bookshop in New Zealand. Interested in the possibility of providing an economic dimension to anthropological data, I found in this book a superb example, based on intimate field experience, of what I had only vaguely dreamed of doing. So in London I was happy not only to have him as a teacher but also to become his research assistant. In 1925 and 1926, under a Laura Spelman Rockefeller Memorial grant, I worked with Malinowski on *Crime and Custom* (1926b), *Myth* (1926c), and *The Father* (1927b)—to use their shorthand titles—as well as the first part of *The Sexual Life of Savages* (1929) and various articles. His work habits were idiosyncratic. He came rarely to the Reading Room of the British Museum, where many academics then did much of their research; when he did I had books ready, marked for him to see. I also abstracted much material for him, read to him sections of work for discussion, and acted as his amanuensis and critic. In London he did much work in bed; in Oberbozen, where he had a villa where he spent most of the summer, he usually worked on the balcony, often nude in the sun, with a green eyeshade, scrubbing himself with a solution of iodized salt in the intervals of discussion about Trobriand myth or family life.

Whether in London or in Oberbozen he led an active social life, moving easily in multilingual conversation in a continental world of scholarly intellectuals, but without that pomposity which so often marked the senior academic of his day. But social life with Malinowski merged very easily into intellectual life. His seminars were famous: penetrating, with a quietly relentless Socratic approach broken by a sudden shaft of wit; impatient of any slick formal textbook definition; insistent on careful statement of a problem; yet generous in acknowledgment of any original contribution, however hesitant. But as much, or more, work with his students was done outside the seminar. Audrey Richards (1943) has noted how "they learned to discuss their theses on bus-tops or dodging the market-barrows down Holborn side-streets." His demands could be exigent. His research assistants could be worked late into the night, writing down many thousands of words—in longhand—more, they knew, than an article could possibly stand, with all protests met by such statement as "First get it all down, then cut." But there were compensations—not only glasses of wine and meals, but also a stimulating flow of conversation, a genuine interest in the assistants' own ideas, and a sense of freedom in sharing a common intellectual atmosphere. Believing firmly in the importance of reciprocity, Malinowski also mobilized the domestic and professional world around him, particularly by exchange of gifts for services. Even his Oberbozen home was brought into the socio-academic orbit. Many of his graduate students stayed at the *Pfarrhaus*, the home of the priest at Maria Himmelfahrt near by, and joined in the teas at the villa, and the walks through pine woods and alpine meadows in the evening, with talk ranging from the latest thesis chapter to more general problems of social theory or more personal problems of agreement and difference.

And at the back of all this, until 1935, was his wife, Elsie Rosaline Masson (the E.R.M. of the diaries). An intelligent, cultured, independent-minded Australian woman, she was very clear-sighted and she had a sense of humor. She realized fully what kind of being she had married, and had accepted this from the start—she married against her parents' wishes and not from their home. She herself had already published a book on North Australia, and she had a fine sense of style and a good critical mind. But she devoted herself to her husband and children; they had three daughters. In the early years she spent much time reading and discussing his work, and he relied very greatly upon her judgment. She appears in his diaries as a person who could heal wounds and absolve from sins—and such she remained for him till the end of her life.

Malinowski's character is not easy to describe briefly. In intellectual matters he was widely if unevenly read, and he commanded a range of continental scholarship unusual in British anthropologists of his period—before European scholars wrote much in English or translations of their works became common. He was a vivid, often very frank conversationalist with very definite views on many social questions, including the effects of national shortcomings. Insistently theoretical in his professional approach, he was yet constantly applying concrete example and pragmatic test. Anthropology was for him a meaningful intellectual discipline which related to everyday life, not just an academic study of "the primitive." As in this discipline, so also in his personal relations—he was not satisfied with superficial appearances but wished to scrutinize motivation and effect. He enjoyed some measure of good living, but was not impressed by wealth. He was careful, even mean, with money and counseled his students accordingly; but he was generous with his time and attention to their problems. He was conscious of the social value of flattery and sometimes used it blatantly, but he was scornful of hypocrisy and quick to identify it in himself and others. In human relations he was apt to be as demanding as he himself gave—sometimes brutally so. Loyalty was a prime virtue in his eyes—and loyalty commonly meant agreement in action, not necessarily in opinion. Himself with a strong ego-drive and more than a touch of hypochondria, he also had an intense interest in the human personality of others, and so tended to make a strong impact on people at the first meeting.

Malinowski's personality then was complex, but it was not protean, not inconstant in change. Rather can he be described as romantic in the sense of subordination of form to theme, both in social action and in the presentation of it in anthropological analysis. He was a romantic not in the sense of sentimentalism—he was a realist, a near-cynic on occasions—but in the sense of having his values in the sphere of human personality rather than in human constructs. He never surrounded himself with choice pictures or other art objects; he liked good food and wine but was no connoisseur. Even books, so important to his intellectual development, were cherished less than people's opinions, and he never built up any very substantial library. He looked for his values in people, not things—friendship, loyalty, truth were prime concepts to him, and overtly appeared in his more personal relationships. Intellectually, he did not reject the principle of order, but order was of less significance to him than the dynamic forces that he saw at work. He was not a classic, not a structuralist in his interests. He was impatient of formalistic statement, and did not always bother to be formally consistent. As part of these dynamic forces he recognized, and used, exaggeration, violence of expression, intellectual shock tactics, as instruments of exploration and understanding.

Introspective, self-exploring, he also had a romantic attitude to faith. A lapsed Catholic who sometimes used his former religion for sociological display, he was actually a skeptic who would have liked to believe. He had a "nostalgia for belief." He felt strongly that in his own circumstances he was subjected to an overshadowing by Fate; in such attitudes his intellect and his emotions went hand in hand. In the aesthetic field he was not artistic in the ordinary sense. He had a strong liking for music, especially the German nineteenth-century composers, including Wagner. But I do not remember that he took much interest in painting—though his second wife was a painter—and in sculpture and architecture he was distinguished by keen sensibility rather than by specialized taste. As for literature, his other pursuits left him little time for lengthy reading, and it is my impression that he was knowledgeable rather than learned in this sphere. (But his recipe for learning a European language, which he himself used for Spanish and urged upon his students for Italian or German, was to invest in an armful of novels and read through them with minimal resort to grammar or dictionary!)

In the field of political and ethical values Malinowski was an internationalist and a humanist. As a product of a cosmopolitan education he spoke Polish, German, French, and English from an early stage, and at various points had added Italian and Spanish. All these he handled fluently, apart from his New Guinea experience of Motu and his command of Trobriand. Rhoda Métraux, in her excellent article on Malinowski, states that he spoke Russian (1968:542). I don't think this is strictly true. When I was travelling with him on a train in North Italy about 1925, he was once away for about an hour, talking with a Russian, he explained. I said I had thought he

did not know Russian. He replied that he did not, but had
"made out" by combining the smattering of what he had
"picked up" with his knowledge of Polish and other Slavic
forms. His spoken Hochdeutsch was perfect—a Gräfin of our
acquaintance whom I asked said that if anything it was too
perfect! In later years he preferred to write in English, and I
think from what he said he would not have wished to write a
literary piece in Polish. But his English pronunciation was
never quite perfect; in some particulars, as in "fud" for "food,"
he continued to betray a continental upbringing. And despite
his amazing linguistic facility he continued to count in his natal
tongue even at a late date in England. (When I caught him once
mumbling to himself what to me were some very odd sounds, he
said rather sheepishly that in private he always counted in
Polish.)

   Given his cosmopolitan outlook, I did not see him as a
Polish nationalist in any active sense. Of course in the '20s and
'30s he was very conscious of the wrongs in Polish history, and
he retained many Polish contacts. But though he had Polish
students—Obrebski and Waligorski, for instance—and perhaps
had special ties with them, he did not give the impression of
being first and foremost a Pole, and I don't think he was ever
interested in returning to Poland academically to stay. In a
generally admirable series of articles, K. Symmons-Symonolewicz has taken me to task for discussing the problem of
Malinowski's relation to Poland and things Polish "in a
somewhat superficial manner" (1958:16n). He cites Malinowski's frequent national self-identification as a Pole before
the war as evidence of his Polish patriotism and nationalism.
Now Symmons-Symonolewicz does add that it is more a question of the meaning of terms such as patriotism and national
consciousness than of real discrepancy in interpretation of
Malinowski's sentiments. But in turn, I think he has failed to
realize how in conversation, as in writing, Malinowski used his
Polishness as he did his Catholicism—as a counter in the play of
argument, a kind of foil to the position he was adopting. There
is no need to doubt the genuineness of his feeling for Poland; the
question is the degree to which this outstripped other feelings,

and my impression is that politically he thought in international rather than narrow national terms. But it seems that Malinowski's sense of Polish identification developed—or revived—quite markedly when he was in the United States during World War II. (I have in corroboration here the opinion of Dr. Feliks Gross, a long-time friend and colleague of Malinowski.) So the appearance in 1973 of Malinowski's portrait in a gold medallion on a 2 zl. stamp of Poland was a justifiable tribute to a Pole of international reputation.[3]

What Malinowski was, unequivocally, was an enemy of fascism and Nazism. Right from the beginning of the Mussolini epoch in Italy, he made no particular secret of his feelings of profound dislike of the regime, and his detestation of Hitlerism was even greater. But his reactions were of an intellectual rather than a political type. He attacked totalitarianism in public lectures, and in the book he was preparing shortly before his death, *Freedom and Civilization* (1947), but as far as I know he joined no political party.

His friends, like his scholarship, were international. Apart from some of his British academic colleagues in anthropology and sociology, and distinguished intellectual figures in Britain and the United States, his real friends included an English statistician and his wife, who was a very talented artistic woman; a Viennese Jewish industrialist (to whom *Sex and Repression* is dedicated) and his wife, with both of whom he had close ties ever since his Australian days; a French pearl buyer whom he had known in the Trobriands and who appears in the diary; a scholarly ex-missionary administrator, who directed the International African Institute; an English landowner of a great county family, who was also something of an anthropologist and an authority on Durkheim and Nietzsche. To these people he opened himself in friendship, which he treated as one of the sacred values.

Ultimate honesty—not superficial honesty—was another such value. He could not stand conventional codes; he used them but despised them. So some of his judgments of people were apt to run athwart of accepted norms. At a time when the French in general were often said to be the most polite people in Europe, Malinowski, seeing as he thought beneath the surface, described them as the rudest, except perhaps the Germans in some moods. The peasants of Italy—not the nobility—he credited with the best manners of all. The English he tolerated, and indeed admired "English" ("British" had not then come so extensively into vogue) democratic institutions. But he sneered at the concept of the English gentleman—"that stinky species" as he once wrote in a letter to me, as a warning. As I have said, he was a flatterer, especially to men and women in positions of power, but he was also quite willing to describe them offensively—mostly with words beginning with "b"—behind their backs. His flattery he treated as a kind of cheerful foible, a social instrument that he did not intend to be taken seriously, except by those stupid enough to believe in it. Also, he was not afraid to mingle flattery with solid criticism. I well remember after we had once called on Marcel Mauss and he had been almost offensively critical, as we left the apartment I queried his manner. He laughed and said, "The thing to do with these people"—he meant the *L'Année sociologique* group—"is every now and again to give them a good sound kick." But underneath all this he attached great value to sincerity, to frankness, to a willingness to put all the intellectual and emotional cards on the table, to admit to one's own ambitions and vanities—and to a capacity to point out those of the other person too. Friendship with Malinowski could be a wearing relationship. It might demand a confrontation every now and again, with no or almost no holds barred. But it had its compensations, not least of which was precisely to have the benefits of this cuttingly analytical realistic scrutiny of act and motive. Of course, every now and then he got it wrong, or the friend committed some blunder, and this could be difficult. (I have indicated elsewhere [Firth 1975:6] one such development in my own case.)

Much has been made of Malinowski's profanity, which was free and, in English at least, at times almost adolescent. People have been shocked by what he said about the Trobrianders—but as one of his friends has said, that is nothing to what he said about, or to, some of his British colleagues. I have no wish to defend the vulgarity and prejudice revealed in some parts of his diary, including the expression translated as "niggers" which apparently might equally have been rendered as "blacks." But two points are worth remembering in this context. The first is that the diaries were written in Polish, for his own private record, as a kind of catharsis in which no ideas or feelings should be kept back; there is no suggestion that they were ever intended as anything more than a frank expression of his personal state of mind. Who among us has the courage to set down his private thoughts, including his grosser thoughts, as openly? The second point is that in his own idiosyncratic way Malinowski was a firm believer in the universality of human rights. His consciousness of ethnicity is not to be simply equated with a racist denial of such rights.

Malinowski was a humanist, in two senses. He had no belief in spiritual powers other than those of man himself, no faith in revealed religion. Though a Catholic when young, he seemed to have lost all trace of this by the time I knew him, in his forties—except for the occasional lighthearted reference for comparative purposes. Even when admiring with him the architectural and sculptural grandeur of Catholic churches in North Italy, I had no hint that he had any nostalgic interest in their rituals, or that their beliefs formed any very active part of his intellectual heritage. Perhaps one of the legacies of his Catholicism was a certain preoccupation with the concept of death—though his intellectual interest in the problem of the fear of death was perhaps more a reflex of his personal temperament than of his religious heritage.

He was a humanist in a broader sense too. He believed intensely in the value of man irrespective of individual status or condition. Superficially perhaps he was a bit of a snob—it amused him to hobnob with a titled person. But it was a game he soon tired of, and it was the quality of the person that he sought. He had plenty of titled peopled—some knights, a princess, a countess, and various continental nobles—in his wider circle of friends, but they stayed there on their merits. Retainers—family cooks, charwomen, college porters—he treated rather regally; he tipped them well, and got them to do services for him (this was in prewar conditions) in an incredibly short space of time after he first met them. But then he also made a point of speaking to them, inquired about them personally, got small gifts for them—so after more than thirty years the face of one of them still lights up when I mention Professor Malinowski to him. He was not a philanthropist in the conventional sense. He contributed to few if any "good causes" that I can remember in the period I knew him best. But he spoke out continually in favour of what he saw as basic human values.

I can exemplify this in a brief reference to his views on sex. He was a pioneer in the advocacy of what may be called modern enlightened sex values. Malinowski himself had strong personal heterosexual interests, which he made no great effort to conceal. But he was actively concerned with more general issues, of the theoretical place of sex in social life, and of the practical significance of anthropology in programs of sex education and social reform. He was a friend of Havelock Ellis—that noble, patriarchal, white-bearded figure (as I knew him in his late years) whose *Psychology of Sex* in six volumes was a more literate Kinsey of the 1920s, when writing scientifically about sex was a more perilous occupation than it is today. He was also a strong supporter of the British Social Hygiene Council, led by its formidable Secretary-General Mrs. C. Neville-Rolfe and counting among its members Julian Huxley, Cyril Burt, and J. Arthur Thomson. He contributed to the conferences of the Council and induced his younger anthropological colleagues to do likewise. Parallel to, and indeed a little earlier than the work of Margaret Mead in the United States, he helped social and cultural anthropology to free itself from the legacy of orgiastic rituals and classical phallic symbolism, of being overly concerned with savagery and nudity. He wrote of "savages" but they were not naked—they were in fact quite prudish about genital exposure. When people said of Malinowski, "Ah yes, I've read his *book*," one never needed to ask which book. Yet the famous *Sexual Life of Savages* (1929) contains almost as much about the status of women, the obligations of marriage, the dogmas of physical resemblance, and relations between different kinds of kin as it does about sexual behavior. Malinowski put forward the Trobriand customs of premarital sex as aids to marital choice of a fairly rational kind.

In an address on "Anthropology and Social Hygiene" (1926a), leveled at modern Western society, he argued against "preaching barren continence" before marriage, and he thought that with the restrictions on divorce then prevailing, many a man and woman would prefer to enter a free union rather than bind themselves in a marriage tie. He was in favor of early marriages, and saw no objection to contraceptives on biological, social, or moral grounds. He held that divorce should be easier, and that the moral tone that in all sexual irregularity penalized the woman rather than the man was unjust and ignoble. In much of this he was well in advance of the public opinion of his day—though his opinions are not outmoded. But central to all his thinking and writing was the view that the full attainment of sexual satisfaction cannot be realized except in a permanent union of deep love and mutual sacrifice. He held that man is neither inevitably promiscuous nor naturally monogamous, that the experimental component in sexual desire leads to new sexual interests and experiences, but that there is also a deep seeking for attachment and fidelity. Assuming, as we all tend to do, the mantle of his science, he declared firmly that "it is evident then that anthropology is a vigourous supporter of all schemes and plans which lead to the strengthening of monogamous marriage and of the individual family" (1926a:84). But he added with a characteristic image, "On the other hand, no student of man can be an absolute follower of Mrs. Grundy—she has never studied anthropology."

This central notion of the basic importance of the individual family, which appears clearly in all his treatment of kinship and which first saw full expression in his book on the Australian aborigines, probably had several roots. It owed something to Edward Westermarck, whose dictum that marriage was rooted in the family rather than the family in marriage Malinowski often quoted. It was also in part a kind of common-sense reaction against the theoretical constructs of primitive promiscuity and group marriage, which earlier anthropologists had invented to explain certain kinship terminologies and associated behavior, and which Malinowski thought were gross misunderstandings of the situation by people who had never studied what actually happened. But I think this notion was also related to his own deeper feelings of the need for stability in human relationships—linked in another aspect to his conception of friendship. There was also perhaps some reflection of his Catholic upbringing in his notion of a high ideal—of beautiful love, a stable marriage and a solidary family—which the weakness of the flesh, "reality," is always threatening to impair.

With his zest for stripping off the superficialities from statements about behavior, it is understandable that Malinowski found much that was stimulating about Freudian theory. I gather that he never met Freud, but Princess Marie Bonaparte, who was analyzed by Freud and did much to help Freud leave Vienna for London when the Nazi occupation of Austria took place, was his friend. So also was J. C. Flugel, author of *The Psycho-Analytic Study of the Family* (1921). Malinowski wrote that the open treatment of sex and of "various shameful meannesses and vanities in man"—the very thing for which psychoanalysis was most hated and reviled—was of the greatest value to science. But he became increasingly impatient of the exorbitant claims of psychoanalysis to explain the origins of human institutions, and he did not accept the full sexual basis advanced by Freudians in their interpretation of symbolism. Together, well after his first reading of psychoanalytical material in the Trobriands, we studied Freud's analysis of dream and delusion in Wilhelm Jensen's novel *Gradiva*, and other Freudian works including the *Drei Abhandlungen zur Sexualtheorie*. On the one hand, Malinowski rejected the idea of a primal horde adopted by Freud from Atkinson and used as a basis for much of the argument of *Totem and Taboo*. On the other hand, he refused to see sexual connotations in many mundane acts of living—he could not believe, he said, that eating a mutton chop was the equivalent of a sexual act. In this as in many other ways he was a pragmatist, not a symbolist.

Malinowski's pragmatism has been examined by Leach (1957), fairly on the whole, though in my view Leach got carried away a bit by his defense of Charles Peirce against William James. Malinowski's formulations were at times a bit naive. But the point is that he was never a rigid doctrinaire, but was willing to be guided by what he saw as the empirical facts of a situation. This comes out in his attitude to psychoanalysis, including his Trobriand modification of the Oedipus complex. Since in the Trobriands the authority over children recognized by Europeans as inherent in the father was exercised by the mother's brother, Malinowski inferred that the hostility expressed in myth for the authority figure could be expected to take on another form—and this he found. It was the rigor of the Freudians, led by Ernest Jones, that helped to alienate him from their theoretical approach as they attacked his interpretation. But note: his was a sociological interpretation, based on a consideration of the structure of social and economic relationships. Malinowski described the Oedipus complex as "essentially patriarchal in character," and the "avuncular complex"—hatred of mother's brother and incest wish for sister—as essentially matrilineal. He reversed the psychoanalytical interpretation: "The nuclear family complex is a functional formation dependent upon the structure and upon the culture of a society." [4] (Note that this is an intensivist rather than an extensionist form of argument!) Malinowski, like later functionalists, has been accused of not looking below the surface of social phenomena, of failing to recognize the abstract systematic qualities of interconnected events. But in Trobriand myths he saw not merely a charter for rights and privileges but also the expression of some deep relations in the structure of the society. He saw the repressed hatred of the mother's brother breaking through in the Tudava myth, which he described as containing a "typical matrilineal drama which forms its core, and which is brought to its logical conclusion" (1927a:105). He even, in language with which we are now much more familiar, said in interpreting the presentation of an ogre's head in a pudding to be eaten by the startled guilty uncle, that the story "contains then in reality one villain and one conflict distributed over two stages and duplicated into two persons" (1927a:105). The reinterpretation by Ernest Jones of Malinowski's views—that a basic hatred of the father had led to a Trobriand denial of him and to transference of the father's role to the mother's brother—seemed to Malinowski a very strained position, and not supported by the symbolic speculative material of the "primal horde" myth type.

Malinowski's relatively straightforward view that the Trobrianders did not know of physiological paternity or at least consistently denied it as an intellectual matter has been borne out by the field experience of Reo Fortune. The interpretation of what such denial means has been modified by commentators such as Radcliffe-Brown, Ashley Montagu, Leach, and David Schneider, but it was Malinowski who first developed the sociological significance of the Trobriand data, from an earlier Australian model.

Malinowski's acute self-awareness was perhaps channeled to some extent by his acquaintance with psychoanalysis. But his almost clinical attitude of exploration of the self was marked, not by the sometimes humorless detachment of the professional analyst, but by a lively expression of self-mockery. This has rarely been understood by his commentators, though his friends knew it well. A few brief extracts from letters to one of his pupils and friends will illustrate this aspect of his character. In April 1939 he acknowledged a letter as "a lovely birthday present on my sad 55th anniversary of the most calamitous event which befell in my life—except perhaps the one which preceded it by 9 months; or else my decision to become an anthropologist." In a letter of May 1940 he disclaimed having taken any offense at what might have seemed a critical note by his correspondent: "Now, as you know, 'Malinowski is as touchy as he is conceited,' to quote the majority of my colleagues, pupils and friends. So the phrase cannot be in any way offensive. At the time I probably reacted to it as an indication that you plan and propose to develop

Malinowski's theory and to replace it by something bigger and better. . . ."[5]

I have mentioned Malinowski's humanism, in regard to religion, to sex, and to international affairs. In the field of applied anthropology too he shared the attitudes of liberal humanists of his day, in believing in the broad developmental and philanthropic aspects of colonial government. He recognized many of the inequalities and injustices in the colonial situation, but he regarded moves to self-government as likely to be distant (as indeed they seemed in prewar days). He accepted that the ultimate political decision lay in the hands of the governing power, and he was more concerned that the local people should have good government than that they should have self-government. (I remember arguing with him strongly on one occasion that in "indirect rule" the "indirectness" was less important than the fact that "rule" was still maintained.) He was on good terms with Lord Lugard, one of the architects of "indirect rule"; and he fought Sir Philip Mitchell, a noted colonial governor, on the issue of the practicality of applied anthropology, rather than on the objectives of government.

"Practical" anthropology to Malinowski was primarily getting an understanding of the facts of a social situation—polygyny, female "circumcision," "bride-price," land tenure, labor migration—by careful functional analysis. It meant also not ignoring the effects and implications of agricultural improvement, medical and educational advance, as well as noting the results of settler greed, bureaucratic ignorance, and missionary intolerance. He was not afraid to draw attention to "race prejudice, political and economic imperialism, the demand for segregation, the safeguarding of a European standard of living" (1945:23) as forces which denied to Africans an equality of treatment with their colonial rulers. He also held that the anthropologist had a moral obligation to be "a fair and true interpreter of the Native." He was very conscious of the rights of indigenous peoples, both material in respect to landholding and immaterial in respect to the dignity of personality. It was no accident that he was associated with

Norman Leys, who wrote bitterly against white policies of land annexation in Kenya, or that both Jomo Kenyatta and Z. K. Matthews, strong African nationalists, owed much to him in their anthropological studies and academic life.[6] But for him the duty of the anthropologist to "speak as the Natives' advocate" stopped at laying bare the sources of maladjustment; he did not envisage any more active political commitment. Hence it has been easy for modern critics, in a very altered situation, to impute to him a tolerance, if not actual support, for colonialism, and a shaping of his anthropological theory accordingly. What the modern revulsion from political imperialism often overlooks is the challenge fairly consistently offered by social anthropologists to any form of intellectual imperialism, that is, to attempts to dominate by organizational and sometimes even by physical means the freedom of opinion and the development of ideas by people under a variety of forms of government. In expressing such challenge Malinowski was unequivocal. He wrote, "The absence of political freedom destroys all other liberties." But at the same time he noted the danger of misuse of words like democracy and freedom, the danger of inflation in ideals, and of contempt for ideas as slogans become commonplace. "The spiritual foundations of public opinion have to be watched with the same eternal vigilance with which we look after the physical foundations of our national defenses" (1947:13, 336).

So far I have tried to sketch some of the salient features of Malinowski's character, as an introduction to a more direct comment upon his theories. But in passing I should perhaps make reference to some rather more adverse opinions of the man and his intellectual contribution, as expressed by colleagues who knew him. The most outspoken of these was by Max Gluckman, in a review of Malinowski's posthumous *Scientific Theory of Culture.*[7] While acknowledging Malinowski's notable services to anthropological fieldwork, Gluckman denigrated his theoretical contributions and linked their inadequacies with Malinowski's personal failings. According to Gluckman, Malinowski, as the only specialized social anthropologist of his "generation" in Britain after the

1914–18 war, stood alone, a solitary king; his dissident pupils had hived off; he either quarreled with or absorbed the views of his juniors. "He is noted for his distortions of the views of preceding or foreign or filial rivals. Power corrupts . . . " (Gluckman 1963:243). The thesis is interesting on structural grounds, but to those who knew Malinowski well it is a travesty. The "solitary king" is a view of hindsight. It is true that Evans-Pritchard, with acute perception, had left Oxford to come to the London School of Economics—an almost unheard-of move in those days. But Gregory Bateson, Reo Fortune, Monica Hunter, and Camilla Wedgwood did their major anthropology at Cambridge; Gluckman himself, with his Rhodes Scholarship, preferred to go to Oxford; and in London itself Daryll Forde studied primarily with W. J. Perry. In the 1920s and 1930s Malinowski was certainly outstanding, but in the contemporary scene he was a leader in a field of choice, not a unique potentate. With entirely different personalities and other monarchs around, any authority position can lead to trouble, with filials becoming rivals, as the history of many anthropology departments has since demonstrated. Moreover, few of those around Malinowski were neutral personalities, and some themselves generated much heat as well as light.

It is no secret, for instance, that Evans-Pritchard and Malinowski were at daggers drawn for personal as well as for professional reasons, and that Evans-Pritchard did his best to destroy Malinowski's reputation long after his death. (In 1934 Malinowski begged me to serve as one of the editors of the Festschrift for C. G. Seligman, so that, he said, his name would not have to stand next to that of Evans-Pritchard on the cover of the book! But Evans-Pritchard was not noted for his charity. He refused after some delay to contribute to the memorial volume for Malinowski.) The point of this is that when, for example, Evans-Pritchard said that Malinowski "seldom made abstractions" and showed "little originality or distinction of thought" in his explicitly theoretical writings, these statements have to be read in the light of such strong personal feelings of antagonism. Evans-Pritchard was an expert in the glancing blow. His dismissal of Malinowski's theory of religion and magic as a pragmatic one which "might have come straight out of the pages of William James, *as indeed it may have done*" (Evans-Pritchard 1965:48; italics mine) carries more than a suggestion of plagiarism, but ignores some basic differences between the approaches of the two men. William James, for example, held that it was certain that the whole system of thought that leads to magic and allied beliefs may just as well be called primitive science as primitive religion; Malinowski, as is well known, insisted that the division between magic and primitive science was clear-cut, each with its own separate function. William James was concerned with the pragmatic value of immediate personal experiences in religion, and regarded these as realities in the fullest sense of the term; Malinowski argued that while the roots of religious experience lie in the individual, the realization of religious acts and beliefs requires collective efforts, the controlling force of society. Again, in criticizing Malinowski's "emotional" theory of magic, Evans-Pritchard suggests the possibility that much of Malinowski's observation of rites was of those performed for his benefit, for payment, in his tent (1965:46). But not only does he cite no evidence for this opinion but he omits to mention, as a dispassionate critic should, that Malinowski specifically states that he was present, by permission of the officiating magician, at every garden rite in Omarakana agriculture, and also witnessed the reciting of spells "in the solemnity of actual performance" in the magician's own house" (Malinowski 1935, 1:86, 94). In other words, more generally, when what are ostensibly scientific judgments—either positive or negative—are passed in a circle of people who have known one another personally, they must be regarded as a function of the total situation and may have to be interpreted in the light of considerations not always immediately apparent.

In considering Malinowski's position in theoretical anthropology, many commentators have separated his fieldwork sharply from his theory. They have praised him for the quality of his fieldwork as if he were an indefatigable collector of facts, in rapport with the Trobrianders because he lived in a tent among them and spoke their language fluently, and had a keen eye for the minutiae of behavior. Such views have ignored Malinowski's cardinal principle—no fact without a theory—as clearly set out in the last section of the "Baloma" essay (1916). As more perceptive analysts have seen, Malinowski's real ethnographic gifts lay deeper. He was keenly aware of the complexity of the sociocultural reality. He had an acute perception of how the meaning of cultural items had to be reached (initially at least, we might add) through an understanding of their functional interrelations. He realized that significant problems lay not only in the study of conformity, but also in that of discrepancy—between what people said and what they did, between the norms of social order and the pursuit of individual interests. In some aspects of his field technique Malinowski may well have been stimulated by the example of Edward Westermarck, by whom he was much influenced in his few years at the London School of Economics. He contributed to Westermarck's *Festskrift* in 1912, and in later years talked of Westermarck with a kind of respectful affection, rather different from his somewhat contemptuous affection for Sir James Frazer, to whom he also felt much indebted. Now Westermarck, a cultivated European, spoke the vernacular of the field in which he worked—unlike either Rivers or Seligman, with whose field experiences Malinowski was well acquainted, or Radcliffe-Brown (then A. R. Brown), who gave Malinowski some useful field advice before he went to the Trobriands. Between 1898 and 1914, when Malinowski left London for Australia and New Guinea, Westermarck had paid at least a dozen visits to Morocco, and accumulated a vast mass of field material in Arabic, as well as engaging in close relations with some sectors of Moroccan society. So Malinowski had the example of a man whom he respected, a theoretical sociologist as well as a vernacular-using fieldworker. In a sense, then, he may be said to have been following one thread of the European Orientalist tradition in his immersion in the field—a point I do not remember to have been noted before.

But what Malinowski certainly did not get from Westermarck were two elements in his work. One was his more lively, more sophisticated sense of a theoretical problem in a systematic social order. (When Malinowski is accused of "lacking the notion of a system," his work should be compared with that of Westermarck, in which the lack of a concept of a systematic framework of society is much more apparent). Here the influence of Durkheim and *L'Année sociologique* was probably very important. Another element was of a much more personal kind—his sense of awareness of the anthropologist as a factor in the total field situation. Clifford Geertz, by no means uncritical of Malinowski, has stated that this was among Malinowski's prime contributions to anthropology. Michel Panoff has seen it as a "demand for authenticity," in clearly analyzing the relation between the perceptions of the ethnographer and the actions and reactions of the people he studies. In more than a superficial sense, Malinowski may be regarded as a precursor of some of the developments of "cognitive anthropology." However this may be, there is no doubt that for those within his ambience, fieldwork was never the same after the publication of *Argonauts* (1922). In particular, the use of the vernacular was necessary not just as an instrument for collecting better data, but also as a means of relating more effectively to the people and so gaining a fuller understanding of their society and culture.

And yet while "participant observation" in field anthropology owes a great debt to Malinowski, I have the impression from my talks with him as well as from his *Diary* and other works, that his participation was almost always secondary to his observation. In his relations with the Mailu and even with the Trobrianders, his cerebral functioning had almost complete ascendancy over his "gut" reactions of involvement. His preoccupation with the intensely personal quality and significance of his experience was not, however, a mere self-absorption. He saw this experience as having a more general quality, as typifying categories of the human condition. With this, I think, is linked his attitude to anthropological theory. He has sometimes been called "a mediocre theoretician" because some of his specific theories no longer fit the modern idiom or have been shown to have clear imperfections. But his major contribution lies not in his specific theories but in his insistence on the need for theory, the relation of the particular to the general, at every stage of anthropological enquiry. So even the most mundane piece of ethnography. for example an article on stone implements, is shot through with suggestions about art, social status, symbolism, and political and economic power. This is why some commentators such as Panoff have been impressed by what he calls the "architecture" of the presentation of material in the *Argonauts*, and why Bateson and others have acknowledged the stimulus of ideas implicit or immanent in Malinowski's work.

Where Malinowski does display weakness, especially by contrast with much modern analysis, is in his failure to supply many "middle-range" generalizations from his studies. Meyer Fortes has pointed out with justice that one of the paradoxes in Malinowski's work is that his theoretical writings are mostly couched in terms of the highest generality, and the specific variability of cultural phenomena tends to disappear. To some extent, I think, this was a response to a very widespread intellectual interest of the time, going far beyond anthropology. There was a strong focus on problems of the concept of a human nature, of what was meant by instinct, of the relation of human culture to innate drives, of the relevance of non-human animal behavior to human behavior. There was much talk of the theories of McDougall and Shand; Malinowski opened his *Sex and Repression* with a quotation from John Dewey's *Human Nature and Conduct;* Julian Huxley lectured to the University of London Anthropological Society on the mating display of great crested grebes; and he and Malinowski had discussions on the role of sexual selection as part of natural selection. It was a period of much speculation and little systematic evidence. With his background of general sociological theory and his recent vivid Trobriand field experience, Malinowski was easily drawn into this seductive but somewhat elusive field of reflection.

Comment on Malinowski's more concrete fields of enquiry is easier. His studies in social and cultural change have attracted much attention, most of it critical, from Africanists who preferred other frameworks for analysis of the material.

His formalist approach by means of charts indeed seems better adapted to preliminary sorting of data than to final conceptualization of results, and his reliance on the notion of "institution" as a unit of culture contact is clumsy. But some of the criticism was rather wide of the mark. Take his attitude to the study of history. It is true that he himself used little historical documentation in his studies of social change. But a broader charge has often been repeated: that he ignored history, that he was confused about what history is, that he had an obscurantist bias against history. It is worth remembering then that on Malinowski's first introduction to New Guinea, he proposed as a possible study the "process of transformation and adaptation of the Koita *iduhu*" involved in the Koita migration from inland to the coast during the last fifty years; and that in the Trobriands he collected material on historical changes in canoe types, in clan chieftainship, in trading patterns and transfer of magic, and in interisland migration. What he said about the value and limitations of history, as cited in the *Dynamics of Culture Change*, can always provide material for argument. But there is no reason to doubt that such expressions as: "I would be the last to underrate the value of historical knowledge"; "To oppose history and science is futile. To neglect either of them makes any humanistic pursuit incomplete"; and "so-called functionalism is not, and cannot be, opposed to the historical approach but is indeed its necessary complement"—represented his considered opinion (1945:33, 34).

In some other spheres there were clearer gaps in Malinowski's approach. He was a pioneer in the study of economic anthropology, but as I have indicated elsewhere, his contribution must be regarded as inadequate in some important respects (Firth 1957:209–27). I do not think he ever really thought about resource allocation and its implications in formal economic terms, or—since "formal" has now become a loaded word in this anthropological context—in a systematic manner. He was too concerned with rebutting the caricatures of primitive economic experience given by Karl Bücher and by the Economic Man stereotype of the classical economists. He did not realize that for a long while this stereotype had never been intended as anything more than a fiction, a model construct for the development of propositions by logical inference. Yet if he himself was not very sophisticated along economic lines, at least he set others off on the path; his contribution on the Trobriand economy in the *Economic Journal* of 1921 was a really new development, remarkable for its freshness and originality. His sociological contribution to concepts of labor organization was limited, but that to the theory of transactions was seminal. In the theory of transactions his presentation was rich in conceptual distinctions—for example, that between levels or spheres of exchange—which I myself, Bohannan, and others later developed.

The concept of reciprocity, of which Malinowski was one of the prime formulators, has borne most fruit. Explicit in the *Argonauts* (1922), it is developed in *Crime and Custom* (1926b) by which time Marcel Mauss had published his "Essai sur le don" (1923-24). I was Malinowski's research assistant during the writing of *Crime and Custom* (see the preface), and with others regarded Mauss' essay as giving a new dress of comparative classical and ethnographic documentation to Malinowski's basic formulation on the Trobrianders. Malinowski had discussed the issues with Mauss, and had accepted Mauss' point about *mapula* being not "free gifts" from husband to wife but diffuse compensation for sexual services. But he did not regard Mauss as an "independent inventor," so to say, of the reciprocity principle—whereas he did so regard Richard Thurnwald. In statements about reciprocity as a weapon for enforcement of rights, and as part and parcel of a whole system of mutualities, it was to Thurnwald alone that he referred. In translation (Malinowski quoted only the German): "We name the symmetry of transactions the principle of recompense (*or* repayment). This lies deeply rooted in human experience (*or* feeling *or* perception) . . . and the greatest meaning attaches to it in social life."[8] After his tribute to Thurnwald, with whose work he was much in sympathy, Malinowski in a prophetic mood stressed the importance of the "inner symmetry of all social transactions, of the reciprocity of services," and foretold that symmetry of structure would be found in every "savage" society, as the indispensable basis of reciprocal obligations.

In political anthropology Malinowski's contribution was quite limited. But there have been some distortions of his handling of Trobriand materials by later commentators. An interesting review of Malinowski's findings has been published by J. P. Singh Uberoi (1962), looking at *kula* relationships as a model of the political organization of small-scale stateless societies. This work does pull out some aspects of the situation to which Malinowski gave too little attention, and provides a useful overview of *kula* politics. But produced under Gluckman's aegis, it tries to treat Trobriand chieftainship as a kind of headmanship of African style, and much underplays the significance of the crouching and other signs of ritual respect paid to Trobriand *guyau* leaders. There was room for reassessment of the status of the officeholder whom Malinowski sometimes dubbed the Paramount Chief, the headman of highest rank in the Trobriands, and H. A. Powell has dealt very adequately with this problem (1960, 1969). But Gluckman's extravagant style of writing led him to the regrettable statement that Malinowski's characterization of the Tabalu chief To'uluwa as a Paramount Chief was "well on the way to becoming social anthropology's Piltdown Man: not that Malinowski was a forger, but he certainly attributed to this man a position which he did not have."[9] Yet if Gluckman had bothered to read Malinowski's own accounts carefully, he would have found that Malinowski had taken over the term—too loosely perhaps—from Seligman and other earlier writers; that he often used it in lowercase initials, not capitals; and that he clearly indicated that it was intended to apply to supremacy of mystical status, not political jurisdiction. He specifically states that the "tributary grasp" of the headman of Omarakana and chief of Kiriwina (i.e., To'uluwa), though considerably restricted by white control, used to reach over all the northern half of the island—i.e., was restricted to this—and that only two miles away lived another chief who though in several respects his vassal, was also his main foe and rival. That Malinowski had no intention of ascribing to the

Omarakana chief a political suzerainty over all the Trobriands is clear from his statement that another district on the western coast of the northern part of the island "possesses no paramount chief." Politically, he clearly meant the term to indicate no more than district headship. That he was sensible of the complexity of the situation is indicated too by his statement that it was impossible "to enter here into all these shades and singularities of political organisation" (1922:65–69; 1932: 112–13; 1935:1:328). In the light of all this, one may borrow a form of expression from Gluckman himself as it appears in his account of the judicial process among the Barotse, and talk of his characterization of Malinowski's "Paramount Chief" as "The Case of the Inappropriate Analogy."

What is more interesting is the contrast between the position of Malinowski and that of Gluckman in the theory of conflict. In reviewing Malinowski's analysis of culture change, with special reference to South Africa, Gluckman (1963: 207–34) said that Malinowski did not recognize the significance of conflict, that he refused to see conflict as a mode of integrating groups and to recognize that hostility between groups is a form of social balance. This is the Radcliffe-Brownian thesis of social opposition in another form, and I think Malinowski would have regarded it as too bland. I think Malinowski did fail to comprehend fully the theory of feud, but I also think Gluckman imported this theory into the interpretation of situations of such heterogeneity that it failed to apply. I myself still cannot understand how Gluckman, with all his knowledge of the South African situation, and his strong reaction against racial discrimination, could write of "the cohesive effect of *conflict* [italics mine] in a modern African situation" (Gluckman 1955:140). Reciprocal economic interest, and shared or parallel aims in education, religion, even friendship have been such that participation in the overall social system has engendered some cohesion, but to juxtapose conflict and cohesion as if one could be translated into the other in South Africa seems to me to be near to absurdity. Malinowski, on sounder ground, regarded conflict as divisive, except where it was ritualized (as in sex antagonism in Trobriand gardening). Gluckman praised Malinowski for his studies of conflict in the Trobriand analyses—as he did more generally for the fruitful hypotheses, suggestions, and implications in his work as a whole (Gluckman 1963:241). But Malinowski's analyses, vivid and enlightening as they were, did tend to depict conflict rather too much in individual focus. The classic dramatic quarrel between To'uluwa's son Namwana Guya'u and his sister's son and heir Mitakata was rendered by Malinowski as occurring largely on personal grounds: Namwana Guya'u the son had received gifts which Mitakata the heir thought should legally have been his; Mitakata had slept with one of Namwana Guya'us wives and Namwana Guya'u had got him jailed therefor (1926b:101–5). Powell has supplied a more sociological focus. He has pointed out (1960:129–31) that Namwana Guya'u was the leader of a political group traditionally rivals of the Tabalu, of which To'uluwa and Mitakata were leaders. Mitakata had scored by marrying a "sister" of Namwana Guya'u, thereby putting himself in a position to demand marriage tribute from the latter; Namwana Guya'u had countered by getting Mitakata jailed for adultery; and the latter's kin had retaliated in turn by expelling Namwana Guya'u from his father's and their village. There was a personal side to the quarrel, but the political dimension was more important.

In kinship too it seems clear that despite Lounsbury's linguistic support, the general point that Fortes and Leach have made about Malinowski's failure to think widely enough in role and category terms is fair. Powell (1969) has reviewed this whole field of argument, bringing in additional Trobriand evidence of great interest and putting forward his own interpretation of the material. Broadly, while somewhat critical of the earlier commentators, who he thinks have departed from Malinowski rather less than they imagined, Powell essentially concurs with the view that Malinowski tended to confuse individual requirement and category response in kinship, to see phylogeny as too much a repetition of a somewhat speculative if plausible ontogeny. At an earlier period I too found myself in disagreement with Malinowski on this issue, in regard to the acquisition of kinship speech by children. Malinowski, as is well known, argued for an extension theory, for an adoption of a term for mother's sister from that for mother, and so on. In my Tikopia study I pointed out to the contrary, that there was no good reason to assume exclusively maternal conditioning of an infant; that a process of definition, of narrowing down of the mother from a wider female universe was as likely as one of extension (Firth 1936:272-76). But Malinowski's focus on what he later called the "initial situation of kinship," from his early work on Australian aborigines, did a great service to anthropological studies. He brought a sense of reality into the discussion of kin relations, a concept of a dimension of service and manipulation of service, of flexibility in verbal and nonverbal behavior, essential to a sophisticated understanding of kinship.

Malinowski's treatment of language, and of symbols, brings out the close relation between his personality and his theories. Able to converse effectively in half a dozen languages, he was very conscious of the power of words as instruments, as stimuli to action as well as communicators of information. Questions of translation were often before him. To him, use of language—even when writing with the help of an amanuensis—was an active involvement in a social situation, not just a mental exercise. Hence his theory of meaning focused upon contextualization. Malinowski's article on meaning in primitive languages (1923), arguing that words have no meaning in themselves but are symbols, was important—even novel at the time—to anthropologists interested in language. His emphasis on speech as a mode of action, in which the meaning of words would be defined by what he called context of situation (broadly equivalent to Ogden and Richards' sign-situation), was stimulating to those engaged in research or interpretation of field material. Malinowski's contextual theory of meaning has been analyzed by Langendoen (1968) in conjunction with that of J. R. Firth. Langendoen's Chomskyan aloofness is at the opposite pole from Malinowski's *engagé* attitude, but his estimate seems basically acceptable to me; a contextual theory of meaning if taken literally is inadequate.

Malinowski's intensely pragmatic attitude to language led him to concentrate upon the use of words in an action frame of reference. Even in the most abstract and theoretical aspects of human thought and verbal usage, it seemed to him that the real understanding of words was ultimately always derived from active experience of those aspects of reality to which the words belong. But his notion of "reality" left many questions open, as did his contention that ultimately all the meaning of all words is derived from bodily experience (1935:2:20-22, 58).

His treatment of the notion of symbolism was curiously uneven. In his article on "Meaning" in 1923 he even said that words must be treated only as symbols, while in the language volume of *Coral Gardens* in 1935 he hardly used the term or the idea of symbol at all. He was much concerned with the mystical and binding power of words, as against their mere communication uses, and gives a vivid illustration of how canoes were guided in complete darkness through intricate channels by instructions shouted from the shore. He was much impressed by the "mysterious" power of speech in such situations, its pragmatic effectiveness as a medium for coordinating action, but not by its symbolic quality. In his Frazer lecture on myth (1926c) he explicitly denied that myths were symbolic. There was little room for symbolism in primitive man's ideas; myth was a hard-working cultural force; we can certainly discard all symbolic interpretations of myths of origin; myths are not symbolic of hidden realities (1926c:14, 79). Only in his article on "The Group and the Individual in Functional Analysis" (1939) did he revert to treatment of words as symbols, and give what he called the "cultural definition of symbolism." It was very general: "symbolism is a component of human culture, with language as its prototype. . . . Symbolism must make its appearance with the earliest appearance of human culture. It is in essence that modification of the human organism which allows it to transform the physiological drive into a cultural value" (1939:955).

What does all this add up to? I am not sure. Malinowski's handling of the "symbol" concept was very elliptical and idiosyncratic. But I think that it embodied a shift of focus rather than of opinion, that he never deserted his early idea of the significance of words as symbols, with their meaning to be got primarily from their context. I think, as Langendoen admits, that Malinowski included in his idea of context the transmitted, traditional elements of language. He stated, "Society and its component groups are the carriers of verbal— that is, symbolic—tradition" (1939:964). (But Langendoen's objection to this, in the work of J. R. Firth, is that it is unusable as a concept—nothing can be said about it in any relevant way.) I think Malinowski's dropping of the term "symbol" in the middle period of his writing was a reaction against intellectualistic interpretations of language. His denial of symbolic interpretations of myth was a rejection of the *particular* symbolic interpretations current in his day. He said he hardly attempted any complicated or symbolic interpretation of myth, any artifical and symbolic rehandling. It was not, then, that myths were asymbolic—after all, they were composed of words—but that what he wanted was a focus on the immediate, overt, instantaneous relationships of what was said, before looking for symbolic values. He put this in another frame by first denying that myths have aetiological/explanatory value and then—in a passage that is often overlooked—saying "once we have realized that myth serves principally to establish a sociological charter . . . it becomes clear that elements both of explanation and of interest in nature must be found in sacred legends" (1926c:121).[10] (In the introduction to a new edition of *Coral Gardens*, Berry has pointed out that Malinowski was dealing with speech rather than with language, which seems to me to be another way of indicating the primary emphasis which Malinowski placed on the here-and-now, and on individual components of a situation.)

The same sense of pragmatic urgency which led Malinowski to transpose the historical dimension of events into the present, to view myth as primarily social charter, and to concentrate on speech even when he wrote about language, emerged in his treatment of Durkheim. Malinowski has been criticized for having distorted or failed to understand the views of Durkheim; I would hold that he simply selected for criticism Durkheim's more reified abstract concepts. He criticized the "collective effervescence" theory of religion and said Durkheim did not distinguish the collective profane from the collective religious. He said (in a final footnote to "Baloma") that he was purposely not using the term "collective idea" introduced by Durkheim and his collaborators—although in the writings of Hubert and Mauss it had proved extremely fertile—because nowhere was there a clear candid statement of just what was meant by a collective idea, nothing approaching a definition (1916:423). The postulate of collective consciousness he felt to be barren and absolutely useless for an ethnographical observer. He criticized too the emphasis which Durkheim laid on the phenomena of material symbolization—the *churinga*, the national flag, the cross—as generating religious attitudes. But Malinowski also wrote of Durkheim as having developed one of the fullest and most inspiring systems of sociology— albeit marred by certain metaphysical speculations and a lack of reference to the biological basis of human behavior (1944:19). He praised Durkheim and his followers for their exploration of the notion of obligation, and of the relation of moral conduct to society. In putting forward his own views about the mystic binding power of words, Malinowski took occasion to reaffirm his debt to Durkheim, saying that his own sociological explanation was obviously a reinterpretation of Durkheim's theory that mysticism is but an expression in belief of man's dependence on society. We can hardly sympathize with Malinowski's view that in one way his whole theory of culture consisted in reducing Durkheimian theory to terms of behavioristic psychology. But his statement that he was trying to reinterpret Durkheimianism in empirical terms is more acceptable and much more positive than he is often credited with being (see 1935:2:235–36).

In the spiral of critical appraisal, the views of Malinowski on Durkheim have in turn been countered by those of Lévi-Strauss on Malinowski. Malinowski criticized Durkheim's metaphysical outlook on social phenomena; Lévi-Strauss has criticized Malinowski's "naturalistic, utilitarian, affective" interpretations of totemism. To Malinowski's critique of Durkheim's theory of religion follows Lévi-Strauss' critique of Malinowski's theory of magic. (Here, we can enter an occasional caveat. Referring to Malinowski's notion of risk as an element in predisposing to magical performance, Lévi-Strauss says there is no objective criterion for deciding which undertakings are held by human societies to be more or less risky, independently of the fact that some of them are accompanied by rituals [1962:82, 96–97]. This seems a little farfetched; what about statistics of automobile accidents and the use made of them by insurance companies?) But Lévi-Strauss has paid tribute to Malinowski's "incomparable" fieldwork, has credited him with the basic materials from which Mauss' "Essai sur le don" emerged, and has praised him, together with Mauss, for truly innovative procedures towards the establishment of proof in the ethnological sciences (1950:xxxii; 1973:16).

On the face of it, the approaches of Malinowski and of Lévi-Strauss to the anthropological scene have been diametrically different, as functionalism has been outmoded by structuralism in a plangent way. Each man has applied a distinguished mind to elucidation of problems of the human condition. But whereas Malinowski explored the subtleties of conduct, in the field, Lévi-Strauss has explored the subtleties of thought, in the study. The conclusions of Malinowski, bold and assertive in their simplicity, had a very narrow ethnographic base; those of Lévi-Strauss, equally challenging, are much more developed and elaborate, and refer to a very wide range of comparative scholarship. Yet I think there is something in common between Lévi-Strauss' grand attempt to chart the unexplored territory of basic human thought, and Malinowski's attempt to lay down a framework for the understanding of the essentials of human culture. Both have been heroic endeavors, the one perhaps more successful than the other. But in the course of their efforts, both have provided new ways of looking at social phenomena which will continue to be of lasting scientific value. Basically, while Malinowski concentrated on modes of action and Lévi-Strauss on modes of thought, there are certain similarities in their approaches. Both have been much preoccupied with the Nature/Culture dichotomy, Malinowski in the bio-social, Lévi-Strauss in the conceptual sphere. Both have been criticized for disparaging history, and both while denying the charge—Lévi-Strauss with a dazzling display of argument—have clearly found totality of social phenomena of more significance than continuity. Both have seen in myth a clue to the nature of society; to Malinowski myth was a differentiating charter, to Lévi-Strauss a differentiating code. Malinowski's idea of symbolism as a process that transforms physiological drive into cultural value seems to me to have something akin to Lévi-Strauss' idea of the "symbolizing function" of the human mind. They start from different sides of the basic problem of human culture, but one wonders whether if Malinowski were alive now the kinship of opposites might not be recognized in subtle debate.

Malinowski died in May 1942. In his obituary notice of Frazer, who died almost exactly a year before, he wrote: "The death of Frazer symbolises the end of an epoch." I think it might have been more truly said of his own. Functional identification and analysis of data had been the basis on which British social anthropology had been built up; in the immediate postwar period it was structural considerations that took over. In her perceptive biography Rhoda Metraux (1968) states that Malinowski's place in anthropology is as yet exceedingly difficult to assess. While there is still much room for argument, I think his role is becoming clearer. Leaving aside the slick comments about his seldom making abstractions or being a superb fieldworker and a poor theorist, and also recognizing the modifications that have been made to most of his theoretical propositions, what he did for anthropology seems to me to be basically comprised in three areas. He directed attention to and powerfully formulated fundamental problems of human social and cultural life, in a manner difficult to avoid—he enforced confrontation with them empirically, and as a personal experience of the anthropologist. He showed with great ingenuity and sophistication how data could be collected to bear upon such problems, systematically and critically. He put forward a range of propositions of theoretical order—on magic, on myth, on matrilineal kinship, on transactional theory—which if overly pragmatic and individual-centered for most modern taste, have still provided jumping-off hypotheses for a great deal of contemporary theory. What he himself said of Frazer can apply to Malinowski: he had an artist's power to create with great integrative capacity a world of his own (an empirical, not a visionary one); and he had the true scientist's intuitive discrimination between relevant and adventitious, fundamental and secondary issues.

Biographical Note

Raymond Firth was born in New Zealand in 1901. He grew up in Auckland, and it was as a schoolboy there that he discovered early accounts of Polynesians and began to nourish ideas of one day studying a traditional island community. At the University of Auckland he concentrated on economics and history, and went on to take an M.A. in economics, However, he joined this work with his interest in the New Zealand Maori, and making use of documentary evidence as well as a brief field trip, began a study of their economic institutions.

In 1924 Firth went to England and began postgraduate anthropological training at the London School of Economics. Malinowski took up his post there the same year, and later said that he began his teaching career with Firth "as chief arbiter of argument and catalyser of discussion." According to Malinowski: "We vindicated the theories of Westermarck and of E. Grosse; we redemolished Morgan and Bachofen; we learned from Rivers and Andrew Lang, without accepting their doctrines" (1936:viii). After taking his Ph.D. in 1927, Firth embarked upon his research on Tikopia, which resulted in one of the great ethnographic classics, *We the Tikopia*, as well as a series of later monographs.

Firth's teaching career began in 1930 at the University of Sydney. Radcliffe-Brown was a professor there at the time, and his structural views influenced Firth—much to Malinowski's disappointment. In 1933 Firth moved to the L.S.E.; in 1944 he was appointed to the chair that had been occupied by Malinowski. After his retirement in 1968, he served as visting professor at the universities of Hawaii, British Columbia, Cornell, Chicago, California (Davis and Berkeley), the City University of New York, the Australian National University, and the University of Auckland.

In addition to his extensive and important studies of Polynesia, Firth did fieldwork in Malaya, beginning in 1939. The book based on this work, *Malay Fishermen: Their Peasant Economy* (1946), represents one of the first analytic uses of the concept of "peasant." Firth was also a pioneer in urban anthropology, having organized two studies of kinship in London during the 1950s and early 1960s.

Firth's theoretical works, especially *Elements of Social Organization* (1951) and the *Essays on Social Organization and Values* (1964), mark significant advances in social anthropology. The major theme of his work is the interest in social process—an organizational approach to problems of social continuity and social change, in which individual choice has a central place. His approach anticipated much of the development in social anthropology of decision-making theory and of attempts to relate structure and process.

Ruth Benedict (c. 1925)

Ruth Benedict 5
Sidney W. Mintz

Ruth Fulton Benedict was almost a contemporary, in age, of Radin and Malinowski, but at the time they were doing their early ethnological studies she was living within the roles available to a well-bred woman of her day. After graduating from Vassar in 1909 she spent a chaperoned year in Europe, did volunteer social work, taught in a girls' school in California, wrote poetry, began some work in biography and, after her marriage in 1914, attempted to be a devoted wife. She became an anthropologist only when she was in her mid-thirties, taking her Ph.D. in 1923. From that time on she worked closely with Boas, training the generation of Columbia anthropologists of the period between the world wars.

Benedict's first anthropological study—her dissertation— was on the distribution of the guardian-spirit theme among North American tribes. Comparative work on American Indian folklore, which followed this, still stressed diffusion, although she was also concerned with the way traits and themes were integrated in different cultures. She had her initial fieldwork experience among the Serrano Indians of California, under Kroeber's supervision; she then worked among the Zuni. It was in 1927, during a field trip to the Pima, that she was struck by the marked differences between Pueblo and Plains cultures and began to think of each culture as a "personality writ large." Her view of cultures as integral configurations—conceiving of a process whereby each culture selects and elaborates upon certain portions of the vast range of human potentialities—was fully developed in the book *Patterns of Culture* (1934). Immensely influential outside of anthropology as well as within it, it formed a link between anthropology and the humanities, on the one hand, and psychology, on the other. This work, along with her papers dealing with the cultural patterning of psychological mechanisms and of behavior defined as "abnormal," became foundations of the field of personality-and-culture.

The advent of World War II drew Benedict into applying her approach to modern cultures. Improvising techniques for the study of culture "at a distance," she produced under government auspices a series of depictions of "national character" relevant to the war effort—most importantly, on Japan. After the war, this interest developed into a large-scale interdisciplinary project on seven national cultures, the Columbia University Research in Contemporary Cultures, which was continued by Margaret Mead after Benedict's death in 1948.

RUTH BENEDICT, whom Margaret Mead described as "one of the first women to attain major stature as a social scientist" (Mead 1974:1), came to anthropology relatively late in life, in comparison with her contemporaries. She discovered anthropology only after a long search, and after having sought fulfillment in many other pursuits, only one of which—writing poetry—seems to have provided her with deep satisfaction. Having discovered anthropology, she was to become one of its most distinguished and distinctive practitioners. It is because certain of her unusual and highly original contributions now appear to have been forgotten or ignored that I will offer here what is only a narrow view of her scholarship.[1]

Benedict was born in 1887, the older of the two daughters of Dr. and Mrs. Frederick S. Fulton. Her father died while she was still a baby, and only a few weeks before the birth of her sister. The girls' mother did not remarry, and grieved her loss unremittingly. The emotional qualities of her widowhood lay very heavily on the children, as did, it appears, the economic constraints it imposed. Reading Benedict's own words, quoted at length in Mead's two books about her (Mead 1959, 1974), one gets the impression of a saddened, often dreary childhood, wherein the moments of happiness came most freely when the little girl could play by herself, and enjoy her own fantasies. She was partially deaf, due to a childhood illness; and Mead gives the impression that most people (including her mother) preferred her more cheerful younger sister, Margery.

Benedict went to Vassar College, where she studied English literature. After graduation she taught school, somewhat desultorily. In 1913, when she was 26, she affianced herself to Stanley Benedict, who is described as a promising young biochemist. The ensuing years, when she lived in a Westchester suburb and worked at being a good housewife, must have been barren and bleak. Mead's citations from Benedict's letters and journal document her attempts to keep up her spirits and to accept her role as a dutiful wife. But she was not happy. At some point she learned that she could not have children, at least not without what Mead calls "a very problematic operation," for which her husband would not give his consent (Mead 1974:18). Though she finished her long-planned essay on Mary Wollstonecraft—a portion of an important work on women she had conceived earlier—it was rejected for publication. Only in her poetry did she manage some early success. There, she concealed her own identity with pen names until well into her anthropological career; and though poetry remained important throughout her life as a form of expression and as a basis for strong bonds of friendship, it never became enough to fulfill her wholly.

It was in 1919 that Benedict happened upon anthropology; she took courses at the New School for Social Research with Alexander Goldenweiser and Elsie Clews Parsons, and was deeply affected by what she began to learn from these two radically different teachers. At that time she had been married for five years; and while neither she nor her husband appears to have been ready to confess failure, their marriage by this time was merely standing still. As Benedict's interest in anthropology grew, her husband's interest in her life seems to have declined the more. Much stimulated by what she was learning, Benedict became Boas' student; he accepted her on Parsons' urging. With Boas' blessing, she completed her doctorate at Columbia in three semesters.

From the publication of her dissertation in 1923 until Boas' retirement in 1936, Benedict remained at his side almost uninterruptedly. After his retirement, she continued to play a key role—though it was often obscured—both at Columbia and in the profession at large. Her work won her an international reputation, especially after the publication of *Patterns of Culture*. But she was not elected president of the American Anthropological Association until 1947–48; and it was only in July, 1948, that Columbia saw fit to bestow upon her a full professorship, in a shamefully tardy attempt to make up for its previous treatment of a great scholar. At that time, Benedict had been teaching at Columbia for twenty-six years, the final twelve of them as an associate professor. She died two months later.

During her lifetime, Benedict's work was the subject of many reviews and evaluations. After her death, Mead wrote two important biographies of her—startlingly different in emphasis and interpretation, it seems to me—and others have also taken Benedict as their subject (see, for instance, Modell 1975, 1978). In the accounts that have been written of her, much has been made of the enigmatic qualities of her character and of the contradictory forces that appear to have governed her—such as the conflict of marriage and motherhood versus a career, and of poetry versus anthropology. I should like to suggest that these contradictory forces are to a large extent played out, enacted as it were, in Benedict's scientific work: not that she "solved" any of her personal conflicts by becoming an anthropologist, so much as that the kind of anthropology she did actualized those conflicts. My feeling is that in Ruth Benedict, as in few others, a consistency of character, of calling, and of theoretical conception can be identified. That is, her anthropology was, in some basic way, her own self embodied.[2]

I will mention three themes of her work to illustrate what I mean. First, the concern with coherence. This reverberates in Benedict's work; she was, from her first papers onward, very sensitive to what looked like coherence or consistency within a cultural system. It would be fair to hazard a guess that Benedict liked it when it all fell into place, that she got aesthetic satisfaction out of closure in her descriptions of culture. Second is the concern with a dominant strain as the expression of that coherence. This reveals itself particularly in *Patterns of Culture*. In Boas' slightly evasive introduction to the book, he indicates his feeling, much as Benedict does herself, that some societies reveal a coherence and a dominant strain, and others do not. I think her work shows that Benedict found it aesthetically more satisfying, intellectually more gratifying, to deal with cultures that could be summed up in rather limited, dense terms. The adjectival renderings that typify her descriptions of the three major cultures in *Patterns of Culture* express this notion of a dominant trend. Finally, and most surprising in view of her training, was Benedict's repeated reversion to the notions of choice—that societies, or cultures, choose some particular direction out of the great arc of human variability, that there is choice for them much as there is choice for individuals.

I suggest, then, that the search for cultural harmony of parts in a single system, the preference for those systems that seemed to her to manifest some single dominant theme, and above all the idea that peoples choose their cultures, get only one, and then sometimes lose it irrevocably—remember her phrase about the cup which is fashioned and the cup being broken—that these views embody the conflicted personality of their inventor and the particular life circumstances in which she found herself. One had the feeling with Dr. Benedict that beauty and calm, and tolerance and humor, and life itself, had been very dearly bought. How was that communicated? I have not the slightest idea. But as with no one else I have known, I had the sense that Ruth Benedict was a person who all along had made choices, and that the notion of making choices was immensely important to her as an integral personality.

I wish to touch on two aspects of Benedict's work, before referring briefly to her personal influence on me. The first has to do with Benedict's contribution to an anthropology of the immediate, the relevant, and—lest it be forgotten—the political; the second relates to Benedict's contributions to an anthropology of modern life, particularly through her efforts to study national states and cultures.

"In the 1930's," writes Mead (1974:49), "Ruth Benedict often chafed at the amount of energy Boas devoted to 'good works' and lamented the time lost to research and writing. But as the Nazi crisis deepened in Europe and World War II approached, she who had so vigorously rejected such good works was in the end drawn into them." Because of her espousal of cultural relativism, Benedict has sometimes been thought to have been politically uncommitted or neutral. This is a misreading, I believe, of her ideas; nor did her cultural relativism mean she was politically naive.

In his paper "American Anthropologists and American Society," Eric Wolf has elegantly described American anthropology of the period during which Benedict's work had its early impact: the faith in human malleability, seen as nearly infinite; the educational process as an Aladdin's lamp of progress; democratic pluralism as the American way; and an unconcern with power and its nature (Wolf 1969). I think Wolf's argument is illuminating, persuasive, and generally accurate. But I don't think Benedict was at all unaware of, or unconcerned with, the nature of power. Indeed, I think both Benedict and Boas were well aware of the problem power posed, and I am not even sure that they were really guilty of an overgenerous optimism about such power, even if they sometimes may have seemed actuated by such optimism. Anthropology at Columbia clearly suffered because Boas was outspoken and willing to take controversial stands—much more would have come his way had he kept his mouth shut—and his colleagues and students suffered with him. Long before Benedict became an anthropologist, Boas had managed to make himself highly unpopular in the United States, particularly in connection with his views on World War I. As a German and a Jew, he was already suspect; the stands he took on war, peace, spies, and nationalism only made him more so. His stress upon the equal potentialities of different races; upon culture as the distinctive attainment of the human species as a whole; upon the difficult social and psychological position of nonwhite people in the United States; and upon other politically sensitive issues earned him the enduring enmity or hostility of many of his professional contemporaries. To a varying degree, his students suffered because of his courageous outspokenness. Some imaginatively enlarged the distance that separated them from his views; others merely ignored the positions he took. Benedict seems to have paid little attention to Boas' public political stance until long after she received her degree. But she emphatically did not seek to disassociate herself from him.

During the years of World War II, Benedict became actively involved in the winning of the war itself; the intellectual achievements of her later years are intimately connected to the war experience. Beyond the meaning to her of personal involvement in a crucial test of American survival, however, in her work and perhaps for the first time, Benedict grasped fully the profound political implications of anthropology. Many of us are, I believe, familiar with the principal limitations of the cultural relativism and pluralism which Benedict espoused and believed in; perhaps we should be equally aware of the very positive aspects of these perspectives.

To begin, Benedict devoted a substantial portion of her intellectual energies from 1940 onward to fighting racial prejudice (e.g., Benedict 1940, 1941, 1942; Benedict and Weltfish 1943). Those of us old enough to remember what the treatment of racial minorities in this country was like at that time (even if we cannot be consoled by the present) ought to be able to see why the positions taken by people such as Boas and Benedict were absolutely essential to change. Yet it will not be enough simply to yea-say their work. Some of Benedict's views (Mead 1959:358–68) are worth citing at length these days—which is to say, the days of Ardrey, Jensen, Schockley, and Herrnstein, not to mention DeFunis, Bakke, and Weber:

Those who hope for better minority relations need to consider equally, when they think out their strategy, the assets as well as the liabilities. The greatest asset we have in the United States is the public policy of the state. This is not to say that our Federal government, our states, our police forces, and our courts have been blameless; of course they have not. But as compared with the grass-roots discriminations and segregations current in the United States, public policy has been a brake, and not an incentive. This would not necessarily be remarkable in a country run, for example, by a benevolent dictator, but in a democracy where the people have a voice in selecting their legislators and their judges, it is something to ponder. The correspondence between popular prejudices and state action has been far from being one-to-one. In states where opinion polls and strong labor unions and powerful industries have been against hiring men without regard to color or creed or national origin, it has still been possible to get Fair Employment Acts passed. In cities where there is a quota for Jewish students in privately endowed colleges, there is no quota for Jews in the tax-supported city colleges. When New York State Negroes protest today that private medical colleges are willing to train such a bare minimum of Negro doctors that the supply is totally inadequate, they unquestioningly propose a state medical college to remedy the situation. In areas where there are restrictive covenants and "Jim Crow" city blocks, city and Federal housing authorities have been able to insist upon and administer housing projects which have both Negro and white tenants. Even in this present postwar year [1947] when the record of civil liberties has been deteriorating, Chicago ruled against a "lily-white" policy in its new veterans' homes, and when a mob attacked the houses let to Negroes, the largest police force Chicago had ever called out was stationed to protect them. In Gary, Indiana, when white school children and their parents struck against allowing Negroes in the schools, the mayor broke the strike by use of the tenancy laws and upheld the city's policy on nonsegregation. On October 30, President Truman accepted as "a charter of human freedom in our times" a strong report on civil liberties for minorities written by the Civil Rights

Committee which he had "created with a feeling of urgency," and which recommended laws to end segregation, poll tax and lynchings, the enactment of permanent Fair Employment Acts and of statutes to prohibit Federal or state financial assistance to public or private agencies "permitting discrimination and segregation based on race, color, creed, or national origin."

This state policy is of the utmost importance in the United States. Of course it cannot be fully implemented in a democracy where there is so much free-floating racial and ethnic prejudice. But the fact that public authorities take such stands, often in the face of public sentiment, is a remarkable fact. For the great crises of racial and ethnic persecution have occurred in all countries precisely when the government gave the green light. From the pogroms of Czarist Russia to the mass murder of Jews in Hitler Germany, the constant precondition was a favorable state policy. The government in power was following a policy of eliminating the minority or was at least allowing matters to take their own course without intervention. The importance of whether the state is on the side of racism or is against it is just as true in matters of discriminatory behavior as it is in pogroms and violence. In a democracy or a dictatorship the state can use law and the police to defend the rights of minorities or to abuse them. When by Federal or city ordinance or by industrial negotiation umpired by the state, a new and less prejudiced situation has become a *fait accompli*, even those who protested most actively against it while it was under consideration tend to accept the arrangement and to become accustomed to it. Certainly in the United States it seems clear that more can be accomplished by these means toward ameliorating the job and housing discriminations than by any amount of work by good-will organizations.

This is not to say that informal, private, and nonlegislative efforts to improve social relations and eliminate prejudice are therefore unimportant. In a democracy laws and court decisions must have the backing of interested citizens, or they become dead letters. The ultimate goals of all who work for better race and ethnic relations can never be achieved merely by enforcing laws, which can forbid only the most blatant and overt acts of discrimination. No fiat has ever made any man over so that he can respect the human dignity of a Negro or a Jew if he has lived all his life in a community which acted on premises of white supremacy and anti-Semitism.

Any strategy for lessening our national shame of race and ethnic discrimination before the eyes of the rest of the world must therefore value interracial meetings of the women's auxiliaries of a Massachusetts town, and the We-Are-All-Americans pageants of a Middle Western city. But unless people who participate in such activities see to it that their efforts feed into a demand for Federal and state and city action they are guilty of bad tactics. For it is clear that the state can be used in America as an asset in their endeavours, and if they overlook this they are neglecting a major resource.

Such workers have often been too idealistic to join hands with politicians who want minority votes, but it is by such means that measures are put through in a democracy such as ours. If the powers that be are not moved to act for the good of the total community, perhaps they can be prevailed upon to court a substantial group of voters. And these voters may be able to press for enforcement also, thereby gaining first hand experience in the business of acting as American citizens. (Benedict n.d. [c.1947]; from Margaret Mead, *An Anthropologist at Work: Writings of Ruth Benedict* [Boston: Houghton Mifflin], copyright © 1959 by Margaret Mead. Reprinted by permission.)

I find it nothing less than remarkable that Benedict should have called attention more than thirty years ago to the fact that the most important force for the elimination of institutionalized racism in America was the United States Government. Perhaps this is obvious; but if it is, we all must be either disposed to forget it or to bury it beneath our catalogue of complaints about that same government. Heaven protect us from the good-will organizations—and I emphatically include here the elite private universities of our fair land, with their eloquent defenders of privilege—whose vaunted struggle against racism appears ultimately to hinge on the pressure, however feeble, to which they are subjected by governmental bodies. What seems, after all, to rise above the pronunciamentos, the indignant denials, and the litanies about quality are the triumphs of the United States Army, the United States Post Office, and the State Department—of all things!—in providing minority citizens with a fair opportunity to perform and to excel.

In 1943, Benedict and Gene Weltfish published the pamphlet entitled *The Races of Mankind*, a delightful item of popular education, to the fate of which an anecdote is attached. This pamphlet set forth a familiar position: it declared that races—insofar as one could speak of such categories in dealing with humankind—were equal in their potentialities. Mead writes that the pamphlet was denounced in Congress as subversive, "mainly because of a tactical error committed in the writing, in stating baldly that some Northern Negroes had scored higher in intelligence tests than had some Southern whites" (Mead 1959:353).[3] In this instance, as in others, Benedict's view turns out to have been very militant for its time, and depressingly apposite today. Who among us has been more outspoken on the issue of racism than she; who has done as much to use his or her professional stature to impel our country toward social justice?

While I believe these materials exemplify Benedict's scientific and political posture in the postwar years, I am struck when I recall now, in the retrospect of three decades, some of the commonly held opinions of the time: that her views were retrograde, unscientific, even irrelevant. Such negative opinions had to do in part, I believe, with the "psychological" determinism she was thought to espouse, and with the lack of congruence between her theoretical positions and the evolutionary and materialist perspectives then in the process of rehabilitation at Columbia University. I am certainly as sure now as I was then that her critics, including some of my friends and classmates, were missing the point; though just as certainly I often found myself in disagreement with her views. No one sought to gainsay Benedict's position on race; but I suspect many persons thought that the belaboring of such views was superfluous. If so, then surely Benedict was right, and we who thought otherwise were wrong—not only was she right in what she thought, but also in her conviction that it had better be said, loudly, clearly, and repeatedly. She is, plainly, still right.

This brings me to another aspect of Benedict's scholarship to which I wish to refer: the studies of national cultures and national character for which she was famous. Her work in this regard is of special interest to me because I was both her student and Julian Steward's. Both of these scholars were interested in the anthropological analysis of large-scale, complex modern societies; their approaches were radically different. Steward's approach was very much in the ascendant in the mid-forties, Benedict's was not. With her death in 1948, research of the kind for which she had fought, and of which she herself was surely the most distinguished practitioner, went into a sort of eclipse. In spite of some work by Mead and others consistent with Benedict's approach, national character studies along the lines Benedict advocated have only grown rarer over the years.

The scientific promise of such research still needs to be evaluated. But my purpose here is rather to point to an aspect of the intellectual history of the time. Both Steward and Benedict were trained in the particularistic study of small-scale, non-Western societies, within some broad Boasian outlook. Though they took markedly different directions in their research, their interests overlapped, sometimes surprisingly. For instance, Steward's doctoral dissertation was on the ceremonial buffoon in native North America; while Benedict's paper on property rights in bilateral societies (1936) was published in the same year that Steward's paper on primitive bands appeared in the Kroeber Festschrift. Their interests intersected, in other words—perhaps even more, at times, than either of them recognized or acknowledged.

Both of these scholars moved from the study of small-scale societies toward the problems posed by big ones, at or about the same time—in the postwar years. Steward's view was ecological and stratificational, emphasizing the environment, the means and relations of production, the organization of institutions, and the role of class, among other features. Benedict's view was configurational, thematic, and value-oriented; differences in values and attitudes were expected to occur both within and between sectors of the same society, but underlying, generally shared understandings were also thought to typify the society at large.

This is not the place to attempt to evaluate or compare these two radically different approaches. But it does seem appropriate—particularly since they have often been seen as mutually exclusive theoretically—to stress that some scholars have benefited from both views, and that time has left the similarity of intentions of Benedict and Steward honestly revealed. Both wished to transfer interpretive procedures from small, relatively homogeneous societies to large, class-divided societies. Both believed such societies might be analyzable in terms of fundamental value orientations. Both were interested in the practical or policy implications of their findings. To note these similarities does not diminish in any way the very important differences, both methodological and theoretical, between the Steward and Benedict approaches—nor should it.

But neither should the differences obscure similarities of intent, or of their aspirations for the future of the profession. The critics of Benedict and the critics of Steward were usually of different sorts; but often they espoused a kind of anthropology equidistant from the work of both of these scholars. On the one hand, Steward was ostensibly not (or no longer) interested in the real subject matter of anthropology (which is to say, "primitives"); and his interests showed a discomfiting concern with what was happening in the real world. On the other, Benedict similarly had supposedly lost her interest in so-called primitive peoples, and had become attracted by real-life problems. Worse, she thought peoples had underlying values or orientations that might not explainable either by class or by ecology—thus managing to be heretical in even more ways than Steward. Though Steward's students continued to work along the lines he had developed—and, of course, he survived Benedict by more than two decades—other anthropologies became the wave of the future in the 1960s and 1970s. Neither Benedictian configurationism nor Stewardian ecology would lead the way in those decades, when it was becoming clear to some that the New Ethnography would soon solve all important anthropological problems. Boas and Benedict were not the only optimists, it seems. Today, it may still be worth-while to touch anew on Benedict's approach to the study of national cultures.

In that work, Benedict revivified concepts she had developed in the study of technically simpler societies, and gave them new meanings: the idea of coherence within one culture;

the presence of some dominant strain or theme as the expression of that coherence; and the relationship between cultural "givens" and the culturally constrained evolution of personality. Readers of *The Chrysanthemum and the Sword* (1946a) are unanimous in the opinion that this is Benedict's crowning achievement in the study of national cultures. There have been innumerable criticisms; but in the light of the methods Benedict had to employ to write the book, few scholars would gainsay the penetrating originality of her analysis. In the years following the publication of that book, Benedict continued to work on national cultures, and provided many graduate students and colleagues with the opportunity to join her in the research.

A short presentation to the New York Academy of Sciences (Benedict 1946b:274–79), made the same year as the publication of *Chrysanthemum*, provides as clear a statement as any of her research aims at the time. In it, she discusses the problems posed by a plentitude of information ("Vast quantities of material are a handicap only when the crucial problems to be investigated are not formulated"); the lack of homogeneity in modern nations ("The conditions do not mean that investigation must be abandoned. The solution is to multiply the number of investigations"); and class differentiation ("The trained anthropologist . . . has to present both parties as actors in a patterned situation. He can see it as a kind of see-saw, and by studying the height of the fulcrum and the length of the board [in the study of classes, laws about property and land, general conditions of social security, and the like], he can show either that the group on the high end of the see-saw is necessarily very far up and the group on the low end very far down, or that they are more nearly balanced"). Most important, it seems to me now, was Benedict's insistence on the study of culture as a way to explain. This may seem obvious to a new generation of scholars; but it is historically interesting to observe how many decades it has taken some of us to discover that understanding class does not obviate the study of culture, and that culture is not reducible to class, when all is said and done.

Her view of the values of a culture as underlying its surface manifestations, resonating in different institutions and providing thematic unity to overt diversity, has been criticized and defended with equivalent zeal. It seems to me that nothing is likely to convince the skeptics; in my own case, I have always been uncertain how Benedict's hypotheses might be tested. But her attempts to distill the value essence of a social group by identifying some core of beliefs, then to show us how those beliefs serve as the mortar of the cultural edifice, impress me all the same with their daring and penetration. I have been unable to find any citation for a remark she once made in passing about the relations between conquering and conquered peoples in the history of European imperialism. She said that she thought the English had always done well with martial and bellicose subjects, like the Masai, the Sikhs, the Maori, the Gurkhas, etc., while the Dutch had always done well with submissive subjects—while neither had ruled wisely those of opposing temperaments. I recall being struck by the observation (without being certain either that it was true or that it could be tested). What impressed me was that it seemed like a way of summing up a very great deal swiftly and neatly—and that it touched on a very important issue, one I had never heard or read a scholar observe upon before. Benedict's unusual gift of providing highly original cameo accounts of this sort, as well as her extraordinary sense of humor—the sense of humor of a great lady—were revealed to me first in her classes, and again in the teacher-student conferences I was privileged to have with her. But perhaps I will be excused for mentioning how I came to be a student of Benedict's.

My first encounter with her in the fall of 1946 was part of my own search for a profession or occupation that would feel worth doing. One has the impression that similar searches have become popular again—or, at least, that they were for a while following the end of the Vietnam War. Like so many of my classmates, recently discharged from the armed forces, I was seeking with some bewilderment a career having "something to do with" the study of society. I cannot now remember who first suggested to me that I attend a lecture by Benedict;

but I remember the lecture well. She was describing the organization of several societies by means of analogies, and I recall her employing "hourglass" and "siphon" designs to dramatize indigenous structures of power for the collection and distribution of valuables. She talked about the *kula* and about *potlatch*—new words for me. (It was a year or two later before the precise images came back to mind, this being when I first heard a lecture by Karl Polanyi.) Benedict stood before us, tall, spare, seeming rather distant, her voice startlingly low and slightly hoarse, plainly dressed, her silver hair short and severe, what I judged to be her shyness heightened by the contrast between the penetration of her ideas and the somewhat absent gaze with which she regarded us. I was astonished by her, and by her lecture. It simply had never occurred to me before that a total culture might be looked upon as if it were a work of art, something to be coolly contemplated, something utterly unique and distinctive, yet available to be studied, analyzed, understood. That any teacher at that time in my life could have impelled me to think of Keats—when I had not so much as looked at a poem in five years—was wonder enough for me. I decided to become an anthropologist because I heard Ruth Benedict give a lecture. And that is about as close to the truth of it as I can come.

Benedict first asked to see me after I had written a short paper for her, comparing the Passover *seder* as it had been observed by my grandfather, my parents, and my siblings. I remember clearly sitting nervously before her, while she explained that she had enjoyed the paper. I made an inane remark about having wanted to make the paper less literary, and more scientific. She smiled and said only: "Oh, I have no objection to good writing!" I was, of course, grateful and very flattered. In the course of the subsequent year-and-a-half, I attended courses given by Benedict, received her advice, and was employed by her in her Research in Contemporary Cultures project. One of the sturdiest memories I have of those times is of her complete evenhandedness with her male and female students, even though we returning male veterans were quite thoughtlessly shouldering out of the way our female contemporaries. While there was—as I remember it—an anti-female bias among many of my male classmates that extended itself to Benedict, it was not reciprocated. Throughout, I recall Benedict as serene, generous and courteous—more so, certainly, than she needed to be.

I have been asked several times whether I can specify how Benedict's anthropology affected my own work, and I have been at a loss to answer, mainly because I never tried seriously to think about it. I think I know the answer now, at least in one particular regard.

In 1948, when Benedict died, I was in Puerto Rico as a member of a graduate student group which, under Julian Steward's direction and John Murra's supervision, was at work on the project Steward had initiated there. I had studied with Benedict in the period 1946–48; but my interest in Steward's perspective and the chance to do fieldwork abroad had led me away from Benedict's research. By the time that I had returned from the field and wrote my dissertation, I had begun to do a kind of anthropology that was heavily historical, with particular emphasis on the economic history of the plantation system, and the evolution of forms of labor. That emphasis emerged when I studied the Puerto Rican south coast community I had chosen in early 1948; in subsequent years, I became a Caribbean specialist.

In the summer of 1953, I returned to Puerto Rico to start a new fieldwork project, this time entirely on my own. My aim then was to record a single life history, but that of a person from the community I thought I already knew fairly well. I did not realize at the time—though I certainly do, now—how much my interest and my theoretical aims had been influenced, partly by my undergraduate training in psychology, but considerably more by the training I had received from Benedict. In her sensitive analytic movement from cultural standard to individual response and back again, Benedict made us aware of the dominant place of culture in the profile of the individual; but she never portrayed culture—nor, I believe, conceived of it—as some impersonal monster, some bloodless computer, "encoding" us, or pouring us into rigid molds.⁴ Because I knew Taso, my chief informant, well, long before our work on the life history began; because I spoke his language comfortably (if not fluently); because I knew his family, friends and neighbors, their work, the place they lived, and a fair amount about its past—for these and other reasons, I hoped that the life history we prepared together would be of a piece with the study of the community that had preceded it. That, at least, was my aim. My search for congruence, though, was not a search for harmony. Benedict's work makes clear that while individuals are certainly "products" of their cultures, they cannot take on their characteristically distinctive identity, while growing up, without strain and suffering. The relationship between culture and individual, then, is neither straightforward nor simple, and Benedict's nuanced view of how cultures work, in and through persons, had surely affected me profoundly. But while I worked with Taso, I had only the dimmest notion of the ways my teacher, the person who had by her words decided me to try to become an anthropologist, had given shape to my ideas, and inspired me to try to test them, years after her passing.

One of Benedict's last published works was her presidential address to the American Anthropological Association, "Anthropology and the Humanities" (1948). She argues here that anthropology, more than any other of the so-called "social sciences," stands at the boundary between science and the humanities, deems this not only proper but necessary, calls her own view "heretical," and concludes: ". . . once anthropologists include the mind of man in their subject matter, the methods of science and the methods of the humanities complement each other. Any commitment to methods which exclude either approach is self-defeating." In this late paper, Benedict waxes particularly eloquent on the illumination provided by fieldwork. She points out that "the humanities . . . were an intense cross-cultural experience . . . their aims were often couched in the same phrases as those of modern anthropological investigation of an alien culture." She argues that "the mind of man . . . man's emotions, his rationalizations, his symbolic structures" are commonly included in American anthropology's definitions of culture—and that this inclusion makes of the humanities anthropology's greatest resource. Her plea is emphatically not an attack on science; though it is perhaps worth mentioning that her science was much damned by some colleagues in the final years of her career as being "no more than" art.

Rereading her presidential address recently, I thought back to the life history I had attempted to record and to fit within what I understood of the history of a community, a region and a class. "For more than a decade," Benedict had written:

anthropologists have agreed upon the value of the life history. Some have said that it was the essential tool in the study of a culture. Many life histories have been collected—many more have been published. Very little, however, has been done even with those which are published, and field workers who collected them have most often merely extracted in their topical monographs bits about marriage or ceremonies or livelihood which they obtained in life histories. The nature of the life history material made this largely inevitable, for I think anyone who has read great numbers of these autobiographies, published and unpublished, will agree that from eighty to ninety-five per cent of most of them are straight ethnographic reporting of culture. It is a time-consuming and repetitious way of obtaining straight ethnography, and if that is all they are to be used for, any field worker knows how to obtain such data more economically. The unique value of life histories lies in that fraction of the material which shows what repercussions the experiences of a man's life— either shared or idiosyncratic—have upon him as a human being molded in that environment. Such information, as it were, tests out a culture by showing its workings in the life of a carrier of that culture; we can watch in an individual case, in Bradley's words, "*what is*, seeing that so it happened and must have happened." (1948:592)

Benedict makes her point again—what she calls "the common ground which is shared by the humanities and by anthropology as soon as it includes the mind and behavior of men in its definition of culture" (1948:593). "But if we are to make our collected life histories count in anthropological theory and understanding," she writes:

we have only one recourse: we must be willing and able to study them according to the best tradition of the humanities. None of the social sciences, not even psychology, has adequate models for such studies. The humanities have. If we are to use life histories for more than items of topical ethnology, we shall have to be willing to do the kind of job on them which has traditionally been done by the great humanists. (1948:592)

But this important plea for anthropology's crossroads does not forget what anthropology itself has to offer. In a prophetic reference, Benedict tells us:

Only with a knowledge of what the current ideas were about ghosts and their communications with their descendants can one judge what Shakespeare was saying in *Hamlet;* one can understand Hamlet's relations with his mother only with an acquaintance with what incest was in Elizabethan times, and what it meant to contract "an o'erhasty marriage" where "funeral baked meats did coldly furnish the marriage tables". (1948:593)

It seems to me that Benedict's insights here about the relation between culture and individual were lessons I had begun to learn from her at an earlier time, quite without realizing it. What Geertz has referred to as "Zola's maxim that character is culture seen through a temperament" (1962:13) is a maxim that was well understood by Benedict, and one she sought repeatedly to teach.

In the three decades since her death, Ruth Benedict and her work have been overshadowed to some extent by the enormous proliferation of anthropologies and anthropologists. I believe that what she offered us, however, is still fresh and penetrating, for those of us willing to contemplate it. That she gloried in diversity seems less and less quaint, in a world the sameness of which grows ever grayer. That she underlined our common humanity seems less and less academic, in a world still so unsure of what makes us human, or whether we are unique. That she wanted an anthropology of modern life made her a pioneer of our profession. That she wanted social justice for all Americans, without regard to gender or race, makes her as modern as our times.

Discussion

SYDEL SILVERMAN: Do you have any thoughts on Ruth Benedict's problems as a woman at Columbia?

MINTZ: There is no question but that she was systematically discriminated against by Columbia University. Among the pictures that hang on the balcony at Fayerweather Hall, hers is the only one of a female. For many years anthropology was not assimilated to the Faculty of Political Sciences because it would have meant that the faculty would have a woman taking lunch with them and participating in the conduct of their affairs. This is stated by Robert Lynd in his memoriam to her. Beyond that, there is the history of her relationship to Boas and to Ralph Linton. I never heard Ruth comment on Linton, but his hostility toward her was intense. After I went to Yale in 1951, he was a colleague of mine until his death on Christmas Eve, 1953, and when he referred to Benedict, it was always with a good deal of animus. He would occasionally boast publicly that he had killed her, and he produced for me, in a small leather pouch, the Tanala material he said he had used to kill Ruth Benedict.

ALEXANDER LESSER: There was another factor at Columbia that caused discrimination against Benedict, namely, that the whole department was discriminated against. For many years Boas was given no opportunity to put anyone into any position; that included Ruth Benedict. If she had been a man she wouldn't have been appointed much earlier. Goldenweiser wasn't. Of course, when the chips were down, the fact that she was a woman was against her too.

MINTZ: I would agree. As you have demonstrated, Boas paid very dearly for the challenges he posed publicly in American life. Benedict was in some ways the unwitting victim of Boas' stands, but I think she suffered in additional ways because she was a woman.

GENE WELTFISH: Before Linton came to Columbia, anthropology was part of the Faculty of Philosophy, Anthropology, and Psychology. It was Linton who engineered it into the social sciences.

Another point about Benedict at Columbia. When Columbia wanted to fire me, Ruth Benedict stopped a meeting of the board of trustees of Columbia to protest. I think it was the only time that the board of trustees at Columbia has had a meeting stopped.

LAURA THOMPSON: We should remember that *The Chrysanthemum and the Sword* was one of the first attempts by an anthropologist to describe the culture of a whole nation. Benedict used all the empirically based information that she could find, and then she filled in the gaps by insightful use of internal evidence from the culture itself in order to describe the configuration or pattern of Japanese culture. In *The Chrysanthemum and the Sword* she shows us how she achieves the pattern at a distance, and she projects it backwards. Then she shows us how to project the pattern forward; that, of course, is prediction—limited prediction within certain boundaries. She's talking about how she thinks a group, a nation in this case, will behave, under certain likely circumstances in the future. At the time she was working for the Office of Strategic Services.[5] I think she was given this assignment in 1944. This work was very important during World War II. The winning of the war in the Pacific depended, we felt, upon this kind of information being accurate, and we can now see that it was. In addition to the military need, there was also the need to know what to do when we won, because by that time we thought we would win and knew we would then have the problem of the occupation. We don't think of Ruth Benedict as an applied anthropologist, but that's the way I'm thinking about her now. The whole last chapter of the book, called "The Japanese Since VJ-Day," deals with predictions. Since that was written thirty years ago, we have thirty years of reported behavior on the part of the Japanese and the Americans, and we can test her predictions against the historical facts. In that way we can judge what kind of a scientist she was and the insights she had. It would be difficult to find any statement she made about what should be done regarding the Japanese that has not been shown to be correct.

MINTZ: I remember being told that a question was put to her that went something as follows: there were about 350,000 Japanese soldiers on the Chinese mainland; on the basis of her analysis of Japanese culture, when the Emperor surrendered would those soldiers put down their arms or continue to fight? answer yes or no. She concluded on the basis of her study that they would surrender, which indeed they did. Now, whether one is able convincingly to demonstrate that her analysis of Japanese culture was the basis for what indeed ensued, is a genuine problem of the social sciences. But one of the things that certainly excited my interest when I was her student was her daring and her willingness to work intuitively. There is a tendency in the more scientific of the sciences to assume that intuition plays no role in scientific hypotheses; I find that view uncongenial. It seems to me that without some capacity to intuit, it is hard to develop operational schemes that allow us then to see whether or not we can either retrodict properly or predict. I think the persisting problem with the work of Ruth Benedict and others who followed in that kind of research has always been the question of confirmation—to what extent can you establish that there is a relationship between the generalizations set forth causally and the events that do in fact occur post hoc?

[*Unidentified*]: I have always been impressed not just by her search for consistency and coherence but also by her awareness of its absence, and by her awareness of the dialectic of culture—for instance, the title of *The Chrysanthemum and the Sword*. She never turned away from contradictions, from paradox. In some ways she even presages structuralism. The reason her books are still read and still exciting to beginning anthropology students is because of the incredible breadth of her vision and the acuity of her insight.

MINTZ: I would agree substantially, and I did not mean to suggest that her search for coherence, her interest in dominant strains, and her emphasis on choice meant that she didn't see a dialectic in this. In fact, I was trying to suggest that the tension that marked Benedict's character persisted throughout her entire life; and that same tension—which is a tension of dialectic, a tension of contradiction—seems to me to mark her attempts to describe how societies are organized and how competing elements function in giving societies their dynamic.

ROGER SANJEK: In the criticism of *The Chrysanthemum and the Sword* on the part of Japanese scholars, one of their main points was her lack of concern with Japanese history. They felt that she had mixed together information from different periods of what was in fact a very changing hundred years before World War II. What were her feelings about history and how did she communicate this in her teaching? This is puzzling, especially considering Boas' interest in history and your own.

MINTZ: So far as I can recall, in the classes I took with her Benedict made absolutely no reference to history. She was, in some very pure way, a functionalist in her explanations, and it was particularly interesting that she took the position she did given the nature of her early work; she had been schooled very carefully in the use of historical inference and in reconstruction. I think she was very much interested in the way things fit and not at all interested in their historicity. She would occasionally make offhand comments about how there are some cultures that aren't very coherent but perhaps at some other time in their history they were. References of this sort always were rather obscure and not helpful. Surely one reason I find difficulty in tracing my own thinking to Benedict directly is that I find her ahistoricity so uncongenial; another reason is her lack of interest in class.

WELTFISH: Benedict took no courses with Boas. She took her work at the New School under Goldenweiser. Boas simply transferred the credits from the New School to Columbia and then she wrote her thesis. Her real thrust was toward religion, mythology, and symbolism, which came from Goldenweiser, who was so interested at that time in totemism and was not really emphasizing history. So she was never exposed to that very strong historical streak in the Columbia department.

PAUL RABINOW: How would you place her importance in American anthropology?

MINTZ: Let me begin to answer that not with Benedict but with someone else. Allow me to refer to what I regard as Robert Redfield's importance in American anthropology. I learned a great deal from reading Robert Redfield. One reason he was so instructive to me—and I don't mean this to be at all depreciatory—was because I thought he was so dead wrong, and he was so eloquent in his wrongness that I always found his books immensely stimulating and continue to find them so. I don't think Benedict was dead wrong, but she was wrong some of the time. One of the important things she did for American anthropology was to pose in a daring new way—much as Robert Redfield did—formulations of an unusual and original kind against which lesser figures could lapidate their own ideas. I was interested to read, for instance, a comment by Herskovits on Redfield's description of the city in relation to the folk-urban idea. Herskovits remarked quite indignantly: Professor Redfield doesn't take into account the fact that cities in West Africa are not heterogeneous, nor disorganized, but that they are mosaics of neighborhoods, composite, that kinship relationships are maintained, and so on. To which Redfield with characteristic graciousness responded, I am so happy to be able to help Professor Herskovits to point that out. When we look at people in the history of science over time, we have to give them credit for what they have done, and one of the things people do is help us get smarter, or at least they help us think better; that may be because we think they are right or it may be because we think they are wrong. One of the things that has haunted me the whole of my professional life is that when I read Benedict I don't know how to operationalize what she says, but over and over again I feel convinced that she is right. I don't know how to deal with that feeling, but it's one of the reasons I don't dwell on the distinction between the humanities and the sciences.

Biographical Note

Sidney W. Mintz was born in 1922 in Dover, New Jersey. His father was a cook; his mother had been a labor organizer before her marriage. The family also included three older children, all girls, one of whom wanted to become an anthropologist. After finishing high school, Mintz went to live with a sister in New York City and attended Brooklyn College. He majored in psychology; in the one anthropology course he took, with Alexander Lesser, he earned a C. The year of his graduation, 1943, he joined the Army Air Forces.

After the war, Mintz took a job as a group worker, hoping to qualify for admission to a school of social work. He also enrolled in a sociology course at Columbia, which he hated. As he describes in his essay, however, a lecture by Benedict influenced him to decide upon anthropology. A student of both Steward and Benedict, he considers his fundamental professional formation to have come also from the M.U.S. and from the collaborative research experience on the Puerto Rico project. Mintz' role in the project was the study of a corporate-owned sugar plantation. This work was the basis for his dissertation, completed in 1951, and then for important theoretical statements on plantation systems, including the earliest anthropological discussion of the "rural proletariat." His subsequent work in this area also resulted in the book *Worker in the Cane* (1960), the life history referred to in his paper.

Mintz' research after Puerto Rico turned to other areas of the Caribbean—Jamaica and Haiti—and led, in both areas, to landmark studies of peasant markets. From his unique vantage point of field experience in Hispanic, French, and English islands, he has written extensively on the comparative ethnology and the political, economic, and cultural history of the Caribbean. He has also done fieldwork in Iran.

Mintz began teaching with temporary appointments at City College, Queens College, and Columbia. In 1951 he became an instructor in anthropology at Yale University, where he remained for twenty-three years, becoming a professor in 1963. In 1972 he was named the best teacher at Yale by the Phi Beta Kappa chapter there. He regards this award as the most important one of his career, for what matters most to him professionally is teaching undergraduates. Mintz moved to the Johns Hopkins University in 1974. He has served as a visiting professor at Wesleyan University (1955–56), the Massachusetts Institute of Technology (1964), the École Pratique des Hautes Études in Paris (1970–71), and Princeton University (1976).

The basic interest of Mintz' work from the beginning has been the relationship between anthropological concepts of culture and materialist philosophy. He has had a major role in the study of Western agricultural systems and in bringing serious historical analysis into the anthropology of complex societies. He is currently writing a book on the history and anthropology of sugar consumption.

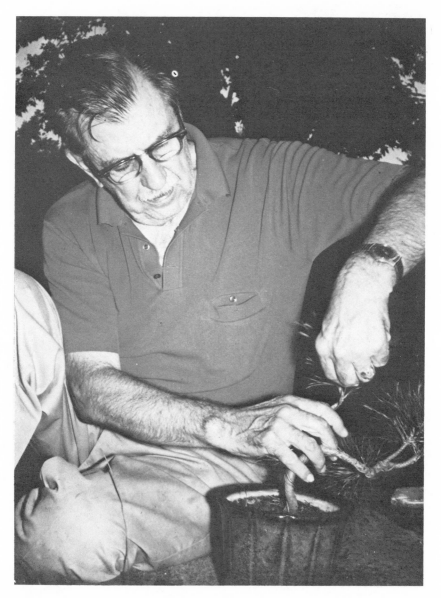

Julian Steward tending bonsais at his farm
at Fithian, Illinois, 1968

Julian Steward 6
Robert F. Murphy

In 1921 the department that Alfred Kroeber had founded at
Berkeley added to its faculty Robert Lowie, one of Boas' first
students, who had spent thirteen years with the American
Museum of Natural History doing ethnological research on North
American Indians. That same year, Berkeley began systematic
graduate training in anthropology. Among the students in the
department during the 1920s was Julian Steward.

Steward was born in 1902 in Washington, D.C., where his
father was an attorney in the government Patent Office. The
family were Christian Scientists. When he was sixteen, Julian
was sent to the Deep Springs Preparatory School, on the
Nevada-California border, near the Owens Paiute reservation. It
was there that he first formed his attachment to American
Indians, and that he developed an interest in both archeology and
ethnology.

Steward began his college studies at Berkeley, where he took
the introductory course in anthropology that was given jointly by
Kroeber, Lowie, and Edward Gifford. After a year at Berkeley he

transferred to Cornell, for financial reasons. There was no anthropology at the time at Cornell, although its president, Livingston Farrand, was an anthropologist trained by Boas. After graduating, Steward returned to Berkeley in 1925 to study anthropology. He received his Ph.D. in 1931 with a dissertion entitled "The Ceremonial Buffoon of the American Indian." The dissertation (which Steward would later claim, incorrectly, to be the first Ph.D. thesis in personality-and-culture) combined distributional study, encouraged by Kroeber, with behaviorist psychological interests stimulated by Lowie.

Steward's teaching career began in 1928 at the University of Michigan, where he initiated instruction in anthropology. In 1930 he was replaced by Leslie White, and Steward moved to the University of Utah, where he instituted programs in both ethnology and archeology. He returned to Berkeley in 1933, teaching there for a year.

Steward began his research career in archeology, working during the late 1920s in the Columbia River Valley. During the Utah years he became the first state archeologist of Utah; he worked on early Shoshoni and desert remains, then shifted his attention to the Pueblo expansion into southern Utah. Steward carried out his ethnological research among the Shoshoni from 1933 to 1935. Thereafter, apart from one summer (1941) among the Carrier Indians in British Columbia, he did no more field research, but he became a research director and promoter. In 1935 he joined the Bureau of American Ethnology of the Smithsonian Institution, where he stayed until 1946. During this period he organized the work on the seven-volume *Handbook of South American Indians*. He also became director of the Smithsonian's Institute of Social Anthropology, in which role he inspired and funded research on Middle American and South American peasantry.

In 1946 Steward went to Columbia University. Along with his teaching and supervision of a large number of doctoral dissertations, he undertook a comprehensive study of the island of Puerto Rico. Steward stayed at Columbia until 1952, when he moved to the University of Illinois. He remained there until his retirement, initiating during this period an ambitious collaborative research on the modernization of traditional societies. Julian Steward died in Illinois in 1972.

Coming into American anthropology at a time when it was dominated by historical particularism, cultural relativism, and functionalism, Steward played a leading role in the revival of interests in generalization and in the development of modern materialist approaches. Regarded as a scientist by some because of his attempts to formulate cultural laws, and as a historian by others because of his limiting comparison to selected cases, Steward himself defined his endeavor as a life-long "search for causality." He brought ecological interests into modern anthropology, through his own studies of Indians in which he sought causal processes in the interactions between culture and environment, his according priority among the elements of culture to "core" features over "secondary" ones, and his explicit concept of cultural ecology. His efforts to define culture types, his concept of levels of integration, and his outline of cross-cultural regularities in the development of civilizations became part of the "new" evolutionism. Finally, his programs for research in complex societies marked a break from folk-urban polarities, global depictions of national character, and the study of communities as microcosms, focusing instead on the relationship of "subcultures" to regional and national contexts.

IT IS a Durkheimian, and Freudian, maxim that the ancestors do live among us; they are imbedded in our thoughts, they motivate us, they limit us, they restrain us, they shape our view of reality, they endow us with the language in which we speak of the world and ourselves. This has long been intuited among many peoples through the institutions of ancestor worship, which speak of the organic and continuing social and psychological links between the generations, links that symbolize the corporate nature of society. The ties between our anthropological teachers and founders and ourselves may not be as primary as those of kinship, but they are commonly modeled on these attachments and share some of their qualities. They are multistranded, or functionally diffuse, they are hierarchical and entail varying degrees of authority, they

are incorporative, and they are ambivalent. We may not follow
the paths set by the ancestors, but our very deviations have
been conditioned by them.[1]

The reality of the ancestral spirits is manifest in Columbia
University's Department of Anthropology, for the department
has spent this entire century centered in the fourth floor of
Schermerhorn Hall. Each office is known for its past
occupants. Alfred Kroeber's office is across the hall from mine,
and the couch on which he took his mandatory afternoon naps
is still exactly where it used to be.[2] At the end of the hall,
Franz Boas' office is currently occupied by Marvin Harris.
Harris, it should be noted, has attacked almost every position
ever taken by Boas, but he does so with a sense of immediacy
and intensity that one would usually extend only to the living.
It might be said that Boas is dead, but this would be irrelevant, for Harris remains inescapably his heir. It could even be
added that Harris' sallies against "historical particularism"
are part of the ritual that keeps Boas alive, at least in spirit.

The office next to my own has had a wooden bench outside its door ever since the Boasian period. On it, generations
of Columbia-trained anthropologists have waited their turn, as
in a doctor's office, to see their professors. The bench is still
there and students still sit in waiting, just as they used to, but
the office's tenants have changed. Julian Steward, a former
occupant of the office, died six years before this writing, and
he left Columbia twenty years before that, but as a true ancestor his intellectual presence continues. It is noteworthy that
the present tenant of the office studied under a Steward
student, and the one before him took courses with Steward in
the early 1950s. Several of the current members of the
Columbia faculty wrote their doctoral theses under Steward's
direction, returning to Columbia to teach, and they help
continue a perspective, if not a specific theory. Beyond this
influence, the department's graduate students seek out Steward's writings year after year, for they still find him lively and
topical. It is indeed hard to realize that over a quarter-century
has passed since he taught at Columbia.

Steward's influence at Columbia is reminiscent of that of A. R. Radcliffe-Brown at the University of Chicago. Both were compelling teachers who attracted devoted followings, and both had an impact upon the local anthropological culture that was out of proportion to their relatively short tenures— Radcliffe-Brown spent but six years at Chicago, from 1931 to 1937, and Steward was at Columbia only six years too, from 1946 to 1952. The persistence of the tradition in each case was due in part to a tendency of both departments at the time to hire their own graduates, a practice that has ended with the diversification of anthropology and the institution of affirmative action programs. But the impetus of the ancestral ideas at both universities has been carried on more vigorously by the students than by their mentors, for Steward and Radcliffe-Brown have had something of lasting importance to say to their respective audiences.

Steward's influence at Columbia was great, but so also was Columbia's upon Steward. He fitted into a preexistent theoretical tradition, which he served to shape and crystallize; it was as if he and Columbia's graduate students had sought and found each other. I will review the salient features of Stewardian anthropology in detail in later pages, and I give here only a few highlights to help clarify Steward's preeminence at Columbia. Its primary characteristic was a naturalism through which cultures and societies were viewed much as a physicist would view matter and energy. Implicit in this positivism was a faith that culture is caused, and causal, and that we can find these chains of determinism, and thus explain culture, through proper methodology. Coupled with this assumption, Steward's anthropology had an earthy and common-sense orientation that regarded the exigencies of work and livelihood as among the most important of these determinants. He was not a systematic philosophical materialist by any means but, more than any anthropologist of his day, he saw the key to much of human culture in food-getting activities. Steward's theories also stressed the active and sensate over the symbolic and conceptual in social life, a logical enough outcome of his preoccupation with work and groupings. The approach was realistic, unetherealized, self-consciously tough-minded and dynamic. It found its subject matter in the more mundane aspects of culture, and it sought explanation in sinew and sweat.

Steward's anthropology would seem, at least superficially, to be a sharp departure from the Columbia tradition set by Boas. There never was a Boasian "school," however, and Columbia's Ph.D.s were remarkable for their diversity of interest and theory. What they did get from "Papa Franz" was a cultural realism that was shared by his students Alfred Kroeber and Robert Lowie, and by their student Julian Steward. Added to this was Boas' politics, expressed in pacifism during World War I and radicalism in his later years. This orientation was also characteristic of most of his students during the 1920s and 1930s, a community of opinion that had nothing to do with Boas' anthropology but which could only have been encouraged by his politics. One of Boas' students fondly recalls a conversation with him in which the dilemma of being young and starting out in life during the Depression '30s was raised. The old man disagreed, saying these were the best times in which to launch a career. Conditions were indeed miserable, he added, "but if I were young, I would do something about it." To the extent that the anthropological theories of the Columbia students reflected their political orientations, Boas must be considered a primary influence. Ironically, it would appear then that Boas was the spiritual founder of Columbia's so-called materialism.

Boas' influence was strongly reenforced by time and place. The Depression era germinated radicalism of thought and action within anthropology, as within all intellectual pursuits. That some departments of anthropology remained unaffected by the mood of the times was symptomatic of moral and physical isolation from their social milieus, a smug aloofness that used to be paraded as "objectivity." Columbia, however, was also located in New York City, then as now a center of intellectual innovation and ferment as well as a staging area for all the malaises of urban society. If the politics of the

Columbia students stressed human exigency and struggle, it was because these were a part of their way of life. And it is not surprising that their anthropology was based upon the same premises and world view. Such was the ambience at the Columbia to which Julian Steward came in 1946.

The specific theoretical heritage of Boas, and that of Ralph Linton and Ruth Benedict, may not have been congenial to the ideas brought by Steward to Columbia, but the basic epistemology was the same and the student culture, as opposed to faculty thought, was even more receptive in 1946 than during the Depression '30s. The Columbia students of the late 1940s were a new breed. As in the past, there was a large contingent of New Yorkers, but the postwar generation differed in significant ways. Most of the students had come of age during the Depression and, haunted by the failures of their parents, were prone to economic anxieties and driven to succeed. They had also gone through a war; a majority had been in combat zones and most had been enlisted men. It may be conjectured that the officer/enlisted-person division contributed to the political climate of the student body and to their affinity for the world's losers, and their overseas experience must surely have whetted their appetites for other cultures. The student body of the period also included a higher proportion from the lower class and lower middle class as opposed to past decades, for their studies were largely supported by the educational benefits of the G. I. Bill of Rights. Finally, the universities of the entire country were inundated by male students who had postponed higher education for up to four or five years and, as a consequence, the Columbia anthropology department had a lower percentage of female students than during any time in its history. The composite picture that emerges from these traits is of a student group that would have no trouble understanding the compelling motivations of an empty stomach or seeing authority to emerge from the muzzle of a gun.

This short sketch does not, of course, do justice to the variety of interests and personalities of Columbia's students, but the characteristics were sufficiently pervasive to set the tone of the department. The materialism of the postwar students ranged from Marxisms of variable orthodoxy through Leslie White's "culturology" to, more commonly, an eclectic concern for economic and environmental factors. At the very least, it was a view of the world that was both agonistic and realistic. There was some division within the student body between the new students and a few who had entered somewhat earlier. The latter were holdovers from Linton and Benedict, were in varying degrees influenced by Freud, and were more interested in symbolic systems than in concrete social action. Having lost Linton by resignation in 1946 and Benedict by death in 1948, they found themselves with a faculty that was uninterested in their work and fellow students who were antagonistic to it. One of the credos of the evolutionists and materialists of the 1940s and '50s was that there is a necessary contradiction between cultural explanations and psychological ones; this is not at all true, of course, but the notion persists to this day.

Steward did not have to establish a "school" at Columbia—he found one waiting for him. The student temper combined with Steward's theories and persuasiveness as a teacher to produce an almost instant following. The Columbia faculty at the time were few in number, consisting of Steward, William Duncan Strong, Harry Shapiro, George Herzog, Ruth Benedict, Gene Weltfish, Marian Smith, and Charles Wagley. The size of the student group was, however, larger than at the present writing, due to the pressure of the returning veterans and a very loose admissions policy at that time. The result was a badly overworked faculty, a situation that was somewhat ameliorated by the fact that the few undergraduate offerings were taught by the junior members, Weltfish and Wagley. The sheer weight of numbers and the attraction of his ideas placed a heavy teaching burden on Steward, a problem that was complicated by bouts of poor health throughout his Columbia tenure. But even in the semesters in which he was unable to teach, he held seminars and discussions at his house in Alpine, New Jersey.

Steward's classes were large, his audiences attentive. He was neither flamboyant nor charismatic in the classroom, but his lectures were masterpieces of integration of fact and theory. Though noted as a theoretician, he held to the principle that theories must be based on facts and the facts, in turn, were unintelligible without theory. I particularly remember his one-year course on the "Greater Southwest Culture Sphere," which was an organizational gem. He covered the standard ethnography and archeology of the Southwest United States in exhaustive detail, but he did it within a framework that he first outlined in his paper "Ecological Aspects of Southwestern Society" (1937). He interwove and contrasted the concepts of culture area and culture type, analyzed the varieties of society in terms of his method of cultural ecology, and attempted to see the entire picture as episodes in evolutionary process, from pre-Basketmaker horizons to the modern period. The empiricism was painless for being placed in context; this also made it retainable in our minds. Only a few members of the class had a deep interest in the area as such, but the course was a better introduction to Steward's thinking than some of his more theoretically slanted seminars.

There was a certain magnetism in Steward's lectures that was created in large part by his remarkable gift for synthesis. He also radiated a sincerity and conviction that welled from a certainty that he was on the right track. This was conveyed without undue dogmatism or authoritarianism, and the students sensed that he wanted them to join him in the quest. The theory was not complete, the answers were not all collected, but, we thought, if we develop the theoretical structure further and flesh it out with the right kind of data, then we would surely break through to a true science of man. Like another great teacher, Leslie White, his closest intellectual associations were with students and he treated them as partners, albeit junior ones. Steward conveyed a sense of excitement and purpose to us, and he took us seriously; the latter was probably his most important gift to his students.

Columbia University, in common with other institutions, was profoundly affected by the political moods of the postwar period. Want and struggle were part of the life experience of many of the Columbia anthropology students, and they were understandably attracted to a theory that took adequate account of this aspect of society. This basic view of social life also contributed to a political climate that, in terms of the ideology of the country, was radical. Although eschewing organizational ties that would involve endless meetings and passing out mimeographed circulars at subway stations, many students of the time were influenced to varying degrees by Marxian thought. They found in Steward's ideas a sympathetic resonance, an alternative to a rigid philosophy that would nonetheless preserve an emphasis on the material conditions of life. Moreover, it was a theory developed in the language of anthropology and using anthropological data. The ponderous terminology and obsessive concern with class struggle of orthodox Marxism were replaced by a more open-ended theory dealing with human labor in its natural setting. To his students, Steward was pioneering a new road to the understanding of history, a road that did not lock them into a fixed system.

The growing tensions of the Cold War in the late 1940s and the appearance of McCarthyism in the early 1950s cast a pall over academic inquiry that drove Marxian thought underground and rendered somewhat suspect even the non-Marxian materialisms of Steward and White. It is difficult for today's students to understand the mood of the period, or to empathize with its victims, for there has been a profound liberalization of moral and intellectual norms since the early 1960s. The subject is certainly beyond the scope of this essay, and I can only note that thought was constrained by fear for livelihood; the 1950s were chill, narrow, rigid, and fearful years, and this had an inevitable effect upon the discipline of anthropology.

To his credit, Steward did not modify his theories under this pressure. It could be argued that it kept him from taking a more avowedly materialistic position, but this would ignore the fact that he had maintained a pluralistic stance throughout his career, as documented by several of his earlier publications (see, e.g., Steward 1941). Actually, Steward was quite frank about the political implications of his theories and used the

Chinese Revolution as an example of an independent evolutionary change, contrasting this to the conspiracy theories of the right, which he saw as a kind of diffusionism. Harmless though this may seem today, it was bold talk in 1951. Contemporary students often note that Steward never referred to Marx's writings, despite some of the common ground between them. This may have been in part a matter of discretion—few other anthropologists of the day mentioned Marx, for that matter—but I believe it arose more from a lack of deep interest in Marxism. He had done his student reading of Marx and was well aware of the theory, but he never gave any indication that he had given it close study. To the best of my knowledge, most of his scholarly reading was restricted to anthropology, and his entire intellectual frame of reference was couched within the discipline. There are, of course, profound differences between Steward's theories and the Marxism of the time, which will come out more clearly in the pages below. It can be stated summarily here, however, that Steward gave greater attention to technology and environment than did Marx, and his view of historical process was wholly nondialectical. The chief area of overlap was a common concern for labor process. In the final analysis, Steward was a liberal, and his anthropology was consistent with his politics.

Steward's Columbia students are now a few years older than was their professor some thirty-odd years ago, a thought that will dismay them. They include Pedro Carrasco, Stanley Diamond, Louis Faron, Morton Fried, Sidney Mintz, Robert Manners, Elena Padilla, Vera Rubin, Elman Service, Elliott Skinner, Eric Wolf, and many more.

Several others were indirectly influenced by Steward. Marshall Sahlins entered the department at about the time Steward was leaving, but his studies with Fried and Service were in the ecological-evolutionary tradition. Marvin Harris was not a Steward follower during his graduate student days, but he later acknowledged him as a principal source of his ideas on "cultural materialism" (Harris 1968). All of these people have pursued their own courses, their own interests, and their own ideas. What unites them, however, is a basic

assumption, a premise and axiom, that social thought ema-
nates from social action and that the imperatives of work,
power, and sex are prior to the symbolic forms that encapsu-
late them. It is this very elemental and general kind of
materialism that prevails to this day at Columbia, and not one
or another particular theory. Despite the departmental so-
briquet as "the cowshit-weighing capital of the Western world"
bestowed by one wit, who will remain nameless as well as
tasteless, its faculty and students display a variety of talents
and inclinations that range the gamut of current anthropological theory. But beneath this diversity there exists a community of understanding and a common language that was
inspired by Franz Boas and crystallized by Julian Steward.

In sketching Steward's influence at Columbia, I do not
mean to underplay his important role in the history of the
Bureau of American Ethnology and the Smithsonian Institution, nor am I ignoring his impact upon another generation of
students at the University of Illinois.[3] I am merely writing
about what I know best, and hope that others will write of
their own experience of the man. Actually, much of the following account of Steward's theories will be based on his work
during the Washington years from 1935 to 1946 and his tenure
as a research professor at Illinois from 1952 until his death in
1972. Thus, I am not at all suggesting a view of his work seen
exclusively from a New Yorker's perspective. (Like the lady
who, when asked what route she had taken on her drive from
New York to California, replied "The Lincoln Tunnel.")
Columbia, however, was a special high point in Steward's
career, for he came into intensive interaction with a large
group of involved and supportive students, most of whom have
become major figures in the profession. Moreoever, fortyish to
fiftyish is a good age for anthropologists, though advanced
senility for physicists and molecular biologists. By the mid-
forties, the anthropologist has acquired the necessary background in empirical research and is ready to start putting it all
together, and by the mid-fifties his talents are best used in
issuing retrospectives and benedictions, such as this paper.
Steward came to Columbia at the age of forty-four and left

when he was fifty. He had come at the right age to the right
people in the right place at the right time.

The appeal of Steward's anthropology to his Columbia
students derived in good part from his approach to culture. He
was not greatly concerned with the concept as such and
generally accepted the classic definition of Tylor, or its modifications by his teachers Kroeber and Lowie. Rather, it was his
basic fieldwork method and the kinds of data he collected that
distinguished his research from that of most of his contemporaries. By the 1930s, when Steward did his principal
ethnographic research, there were no autonomous native social
systems left in the United States. Indian culture was carried
about in the memories of the aged and was unevenly and frag-
mentarily transmitted to the young. However well or poorly
remembered, traditional cultures found little expression in
concrete social behavior. Many practices, such as those connected with etiquette, child rearing, body usage, household
ritual, and the like, continued with only moderate alteration,
but other areas of social behavior had lapsed, leaving only
disembodied traditions. The economic life of most Indian
societies had been disrupted and totally transformed, reducing
groups to absolute dependence on the whites. The native
political orders had been smashed with the defeat of the Indian
nations, and the political patterns remaining were usually
either creations of government officials or responses to reservation life. Religious practices had been suppressed by the
Bureau of Indian Affairs, the people proseletyzed by Christian
missionaries. What was left of native American life was little
more than memories.

Due to the historical situation of the American Indian,
most attempts to document aboriginal cultures were based on
informant interviews, and not on direct observation. An old
man could tell the ethnographer how buffalo were hunted, but
there was no way that such an event could ever again be
observed. The result was that the researchers collected skewed
data. The informants idealized and rationalized past custom,
and they also standardized it. What was often elicited was not

how a certain practice was done, but how it should have been done. The varieties of situation and expression were reduced to neat normative systems, a process of reduction that was aided and abetted by the investigator's own search for regularity and order. As most ethnographers have learned, it is extremely difficult to achieve even the most rudimentary quantification from an interview and virtually impossible when the informant's culture lacked developed systems of enumeration. This same problem extends to the collection of case material, or slices of real life, from interviews. The informant may know that there was once a preference for cross-cousin marriage, but he will usually be hard-pressed to supply instances of such unions from the past. In short, the entire realm of concrete social behavior was of necessity underreported in Americanist research. But this was exactly the kind of data needed for Steward's theories—and it was the kind he gathered in the field.

The primary characteristics of Steward's classic monograph *Basin-Plateau Aboriginal Sociopolitical Groups* (1938) are its meticulously detailed descriptions of local groups, their subsistence-seeking activities, and seasonal changes in their composition and organization. I retraced some of Steward's footsteps when doing research among the Shoshoni in 1954, and found myself unable to collect the same kind of material. The twenty years that had elasped had taken their toll of older informants, but I believe that other factors were also responsible for Steward's striking compendium of behavioral data, as opposed to normative information.

The Shoshoni had not all been settled on reservations, and there were small Indian settlements scattered throughout the towns and ranches of Nevada. This not only continued the dispersed settlement pattern of native times, but kept the people in contact with the land. Not all of the old subsistence activities had disappeared. People still went out each fall to gather pine nuts, some of which were sold to be marketed as "Indian nuts." The native wildlife had been reduced by the whites, but deer, rabbit, and antelope were still taken and constituted an important source of meat during the Depression

'30s. People still knew where to find roots, they still used the old springs for water, and even their work for the whites took them into the land. They had not been as completely uprooted as most American Indians. Moreover, their aboriginal groups had been small, their memberships more easily remembered than would be true of societies based on large bands or villages. All these factors made the behavioral data accessible, but it took hard work to get it all.

Steward crisscrossed the Great Basin, visiting every part of it, no matter how remote, and interviewed every single Shoshoni with knowledge of times past. Paradoxically, this geographical exhaustiveness, so essential to the development of cultural ecology, was made necessary partly because Steward was also doing a culture element survey of the region as part of Kroeber's distribution studies. Whatever the motive, in doing so, he pioneered a brand of social anthropology that was based on behavioral observation and that saw the normative order to be derivative from this matrix of social action.

Steward's concern with behavior, and with the environmental and situational restraints on that behavior, is often overlooked by commentators, though it lies at the heart of his theory. Steward's peers considered the concept of "culture" to be the governing principle of anthropological research and its main contribution to the social sciences. This is fair enough, but most went on to stress the normative, symbolic nature of culture and its unidirectional determination of conduct. There was little scope in the concept for dynamic interplay between norms and behavior, for the path between them was a one-way street. As for the mechanisms by which culture was derived, it was no less a materialist than Leslie White who wrote that "culture causes culture." And if culture is a symbolic and not a behavioral affair, which White also maintained, then symbols are the causes of other symbols. Finally, given the fact that symbols are ideational, we are led into a total idealism. But it was an idealism which was well adapted to the normative memory-data being collected on the American Indian reservations. Paradoxically, the students closest to a dialectic between norm and action, at the time, were those identified with the personality-and-culture school, a group that was commonly charged with idealism. But a basic sociological materialism—as opposed to simple economic determinism—places activity as prior to idea, and finds norms to be crystallizations of behavior; Steward's approach did exactly this.

Any focus upon social activity per se must account for the fact that behavior is carried out within the framework of constraints both internal and external to the social system, for failure to place it in context would result in complete nominalism. And it was Steward's isolation and analysis of these constraints—notably the external ones—that produced the theory of cultural ecology. One of the concomitants of anthropological positivism is a view of society and culture that posits inherent tendencies toward stability—if not toward outright homeostasis. The result has been that the roots of most social and cultural evolution and change have been traced to exogenous factors—to diffused technology, population growth, contact with other societies, and relations with the natural environment. Steward's theory was concerned with all of these, for he found a principal source of constraint upon, or determination of, behavior to be the patterns of work called for in the pursuit of subsistence.

The behavioral outcome of any social situation is partially governed by norms and partially by sheer necessity, by accommodation to certain inescapable facts within situational reality. In recent years, anthropologists have come to recognize that actors are by no means blindly impelled by the dictates of culture but, rather, often look to culture for meaning and rationalization of prior acts. Among primitives practicing cross-cousin marriage, it has been discovered that most everybody has far more cross-cousins than parallel ones, a phenomenon which would be remarkable if it were genetically true. What happens, of course, is that a nice girl meets a suitable boy and the genealogies are brought into line with the romance. In our own society it has been found that, despite clichés to the contrary, morality can be legislated, as in antidiscrimination laws. All of this is to say that people often do what they have to do and then manipulate the symbolic system to give justification and meaning to their actions. In the cultural ecological method, the necessity of certain ways of behaving is imposed by the absolute imperatives of subsistence and survival and the limited ways in which these imperatives can be satisfied.

Steward's effort to escape the whimsical arbitrariness of cultural relativity and unilateral normative determinism led him to search for the less flexible factors within any social situation. Symbols and groupings are capable of endless permutations, but other elements are given; culture must adjust to them rather than vice versa. One of these given elements is technology. Most of the tools and techniques of any culture are derived from other societies, and the material inventory of a group is highly dependent upon its position along routes of cultural diffusion. The presence or absence of items of technology is not, of course, wholly a matter of historical accident, for every culture screens and selects diffused traits, and some inventions are autochthonous. But however much necessity may be the mother of invention, the reverse proposition is more commonly the case: needs are defined by available technology—and resources. The resources offered by the natural environment are the second important given category in Steward's theories. Resources and technology cannot, however, be considered separately, for it is through tools and knowledge that natural features become culturally useful and humanly accessible. Thus, if there are no metallic ores in a region, one would hardly expect metallurgy to arise there. On the other hand, unless a group has a knowledge of metallurgy, the ore-bearing strata are just so much useless rock. This is all very rudimentary, of course, but it is well to remember that technology and environment are not completely independent variables and that the two together define the life chances of societies.

The heart of Steward's anthropology is the analysis of the ways that the two givens, technology and resources, are brought together through human labor. Just as the possibilities of any society are promoted or inhibited by the natural environment, and just as technology is contingent upon history, so also are there limited ways in which specific tools can be used on specific resources. That is, certain operations may entail quite delimited and narrowly defined forms of labor, involving characteristic patterns of collectivization and individuation of work, cycling of activities, specialization of tasks, and so on. This does not imply that one and only one form of labor is effective in any operation, but rather that there are limits of variability in patterns of work contingent upon tools and resources exploited.

A few examples may be in order. There are many kinds of fish and many devices for catching them, but how people go about fishing depends much upon the instruments and the type of fish being sought. In the Amazon basin, the main aboriginal fishing techniques were with the bow and arrow and with fish poisons. Bow and arrow fishing is usually done from a canoe and requires at least two people, one to shoot the fish and the other to paddle. The paddling can be done by a woman or young boy, whereas the bow and arrow is always handled by men; this type of fishing can thus entail cooperation within the conjugal family. Fish poisoning, to the contrary, often draws entire villages into cooperation. The poisonous sap of certain vines and roots is released into smaller streams or lagoons by men who beat sheaves of the vines with clubs. The toxic substance drifts downstream with the current and paralyzes the gills of the fish which, dead or stunned, are easily taken from the water by other men and by women and children. The operation involves the coordinated labor of many people. There must be enough men pounding the vines to achieve a certain level of concentration of the poison in the water, and large numbers of people must be stationed downstream to prevent the stunned fish from escaping. In contrast, hook and line fishing, introduced by the whites, can be carried out by solitary individuals. Most species of fish can be caught by any of these means. The giant pirarucu fish, however, is best taken with hook and line, though the latter technique cannot be used for piranha, which are able to bite through the leaders.

The constraints upon labor imposed by certain technologies when applied to specific resources are evident in hunting as well as in fishing. Herd animals, such as peccary, bison, and antelope, are usually hunted by collective means, for a lone hunter may kill only one animal before frightening away the herd, whereas a group of men may dispatch enough to provide meat for an entire community. The Plains Indians hunted bison from horseback, the riders flanking the running herd and killing the outliers with bow and arrow or lance. Groups of unmounted Shoshoni hunted the fleet antelope by driving herds down valley floors to pens, and hunting parties in the South American forests bring peccary bands to bay with dogs. Deer, mountain sheep, and other nonherd animals are, to the contrary, most commonly taken by individual hunters through stalking and ambush. The weapons used are also critical in determining the organization of work. In almost every instance in which firearms have been introduced, there has been a tendency toward more individualized hunting. The greater range and striking power of guns make it less necessary to bring a concentration of firepower to bear upon the animals. White bison hunters, for example, used powerful rifles to pick off the lead animals in a herd from a long distance; the systematic killing of the lead bisons kept the herds from stampeding.

The above are not invariant patterns, for collective hunting parties often encountered and killed nonherd game, and individuals could and did prey upon herds. Rather, a strain was set up toward a certain mode and organization of work which conformed to the practical needs of the task. Steward sometimes referred to this simple process as "adaptation" to the environment, a choice of words unfortunate for its rather biological and Darwinian overtones. We need not, however, posit blind mechanisms of natural selection of the most efficient forms of work, for the matter is more simple. The subjects of anthropological inquiry, be they primitives, peasants, or whatever, must be assumed to possess a good store of pragmatic common sense and a comprehension of their situation at least equal to that enjoyed by the ethnographer. They are

perfectly capable of understanding and acting upon the useful-
ness of certain modes of work. This does not necessarily lead to
the single most effective way of getting a job done, but it sets a
sharp limit on the alternatives.

In my own experience among the Mundurucú Indians, I
watched large collective garden clearing ventures fritter away
time in sociability and side diversions, clearly sacrificing effi-
ciency for social solidarity. But the Mundurucú saw this just
as clearly as I did, for they knew very well that in some villages
the work of clearing was effectively carried out by two or so
men. This was regarded, however, as further evidence of the
abandonment of proper traditional ways by such people. What
must be remembered in interpreting seemingly wasted time is
that the Mundurucú had the time to waste—there was nothing
else that they urgently needed to be doing, the job eventually
got done, and they had a good time doing it. With the general
erosion of social solidarity, however, the pattern of garden
clearing work became more individualized, as befitted the new
social system and the technology of steel axe and machete. It
also fitted into a new economic order in which work had
become intensified due to the demands placed upon labor by
trade with the whites. As the Indians' appetites for Western
goods increased, "spare time" became scarce and pressure
grew to carry out tasks in the most expeditious ways possible.
One result has been the attrition of forms of collective activity
that had their source in the social system rather than in
technical necessity.

That most subsistence operations were seen to allow for a
degree of flexibility kept Steward's ecological approach from
being monistic and rigid, while empirically demonstrating the
limits of this flexibility. Steward recognized that the range of
such variation was itself dependent upon environmental and
technical factors. A crude technology permits small latitude;
conversely, the extent to which a society can control and alter
the environment is a measure of freedom from some of its
constraints. And environments that offer fewest resources and
are most forbidding to human occupation will be those that
allow for least flexibility. This was brilliantly demonstrated in

Steward's study of the Great Basin Shoshoneans, a people possessing only a rudimentary technology and living in a harsh landscape.

Steward's study is too well known to warrant detailed recapitulation, but its main argument is that the very structure of Shoshoni society was a reflex of its habitat and exploitative patterns. Possessing none of the technology needed to realize the full potential of the environment, the Shoshoni scavenged from it, subsisting on its sparse game population and its thinly distributed wild vegetation. Steward painted a picture of a people reduced to the bare essentials of life, living in a society that was all infrastructure. The Basin Shoshoni had no stable political organization beyond parental authority and the prestige given by age. There were no chiefs, and leadership was a temporary and ad hoc matter, a situation that was consistent with the fact that there were no stable or formally defined sociopolitical units beyond the conjugal family. The Shoshoni had no tribes, no bands, no villages, no clans, no lineages. They were found scattered in small clusters of a few families each across an enormous terrain extending from southern California to Idaho and Utah; egalitarianism, individuation, and amorphousness characterized the social system.

Steward found the roots of this system in the processes of work, as shaped by tools and resources. The division of labor was along sex lines, the women gathering wild vegetables and grains, and the men responsible for the protein in the diet. The female labor of root digging and seed gathering scattered the women out, for the plants were thinly distributed and the work completely individual. No help was needed, nor was there any division of tasks, in unearthing roots with a digging stick or beating seeds from grass with a basketry flail. Most hunting was similarly pursued by individual men. Deer, rodents, and other small game were taken by lone hunters by stalking and ambush. Large-scale, cooperative, and organized hunts for antelope and rabbits took place, but these were infrequent and occurred in shifting locales. Leadership was temporary and the roster of participants always different, and stable cooperating groups did not emerge from these occasional and moveable feasts.

The cultural ecological method took Steward from a consideration of known and useful resources and technology to the labor involved in exploitation of the environment to a final consideration of the causal influence of that labor on other social institutions. The latter involved a kind of functional analysis that, unlike some varities, always took the organization of work—the cultural ecological nexus—as its starting point. In the case of the Shoshoni, it would be almost tautologous to say that work was a determinant of social structure, for the foraging units were the principal segments of society. Work is a social activity in the strictest sense, and work groups are preeminently social groups. There is interchange and equivalency by definition between the artificial categories of the "social" and the "economic," and it is an artifact of the anthropological imagination that reifies the two classes and attributes a sort of causal energy to them. Of course, they are related! In terms of concrete social behavior, they are the same. Nonetheless, Steward took the trinity of resources, technology, and labor to be a priori, for they were acted upon by elements exogenous to the social system, and they involved a kind of inflexibility and necessity. There were strict limits to the extent that this nexus could be shaped to fit other institutions; in the final analysis, most of the accommodation would be *to* the cultural-ecological situation and not *by* it.

The key element in Steward's anthropology, then, is not economic or environmental determinism, but a view of social life that sees social behavior as situationally shaped and constrained, and that then goes on to derive cultural norms from regularities in that concrete behavior—this is a point I made before, but its importance merits repetition. It is this underlying principle that guided Steward's Shoshoni work and most of his subsequent writing. The approach was not unique to Steward, nor was it originated by him. Germs of it can even be found in the writings of his old teacher, Robert Lowie. For all of Lowie's fulminations against materialism, he was among the first anthropologists to understand the central importance of rules of residence in the formation of descent principles. In another context, a critique of the evolutionists' idea that kinship and territory are mutually exclusive criteria of organization, Lowie declared flatly that kinship may simply be the language in which territorial, or spatial, relationships are phrased. People are kin because they are brought together and not the reverse. And the reasons for bringing them together, or keeping some of them apart, may lie in the necessities of livelihood. Lowie attacked Morgan's notions that the American Indians were at a higher evolutionary stage than the Hawaiians and that matrilineality preceded bilaterality by citing the bilateral Shoshoni, whom he put at the bottom of the evolutionary ladder, and certainly below the complex societies of Polynesia, for essentially technological reasons. Lowie's thoughts were phrased in cautious and hesitant hints typical of his style, but Steward went far beyond them, erecting a theoretical edifice that was uniquely his.

Labels are ways of aborting thought and of endowing the complex with a counterfeit simplicity. Cultural ecology, from its sound, connotes a kind of environmentalism that was not at all a part of Steward's anthropology. He had little patience for some latter-day ecological approaches that embed their human subjects in ecosystems, rather than sociocultural ones, or that are concerned with biological populations rather than societies. He did not see the ultimate goal of cultural ecology to be a systematic statement of humanity's relation to nature. Rather, he saw cultural ecology as a method for studying and understanding the causal processes by which societies are formed. And the key element in these processes was the very social factor of work.

In a similar vein, Steward's name has been associated with cultural evolutionism, but he was never much concerned with developing general evolutionary schemes; evolutionism, too, was a method and not an end in itself of study. His approach, commonly known as "multilinear" evolutionism, was an extension of anthropology's comparative method into the temporal dimension. Steward was already combining his cultural ecological method with comparison by the mid-1930s, when he wrote a well-known article on patrilineal hunting bands (1936). In it, he argued that a type of exogamic, territory-holding, patrilocal and patrilineal band tended to be associated with the hunting of nongregarious, nonmigratory animals. The regular recurrence of this basic pattern in a number of societies, he argued, demonstrated that a common causality was at work. This was a fair conclusion at the time, although later research showed that most of his representative groups were not formally patrilineal, and that some were bilocal or even tended toward matrilocality.

Whatever the results, Steward's methodology was clear. One can examine a series of societies having common social structural features to see if their ecological situations are similar, and one can also scrutinize societies living in similar environments under similar technological regimes to ascertain whether they have common features of social structure. As in his article on patrilineal bands, Steward preferred the former strategy, for it was consistent with the fact that he considered societies to be the proper units of analysis and regular recurrence of social institutions to be the basis for their scientific study. Moreover, he was not an environmental determinist, a position he sought to stress in "Tappers and Trappers" (Murphy and Steward 1956). In this article, we showed that similar processes of social change had occurred among the Mundurucú Indians of Amazonian Brazil and Canadian Algonkians. Despite radical differences of environment, contact with the whites had resulted in native dependence on trade goods, which were bought by the Mundurucú with latex rubber and by the Algonkians with animal pelts. The exploitation of each resource involved individualized work in small delimited territories and resulted in both cases in the fragmentation of the population into residence on these holdings and their reorientation from village or band life to the trading stores.

The "Tappers and Trappers" essay sought to show the causal influence in social change of new economic pursuits and new forms of labor. And since the piece was both comparative and historical, it was also an exercise in the methodology of multilinear evolution, although I do not believe we used the term at all. The article most commonly associated with Steward's kind of evolutionism is "Cultural Causality and Law" (Steward 1949), perhaps his single most influential paper. Starting from the writings of Karl Wittfogel, who found in the history of China an association between the practice of irrigation agriculture and the rise of the despotic state, Steward extended the inquiry into other areas in which there had been autochthonous development of the state—that is, of states that were not spinoffs or derivative phenomena from other states—including those of the Indus Valley, the basin of the Tigris and Euphrates Rivers, the Nile Valley, the Valley of Mexico, Yucatán, and coastal Peru. The recurrence of large-scale irrigation agriculture and the intimate association of this mode of production with centralized political power were striking in most of the areas. There has been some evidence that the state preceded irrigation in the Valley of Mexico and it was clearly not a factor in the Mayan development, but the case for the rest of the world was strong.

In its essence, the methodology of "Cultural Causality and Law" followed the same lines as Steward's previous work. A relationship between irrigation and the state was posited for China and found to be recurrent in other parts of the world—a demonstration, to Steward, of similarity of cause. To clinch the argument, he took each society in his study from its earliest beginnings through the development of agriculture and on to the rise of cities and states, showing in each phase a causal sequence that explained it and paralleled the others. The actual method of analysis was much the same as that used in his Shoshoni work, however different the subjects; multi-linear evolution had merely added new controls and criteria of proof. In his analysis, Steward started from certain characteristics of the natural environment, in these cases climatic aridity and highly fertile soils, which provided the need for irrigation and the potential for great productivity. The technological factor was agriculture, which originated in dry farming and then became coupled with the new techniques of irrigation as cultivation spread into the arid zones. Given these elements, certain forms of organization were needed to carry out production. First, large concentrations of collective labor were required to build canals, weirs, flood control works, and to maintain these facilities. The control and direction of this labor force, and the expertise needed to undertake these complex engineering projects, called for a specialized leadership group having coercive powers over the population. Such an elite would also have the responsibility of allocating the water to the communities served by the irrigation systems. The process inevitably produced class stratification and the state. It was not the only way the state could evolve, but it was indeed the source of much of civilization.

As in his labeling of the comparative-historical method as "multilinear evolution," Steward always sought new concepts and nomenclature to delineate what he was doing. Thus, there were "levels of sociocultural integration," "sociocultural types," and "culture cores," all of which had the heuristic value of communicating a complex set of premises or strategies under a single rubric. At times, the terminology acquired an ultimate reality that it never truly had. Steward, Eric Wolf, and I spent hours and days discussing whether the "culture core" contained other institutional features than those relating to the productive system—until we finally recalled that "core" had no meaning other than what we thought useful. Rubrics and labels can block thought as well as facilitate it, but Steward's methodological lexicon had the merit of glossing and stressing his ideas and making them more communicable. We should not, however, allow the verbiage to overlay and hide the fact that there was an amazing consistency of method and purpose in Steward's writings, from his first articles on the Shoshoni to the mature reflections of his retirement. This consistency centered on the mode of production as a mediating activity between environment and culture and on the socializing effects of labor.

It is through their ideas that the ancestors live on, and Steward's legacy has a vitality that derives from its continued relevance to anthropology, and to our society in general. But the special quality of excitement and discovery that Steward's students of thirty years ago experienced has passed and can never be recaptured—by them. Anthropology's special deliciousness is based upon a continuing opening up of new vistas, a finding of the totally new or a refinding and a different perspective on something familiar. We are constrained always to press on, to seek progress through research and imagination, but it is necessary to remember that the bases of our concepts were laid in the past. Under every innovative and heady idea lies the shadow of past thought, and some of our greatest discoveries are restatements of what had been known before. Students will be rediscovering Steward, in spite of themselves, for generations to come.

Discussion

GENE WELTFISH: You say that Steward was not a dialectician, but I wonder if you wouldn't admit some kind of dialectics, that I do see in Steward, and that to a certain extent explains Marvin Harris' unwillingness to let Steward fully into the materialist cadre. If you are going to allow ideology a causative role in a model of causality in culture, then I think that constitutes a trap door—the kind of trap door that Harris would hate to see opened—that once opened allows for all kinds of theoretical jumping around in a dialectical way.

MURPHY: I suppose you could reinterpret or help him along a bit; for example, in "Cultural Causality and Law," the progression from the Formative Period to the period that he called Cyclical Conquests comes about with the growth and development of irrigation agriculture and with the soaring of population until the previous forms of society are inadequate. But I'm not sure that this is the kind of dialectics that either Hegel or Marx had in mind. For example, the idea of the growth of population being an outcome of increased subsistence causing certain changes can be handled in straight mechanical causal terms. This is the way Steward tried to handle it. There was no necessary development of contradictions within the social systems themselves in Steward's work, although maybe you could supply it for him.

Incidentally, Steward's convictions about the causal role of subsistence did not always carry over into his view of things in his own life. During the years that Eric Wolf and I were his research associates at the University of Illinois, we occupied a little suite in a corner of one floor of the College of Agriculture, space released only because the main part of the College of Agriculture had moved into more sumptuous quarters. Down the hall from us was the office of the Department of Meats, which was chaired by a gentleman named Sleeter Bull. Julian had a series of secretaries, none of whom could spell. Finally he got a young lady who could spell beautifully, type perfectly, an absolute gem. He treated her with the greatest of care, he pampered her. But the Department of Meats would cook up rashers of bacon every morning; and as Eric and I would sit in our office going out of our minds at the smells, Sleeter Bull would come tip-toeing down the hall and say to the secretary, "Why don't you come down and have a little bit of breakfast, dear?" and she would go. Every now and then he'd say, "You look sort of peaked, looks like you could use a steak tonight for dinner," and he would take a great big thick T-bone out of his locker and give it to her. She left Julian for him. Julian was very cut up about this, and thought this was manifest disloyalty, poor repayment for all the consideration he had given her. Eric and I tried to tell him, "Look, this fits very well with all of your theories. First things first. There is a bit of the Shoshoni in every one of us." Julian said, "Well, that may very well be, but people should have some principles before thinking of their stomachs all the time."

ALEXANDER LESSER: I would like to go back to the question of what Steward meant by multilinear and unilinear evolution. It seems to me that biological evolution is inevitably multilinear; that's what it was in Darwin, and that's what it always has been. The interpretations of the term "evolution" as unilinear have nothing to do with factual work in biological evolution. Multilinear evolution would mean that evolution takes place differently in relation to different forms; for instance, the bird is an end of evolution, just as man, but the bird is not on the way to man, nor man on the way to the bird. Julian's use of "multilinear," as you have explained it, ends in an effort to find a single cause of cultural evolution. In his studies of the comparisons of high civilizations, or the conception of levels of sociocultural integration, what he seeks is actually a unilinear development, *one way* in which basic evolution is taking place. I can't see that "multilinear evolution" has anything to do with his effort, except insofar as he was trying to get away from oversimplified conceptions of unilinear evolution.

MURPHY: You might see a multilinear evolutionism becoming a unilinear thing, in the phase of the development of civilization. The question then becomes, what are the ways of getting primary states other than through the development of irrigation? I'm not sure that Steward had a hard time dealing with the fact that all the evidence indicated the influence of irrigation was problematic in the Valley of Mexico, and certainly absent in the Maya case, and that there might be other ways that the state could be reached. I think that the only person in anthropology who used a Darwinian model, a biological evolutionary model, was Fred Eggan. This appears in Eggan's "Method of Controlled Comparison," even though he doesn't look upon that approach as an evolutionism. In his original attempt to understand Siouan kinship, Eggan always tried to deal with what happened: he started off with a linguistic group, such as the Sioux, and he then tried to see what were the ramifications of Siouan kinship, what various lines it took, how it diverged from what was presumably a uniform proto-Siouan kinship. Some people have called that a genetic model.

LESSER: But the ways in which Steward worked at, say, the development of the state, are unilinear and not multilinear evolution. The concept of multilinear evolution which he developed has really nothing to do with his work on the development of types, because he always looked for a unilinear pattern of development: one way in which bands changed, kinship forms changed, states developed. Maybe his procedures and his derivations are correct, but they are unilinear, and his concept of multilinear evolution is irrelevant.

MURPHY: The nearest that you come to a really unilinear scheme in Steward is in the idea of levels of sociocultural integration, the idea that there are, within any system, certain levels: within the state, for example, are certain regions, within the regions communities, within the communities kin groups, within the kin groups families. Many people tried to make that into a unilinear evolutionism. He developed the notion of levels of sociocultural integration in his book on area research (1950), and he proposed it as a means of trying to handle the study of acculturation. The point he made was that the history of contact in South America indicates that those institutions and aspects of culture that went first were the ones related to the broadest levels of integration, while the narrowest, most parochial levels of integration were least affected in the acculturation process. The Spaniards came into Peru and smashed all the idols, completely destroyed the state cult and substituted Catholicism, but afterwards there were left local shrines. As the Spaniards consolidated their control, they eliminated the local shrines; there were still family practices left, and so forth. Three or four hundred years after conquest the people were still being socialized as Indians; they were still sitting and walking like Indians, because these are things that you learn earliest and in the most primary, localized level of integration. Now this was very much like a unilinear evolutionism. I think that the idea of a progression from family level of integration to band level of integration to chiefdoms to states—for example in the work of Elman Service—these evolutionary taxonomies, I think, derived straight from Steward's levels of sociocultural integration. I do believe this is a kind of unilinear evolutionism. But not Steward's other ideas.

ROBERT CARNEIRO: I think Professor Lesser is right in thinking of "Cultural Causality and Law" as essentially the expression of unilinear evolutionism. Even though Steward originally meant it to apply to areas that were arid or semi-arid, since he was using the Wittfogel hypothesis, he nevertheless pointed out that he had six or seven stages by which he could accurately characterize cultural development in various areas. He pointed out that in the Maya lowlands and in Southeast Asia, which were not arid areas, these stages still applied. He thus discovered that he had a unilinear sequence. But something surprising happened, and I wonder if you can shed any light on it. The article had created a sensation in 1949, and a few years later there was a symposium at the AAA meeting in Tucson, at which a number of scholars familiar with each of the areas that Steward had dealt with examined his sequence and his theory of causation in detail. The result was as you suggested: in the Valley of Mexico there did not seem to be evidence of irrigation very early, and in Mesopotamia too, large-scale irrigation came after the state was formed. The causal basis for Steward's developmental theory was severely undercut. Steward, reacting to this, backed away from the sequence of stages he had proposed to characterize development. One archeologist on the panel was displeased at this and told Steward, "You should not throw out the baby with the irrigation water." "Cultural Causality and Law" was the high-water mark of Steward's evolutionism. From then on he began a retreat, which became very marked by 1953. He made such an enormous advance. Why did he back away from trying to consolidate it and from finding as much order and coherence as he could? The rest of his life was retreat, as far as cultural evolution was concerned.

MURPHY: I think this gets back to my point that fundamentally he wasn't really interested in evolutionism. He didn't consider himself an evolutionist. To the extent that he found it useful for discovering laws, yes, he was an evolutionist. To the extent that he looked upon history as not being a hodge-podge concatenation of events one after another but as involving some orderly unfolding, yes, he was an evolutionist. He was an evolutionist in many ways. Everybody is a unilinear evolutionist, if you use the basic premise that evolution is characterized by a progression from simplicity to complexity. But it depends on how you define evolutionism.

MICHAEL HARNER: Something that is very distinctive about Steward is his preoccupation with causality, which I think was at least as important, if not more so, than his search for law. I wonder about the origins of this preoccupation. Certainly the Berkeley academic scene may have played a role in this, if only in a negative way. For example, Gifford's famous required course, "World Ethnography." Edward provided the students with the annual rainfall, temperature ranges, and many other environmental facts related to perhaps twenty cultures in the world, and the students were left to absorb it all and were not given any explanation as to why these facts might be significant. This was typical of the Berkeley undergraduate program; there was a tremendous variety of area courses and virtually no theories to explain why all this cultural diversity developed. I wonder if you have any insights into this very salient aspect of Steward's character, his search for causality.

MURPHY: I really don't. I know Gifford's course contained every known fact; people learned more about world ethnography than they ever wanted to know. (After Gifford retired, the course was always given to the youngest faculty member joining the Berkeley department. Very optimistic, bright young people used to be driven into absolute despondency by the information that they were to teach "World Ethnography." Then somebody would take them aside and say, "It consists of the group you're studying and anything else you want to throw in.")

Certainly Steward never got this preoccupation from Kroeber, who was concerned only with culture, not with social institutions qua social and not with social activity qua activity. He didn't really get it from Lowie, who said he was interested in causality but then imposed such strict scientific canons for determining causality that they simply couldn't be met in most of anthropology. But at the same time this aspect of Steward's work began to show up early. It might partially have come out of Steward's work in the natural sciences at

Cornell. In part it may have been a reaction to his Christian Science mother. In part it derived from the Shoshoni experience, in which he saw the direct, dramatic, and irrevocable impact of the limitations of environment on an entire way of life.

LESSER: I don't see that an interest in causality needs to be explained. It seems to me that to be a scientist you have to be interested in causal relations, otherwise you're not doing anything. The fact that Steward followed the interest up in a particular way was the particular theory that he had, but even functionalists doing synchronic studies are interested in finding causes and effects and influences and interrelationships, when they look for connections that involve interinfluence. I don't see any problem with an interest in causality. The fact that he—unlike other people—tried to pursue it through broad cultural comparisons is one of the things that he added, but he didn't have to expound multilineality, because that was irrelevant to what he was trying to do. When Lowie used the *Kulturkreise* as an illustration of multilineality he had a good point, because that was supposed to describe different developments. But when you are looking for similar or parallel development you are looking for some kind of unilineality, and you have to use causality; otherwise you've got nothing.

MURPHY: Obviously there are all sorts of causes; Steward was interested especially in a causal sequence that showed some organic and regular unfolding of tendencies. He was interested in those causes that could be adduced from, that were contained in, autochthonous internal developments in societies. It was that interest that led him to engage in long dialogues about diffusion versus independent invention (which was one of the favorite problems of anthropologists of that time, of course). Steward always came down on the side of internal development as the thing to look for in the first place, because diffusion always seemed to him too adventitious and accidental. He wasn't denying its importance, but he always took the attitude that any society that was going to adopt some very important trait was probably ready for it anyhow. It was this attempt to see causal developments as emanating internally, autochthonously, within the society, as having some sort of inevitability, and as being connected in some organic way with the unfolding of the society, that made him, in a real sense, an evolutionist as well as a student of causality.

Biographical Note

Robert F. Murphy was born in 1924 in Rockaway Beach, Queens, where he grew up. He attended Far Rockaway High School—a school that produced an exceptionally large number of anthropologists, among them Alexander Lesser. His first exposure to other cultures (apart from growing up as an Irish Catholic in a Jewish neighborhood) came through naval service in the Pacific during World War II. After the war, he enrolled in Columbia College under the G.I. Bill, and a course in anthropology (chosen because he had heard it was easy) introduced him to the subject. His interest aroused by his teacher, Charles Wagley, he went on in 1949 to do graduate work at Columbia; although at the time it seemed unlikely that one could make a living out of anthropology, he "found the university to be more agreeable than was either home or the navy."

At Columbia Murphy worked closely with both Steward and Wagley (a student of Ruth Bunzel and Ralph Linton, and Marvin Harris' teacher as well). These professors led Murphy to do his initial fieldwork in South America among the Mundurucú Indians of Brazil (1952-53), whom he describes as the most persuasive of all his teachers. While completing work on his dissertation (the Ph.D. was awarded in 1954) he joined Steward at Illinois, one of a series of research associates Steward brought to work with him there. In 1955 Murphy was appointed an assistant professor at Berkeley, where he came to know Robert Lowie (see Murphy 1972). He remained at Berkeley until 1963, when he returned to Columbia as a professor. He served as chairman of the anthropology department from 1969 to 1972.

Murphy's varied fieldwork has addressed a series of basic problems in ethnology, exploring a number of anthropological contradictions: the Mundurucú were patrilineal and matrilocal, the Shoshoni (1954) survived near starvation, the Tuareg of North Africa (1959-60) were Moslems and matrilineal. His theoretical orientation is (by his own description) "deliberately and happily eclectic," combining an early and persistent cultural-ecological bent, a strong dash of Freud (who attracted him since his undergraduate days), a middle period of structural-functional influence, and a later absorption with Lévi-Strauss—interests that "were cumulative, not substitutive"—and that resulted in "an intellectual stew, well seasoned with Marx." The combination was expressed in his theoretical synthesis, *The Dialectics of Social Life* (1971). Murphy continues to think of himself first as a teacher and second as an anthropologist, and to do both because he likes to.

Leslie White in 1967

Leslie A. White 7
Robert L. Carneiro

A contemporary of Steward's, Leslie White, was equally instrumental in moving American anthropology toward generalizing
theories of culture and toward materialist explanations. Like
Steward, White was educated by students of Boas: Alexander
Goldenweiser, with whom he took courses at the New School for
Social Research, and then, at the University of Chicago, Edward
Sapir and Fay-Cooper Cole (an ethnologist-archeologist who had
studied under George A. Dorsey at the Field Museum before taking his degree with Boas). Like Steward, White had an early flirtation with psychology, and then fieldwork experience among
Indians in the American Southwest. While the two men are
linked for their both having departed from the Boasian tradition,
for their interests in formulating laws of culture, and for their
respective contributions to the revival of cultural evolution, their
concerns and their approaches were very different—often at odds
with each other—and there was little direct contact between
them.

Although White got his Ph.D. a few years earlier than
Steward, his breaking of new theoretical ground began

somewhat later. Until the late 1930s his writings dealt with Pueblo Indian ethnology and were fully consistent with his Boasian training. During the 1940s, however, White produced a series of seminal statements setting forth a comprehensive theory of the evolution of culture and redefining anthropology as a science of culture—"culturology." Iconoclastic and bitterly opposed at the time, White's ideas on evolution, energy, and the concept of culture eventually came to be widely accepted.

Like Steward, White was at the height of his development as a scholar and teacher when anthropology entered a period of explosive growth after World War II. Thus, the two men had a profound influence in shaping contemporary anthropology—including the shaping of reactions to their views.

LESLIE WHITE was, without question, one of the intellectual leaders of contemporary anthropology. But he was more than this. He was one of the major instruments by means of which anthropology became a full-fledged science. When he entered it, anthropology was dominated by a negative and critical particularism. When he left it, it had become a positive, expanding, and generalizing discipline. And this transformation was due in no small part to White's own efforts. He gave anthropology powerful concepts and invigorating theories. In a word, he gave it propulsion.

My purpose in writing this paper is to show how this came about. In doing so I will draw not only on published writings, but also on my personal experiences as a student, follower, and friend of Leslie White. [1]

Leslie Alvin White was born in Salida, Colorado, on January 19, 1900. His father, Alvin Lincoln White, was a civil engineer who did location and construction work for the railroads, and because of the requirements of this work, the family moved frequently. When Leslie was five years old his father and mother were divorced, and his father was awarded custody of the three children. Two years later, in 1907, because of ill health, Alvin White decided to give up the desk job he then held in Kansas City and move to a farm near Greeley,

Kansas, some sixty miles to the southwest. There they lived, Leslie, his older sister, and his younger brother, in a house that, "as was the case of all houses in that community at that time . . . was without running water, plumbing, or electric lights" (White n.d.:3). One night in 1910, Leslie's father took him outside and showed him Halley's comet, which was then blazing across the sky; this event seems to have been a turning point in his life. Leslie became very much interested in astronomy, and later read a book entitled *Natural Philosophy* that his father had used in college. As a result, he decided to become an astronomer or a physicist.

In 1914, the family moved to a farm near Zachary, Louisiana, where Leslie finished high school at the age of sixteen. He would have enrolled in Louisiana State University immediately thereafter, but illness, and then in 1918 enlistment in the United States Navy, delayed his entry into college.

Of the effect the war had on him, White wrote:

The War changed my life purpose and outlook profoundly. I discovered somehow, during the War, that all I had been taught, formally and informally, about my society, my country, and related subjects, was a gross distortion of reality. I therefore determined, when I entered college, to find out why *peoples* behave as they do. My love for physics was not extinguished; it was merely pushed into the background. I majored in history and political science during my freshman and sophomore years at Louisiana State University, thinking they would answer my new and big questions for me. They did not, and I turned to psychology, sociology and philosophy during my junior and senior years at Columbia University, to which I had transferred. (Quoted in Barnes 1960:xvi)

White was a student at LSU from 1919 to 1921, and at Columbia College from 1921 to 1923. He received his bachelor's degree in psychology from Columbia in February, 1923, and stayed on to do graduate work in the same field under Robert Woodworth, receiving his M.A. in June, 1924. During his three years at Columbia, White did not take a single course in anthropology, despite the fact that Franz Boas was at the height of his fame there as a teacher.

At the same time that he was formally in residence at Columbia, White was taking courses at the New School for Social Research. He took his first anthropology course there under Boas' student Alexander Goldenweiser, as well as courses from John B. Watson, the behaviorist psychologist, W. I. Thomas, the sociologist, and Thorstein Veblen, the economist.[2]

After receiving his master's degree from Columbia, White decided to go to the University of Chicago and enroll in the joint department of sociology and anthropology. About this move he wrote:

I still remained interested in what I then called "peoples" (rather than "culture"). Therefore, I went to the University of Chicago to study sociology. I quit sociology because I found that it seemed to me all theory and little fact. I jumped out of the sociological frying pan into the fire of anthropology only to find that the anthropologists had plenty of facts but no ideas. (Quoted in Barnes 1960:xvii)

In 1925, a year after transferring to the University of Chicago, White published his first professional article, entitled "Personality and Culture." This appears to have been the first article ever written bearing this title (Aberle 1960:2). It is ironic that it should have been Leslie White who "pioneered" this field, since he came to abandon psychology as the master key to an understanding of human behavior. Indeed, he is often regarded as the archenemy of the personality-and-culture movement in anthropology. (He once remarked that those anthropologists who had been seduced by this approach were "selling their culturological birthright for a mess of psychological pottage" [1946:86].)

It is clear from a book review White wrote of John Dewey's *Human Nature and Conduct* for Robert Woodworth's course in social psychology in 1922 that he had found in Dewey the germ of the idea of culture as an external class of phenomena which exerted a powerful influence on human behavior.[3] When considering a topic for his doctoral dissertation at Chicago, White first proposed to write a library thesis, highly theoretical and philosophical in nature, which foreshadowed a number of his later interests and views, including culturology.⁴ The thesis proposal was submitted to Benjamin Faris, chairman of the department and a sociologist, who rejected it as too theoretical and ambitious. (This rejection precipitated a dispute within the department, in which Faris was ranged against Fay-Cooper Cole, the senior anthropologist. The result was a split which ultimately led to the formation of separate departments of anthropology and sociology.)

His theoretical thesis topic rejected, White had to look elsewhere for material for his dissertation. The year before, 1925, he had gotten his first taste of fieldwork when he spent a few weeks among the Menomini and Winnebago in Wisconsin. This experience, he later wrote, "made a firm and lasting impression on me" (White 1973a:v). But his first real fieldwork came in 1926 in Acoma Pueblo, New Mexico. White (1973a:v) described the circumstances leading up to this field trip as follows:

After having taken courses for six consecutive quarters at Chicago I became restive, and Professor Sapir "prescribed" a field trip. He wrote to Dr. Elsie Clews Parsons, who was then in Egypt, to inquire if I might receive financial support from the Southwest Society (i.e., Dr. E. C. P.). She replied that financial support would be forthcoming, but said that I should not go to Acoma until she had briefed me fully with regard to the difficulties confronting a would-be ethnographer among the Pueblo Indians of New Mexico. But I was too restless to await my indoctrination and set out on my own before Dr. Parsons returned to the United States. During my first few weeks in the field, I received rather severe letters from her, chiding me for rashness in going into the field ignorant and unprepared.

In those days it was difficult to do fieldwork openly among the eastern Pueblos, and when Franz Boas learned of White's field plans, he was concerned lest he be unable to obtain informants at Acoma. Boas wrote to Sapir solicitously that "it would seem very undesirable that a young man on his first expedition should fail to get any material," and passed on

Elsie Parsons' advice that in such an event he should try working among the Pima (White 1973a:v-vi).

White's Ph.D. dissertation, "Medicine Societies of the
Southwest," was written in 1927 and was based on his year of
fieldwork at Acoma.

In the fall of 1927, degree in hand, White began his teaching career as an instructor in anthropology at the University of
Buffalo. At the time, he was still a Boasian in outlook, at least
as far as cultural evolution was concerned. Although he had
never taken a course under Boas, he had been taught by
Goldenweiser and Sapir, both students of Boas, and he had
read and absorbed Robert H. Lowie's antievolutionary mani-
festo, *Primitive Society* (1920). "I was trained in the Boasian
tradition of anti-evolutionism," he later wrote (White, in
press). He had not yet read anything by Lewis H. Morgan or
the other classical evolutionists, having been discouraged from
doing so by his teachers, who represented their work as
"obsolete" (Barnes 1960:xxv).

However, an experience White had while teaching at the
University of Buffalo began to change his attitude toward
cultural evolutionism. He described this experience as follows:

I taught my students anti-evolutionism. But I had some very
intelligent and alert students in my courses. They had never heard
that the theory of evolution—so fundamental in biology—was out of
place in ethnology. They challenged me on this issue. I repeated all
the reasons the Boasians offered for rejecting the theory of cultural
evolution. My teaching may have been acceptable to some of my
students, but certainly not to all. They pushed me into a corner.
Before long I realized that I could not defend the doctrines of anti-
evolutionism; then I realized that I could no longer hold them; they
were untenable. (White, in press)

Not far from Buffalo was the Tonawanda Indian Reservation where Lewis H. Morgan had studied the Seneca Iroquois.
This prompted White to read Morgan, first *The League of the
Iroquois* and then *Ancient Society*. And as he did so he found
that Morgan was not as benighted or archaic as he had been

painted, and that much of the evolutionism presented in *Ancient Society* was still valid and fruitful. Over the years, White continued to study Morgan's work and eventually edited some of Morgan's letters and journals, as well as the definitive edition of *Ancient Society* (see White, ed., 1937, 1940, 1959; White 1942b, 1944, 1951, 1957a, 1957b, 1964). At the time of his death, he was undoubtedly the leading Morgan scholar in the world.[5]

According to Harry Elmer Barnes (1960:xxv), another important influence that led White to reassess the merits of cultural evolutionism "was that of a young colleague, the brilliant and learned philosopher Marvin Farber, who had joined the staff of the University of Buffalo the year before Dr. White came there. Farber had taken some anthropology as a student at Harvard and in extensive foreign study thereafter and was especially interested in the subject of evolution in general. He did much to undermine Dr. White's already fading confidence in the extreme anti-evolutionary arguments advanced by Lowie in *Primitive Society*."

Still another factor in White's acceptance of evolutionism was his visit to Russia in the summer of 1929. This experience exposed him to the writings of Karl Marx and Friedrich Engels, who themselves had been very much interested in Morgan's work, especially as it bore on the transformation of primitive society into civil society.[6]

As a result of his trip to Russia and the reading it led him to do, White became convinced that socialism would ultimately prevail in Western society. Toward the end of the following year, 1930, at the annual meeting of the American Association for the Advancement of Science in Cleveland, he presented a paper entitled "An Anthropological Appraisal of the Russian Revolution" in which he predicted the collapse of the capitalist system and the eventual triumph of socialism. The paper received world-wide attention, including front-page coverage by *The New York Times* and *Pravda*. Some weeks later, in another article in *Pravda*, Maxim Gorki took favorable notice of White's remarks. Years later, recalling this incident, White remarked, "This didn't endear me to anyone in the United States except the Communists." He was asked to meet with the dean at the University of Michigan, where he had been teaching less than a year, and was told of the letters, phone calls, and telegrams the university had received demanding he be fired. "The dean told me I was indiscreet, and didn't predict long tenure for me," White later observed (Weiner 1969:4).

In reviewing the intellectual influences on Leslie White we must recognize that while White never cited his indebtedness to Karl Marx in print, he was certainly influenced by Marx. He once told me he had read the first chapter of *Capital* sixteen times, and learned something from it each time. In this era of "Marxist chic," when young anthropologists vie with one another in quoting Marx, it may be difficult for some to understand White's failure to acknowledge this influence. But one must remember that until relatively recently, citing Marx with approval might jeopardize an American scholar's academic career, as in fact White had already learned. White expressed heretical views so freely during his lifetime, among both his students and his colleagues, and felt the sting of their reproach so often, that one can hardly accuse him of academic timidity. On the contrary, his career was marked by the outspoken espousal of unpopular ideas.[7]

What White found most fruitful in Marxism was the concept of historical materialism—the idea that technological and economic factors play the primary role in molding a society. He took up this notion wholeheartedly and expressed it many times in his writings.[8] Another Marxist concept he found useful was that major cultural changes occur through the accumulation of small, quantitative increments that lead, once a certain point is reached, to a qualitative transformation.

However, it is important to note that White made no use at all of the dialectical method, making him, in Stanley Diamond's view, "a mechanical or mechanistic, as opposed to a dialectical materialist." As a result, Diamond concluded that White, "although obviously influenced by Marx, is not a Marxist in the traditional sense at all" (1974:341).[9]

Among White's other intellectual debts, that to Morgan

has already been mentioned. He absorbed Morgan's evolutionism, his appreciation of the role of property in determining social relations, and his deep interest in kinship systems. From E. B. Tylor, White derived the concept of culture and the idea of a science of culture, as well as Tylor's more limited evolutionism.[10]

From Herbert Spencer, White adopted the notion of evolution as consisting essentially of differentiation of structure and specialization of function. He also seems to have derived from him the idea of society as a system, which he developed so beautifully in chapters 7 and 8 of *The Evolution of Culture* (1959a),[11] and returned to in his posthumously published volume, *The Concept of Cultural Systems* (1975). White's critical views of the Great Man theory of history also stem from Spencer, who vigorously attacked this theory, especially in *The Study of Sociology* (1873; *see also* Carneiro 1974a:553), which White once said was his favorite of Spencer's work. "But above all," he once wrote to me, "from Herbert Spencer I learned how to think." (For some time I assumed he had told me this because he knew of my own deep involvement with Spencer's work, but later I heard from Napoleon Chagnon and Beth Dillingham that White told them the same thing.)

From Émile Durkheim, whose work he greatly admired and whom he considered a culturologist, White derived the idea of a science of culture, cultural determinism, and the functional approach in general. This acceptance of functionalism may have been strengthened later by his reading of Malinowski and Radcliffe-Brown (see White 1947a:183). White used to say in class that what was sound and illuminating in functionalism had been absorbed into the intellectual bloodstream of anthropology, and he was no doubt speaking for himself as well as for the profession at large. Certainly his article "History, Evolutionism, and Functionalism: Three Types of Interpretation of Culture," published in 1945, portrayed functionalism as equally valid with evolutionism.

Thus, in assessing Leslie White's intellectual debts, we see that he had several major ones. But he rendered no mentor full allegiance. He was not a disciple. He was not wedded to anyone else's system. Rather, he was an independent thinker concerned with building his own. And though in doing so he took disparate elements from various sources, he carefully articulated them into a unique and distinctive end-product. His total philosophy, eclectic in its origins, was, once assembled, solid, unified, and integrated.

Let us return now to White's academic career. In 1930 he left Buffalo and began teaching at the University of Michigan, replacing Julian H. Steward, who had moved to the University of Utah. The following year he married Mary Pattison, who had been his student at the University of Buffalo.[12] In 1932 White was promoted to associate professor and was made acting chairman of the department. However, largely because of the controversy that surrounded him at Michigan, promotion to full professor was delayed until 1943, and he was not made chairman (with the "acting" dropped) until 1945. He remained chairman until 1957 when he voluntarily stepped down from the position. In the twenty-five years he headed the department he built up its strength from one full-time anthropologist to twenty (Beardsley 1976:618). The department increased not only in size but in renown, and when White resigned as chairman, it was one of the most distinguished in the world.

Academic honors were slow in coming to White, but eventually they did come. When the University of Michigan instituted a Distinguished Faculty Achievement Award in 1957, White was one of the five professors out of the entire university to receive it the first year. The same year he was elected a vice-president of the American Association for the Advancement of Science and chairman of Section H, the Anthropology section. In 1959 he received the Viking Fund Medal in general anthropology. In 1960, in honor of his sixtieth birthday and his thirty years of teaching at the University of Michigan, he was presented with a Festschrift by his students and colleagues (Dole and Carneiro 1960). In 1964 White was given one of the highest honors in his profession when he was elected president of the American Anthropological Association. He received two honorary degrees, an Sc.D. from the University of Buffalo in 1962 and an LL.D. from the University of Colorado in 1970.

Because of his provocative views and his acknowledged ability as a teacher, White was invited to lecture at a number of other institutions. He served as visiting professor at Yenching University in Peiping in 1936, at Yale in 1947, at Columbia in 1948, at Harvard in 1949, and at the University of California at Berkeley in 1957. In later years, after his retirement from Michigan, he taught at Rice, San Francisco State, and the University of California at Santa Barbara.

In 1970, after forty years of teaching at Michigan, Leslie White retired. Later he found a second home at the University of California at Santa Barbara, where he received a staff appointment and an office. There he was among former students and colleagues: Elman Service, Albert Spaulding, Thomas Harding, and the mathematician and his close friend, Raymond L. Wilder. Still trying to complete a manuscript, "Modern Capitalist Culture," which he had begun more than twenty years earlier, Leslie White died of a heart attack in Lone Pine, California, on March 31, 1975.

I would like now to convey something of what White was like as a teacher. If that much-overused term "charisma" ever applied to a teacher, it did to Leslie White. Rather than personal, though, his charisma was intellectual. Students were drawn not so much to the man as to his ideas. As a lecturer, White did not have a smooth and polished delivery, but that did not matter. He was able to command attention as no other lecturer I have ever heard. There was an intensity in his manner, an incisiveness in his ideas, and a force to his personality that arrested the listener. His lectures before large undergraduate classes at Michigan were charged with electricity. Always there was an air of expectancy in those classes as students waited for lightning to strike. One of his former students, the late William Masters, described the atmosphere in White's classes as follows:

At Michigan, Leslie White came to teach two kinds of courses. The first consisted of the immensely popular offerings with titles such as *The Evolution of Culture* and *The Mind of Primitive Man*. Students from every walk of campus life flocked to these lectures and formed a large, if sometimes tense, audience. Now any large school has its share of prima donnas, and the University of Michigan is no exception. Some of these gentlemen—notably heavenstorming romantics out of literature, converted Thomists out of philosophy, and the moodier type of analyst out of psychology—bridled at certain arguments in White's brand of anthropology. So they told their students, and the students, very naturally, attempted to carry the war to the floor of White's classroom. These students were in for a painful surprise. Over the years, White developed the lightning-witted acidity one usually associates with the House of Commons. A student, equipped with a loaded question that he thought would demolish White . . . was outmanned, outgunned, and usually outflanked. Some of them probably still carry the scars. (Quoted in Barnes 1960:xxiii)

"The Mind of Primitive Man" was a course White had first taught at the University of Buffalo and had brought with him to Michigan. It was by far his largest undergraduate course, and though it was not required, the enrollment in it often exceeded 300. Some students, seeking intellectual challenge and excitement, took it because it was the most heretical course offered on campus. Others, with that perversity that draws people to what they dislike, took it to be offended and outraged. But despite the fact that White trampled underfoot their most cherished values, sparing neither God nor soul nor freedom of the will, most of these students enjoyed the course tremendously.

It is the custom at Michigan for students to applaud a professor after the last lecture of his course, the volume and duration of the applause being a measure of their esteem. Invariably, following White's last lecture in "The Mind of Primitive Man," there was a thunderous ovation. Because of my secular and deterministic background, I was drawn from the beginning to White's arguments and considered myself as staunch an adherent of his views as there could possibly be in the class. Accordingly, I was amazed that long after I had finished expressing my enthusiastic appreciation for the course, most of the other students were still clapping.

One day in class White remarked, offhandedly, that there was nothing original in the course. I was dumbfounded. As far as I was concerned, everything in it was original. Moreover, as an eager young disciple, I *wanted* everything to be original. It took me years to learn that White was right. In one way or another, every idea he had expressed in that class had been expressed by someone else before. But I have never found anyone who said these things so clearly, forcefully, and convincingly as Leslie White.

In his large undergraduate lectures, White would tolerate no nonsense. Those who offered only captious or frivolous objections received short shrift. He also expected full attention while he was lecturing. One day in the middle of class a student opened a newspaper and began to read it. White immediately stopped lecturing and summarily ordered him out of the room.

White never suppressed his opinions in the classroom, regardless of the consequences. This led to a certain amount of ill feeling when word of White's latest pronouncement filtered back to some other members of the faculty. For example, White used to refer to philosophy as "intellectual thumb-sucking," a remark that did not sit well with William Frankena, one of the leading philosophers on campus.

White's unequivocal rejection of theism, while routine to professional anthropologists, was not so readily accepted in the university community. Indeed, it brought him into repeated and bitter conflict with the clergy in Ann Arbor, and drew down on him the full force of *odium theologicum*. The Catholic Church assigned nuns to enroll in "The Mind of Primitive Man" and to take stenographic notes so there would be a verbatim transcript of White's remarks to use against him. In 1942, the Catholic chaplain on campus went to see Alexander Ruthven, then president of the University, to inform him of the antireligious nature of White's lectures (*The Michigan Catholic*, January 2, 1958). On another occasion, Catholic and

Lutheran clergymen together drew up an eight-page indict-
ment which they took to President Ruthven, demanding that
White be fired. "They said I was guilty of robbing young
people of their faith and ideals," White later recalled (Weiner
1969:4). The tradition of academic freedom was strong enough
at Michigan to prevent White's dismissal, but the long delay
in his promotion to full professor and in his designation as
chairman suggests that clerical opposition to White impeded
the normal progress of his career.

The biggest uproar of all resulted from a paper entitled
"Anthropological Approaches to Religion," which White read at
the annual meeting of the American Anthropological Association in Chicago in December of 1957. Ruth Benedict (1948:589)
had once written: "Man is a creature of such freedom of action
that he can . . . at any stage of technological development
create his gods in the most diverse forms." White disagreed
with this assertion, and his paper was designed to show that a
society's religious system was not idiosyncratic at all but
reflected its socioeconomic system. He pointed out that the
notion "the Lord is my Shepherd" reflected a pastoral
economy. He argued that a society subsisting on wild food,
with no knowledge of monarchy, could hardly have a conception of "Great God, our King," or speak of "Christ, our Royal
Master." "Contrariwise," he continued, "a monarchical cultural system is not likely to have a bear . . . for a god." A few
months earlier the Russians had placed the first Sputnik into
orbit, and White concluded his paper saying, "A cultural
system that can launch earth satellites can dispense with gods
entirely."

The next day, the *New York Times* carried a full-column
story of the meetings, mentioning a number of the papers
presented. In the middle of the article was a paragraph about
White's paper which quoted the above line without comment.
The Detroit papers, with a ready eye for an issue they could
sensationalize, picked up the story from the *Times*. They
called various clergymen in the state, asking them to comment
on the fateful line. The clergy were only too happy to oblige,
and denounced White for his irreligion. The Episcopal Bishop

of Michigan accused White of "playing into the hands of people who would undermine the spiritual heritage of the Western world" (*The Detroit News*, December 28, 1957). *The Michigan Catholic* of January 2, 1958 headlined a front-page editorial, "How Long Will UM Let White Deride God?" Once again, pressure was mounted to dismiss White, but discomfited though the university administration was, it again held firm.

In a reply to his critics, which White prepared for private circulation, he commented wryly: "One wonders . . . at the vehemence of the clergy. If a puny anthropologist should in fact 'deride God,' does He need a protective clergyman to defend Him? Did the reaction of the clergy, their unwillingness to countenance a free competition of ideas, express a sense of insecurity on their part? Or, was it, perhaps, . . . the prospect . . . of technological unemployment?"

In his graduate courses, Leslie White was very different than he was in his undergraduate classes. In the latter, he often faced open antagonism and at times reacted in kind. With graduate students, though, most of whom already accepted his views, he was more relaxed and at times even jovial. His manner of teaching was different too. Here is how Lewis Binford (1972:6–7) recalls his first impression of White in a graduate course:

Leslie White—the dragon slayer of Boasianism, the terror in debate, the irascible "deviant" who insisted that science was not a popularity poll—was my teacher. Every student had to take his History of Anthropology. I had pictured a large man with a strong voice, stern face, and cold, forbidding exterior. I walked into class, seating myself in the third chair from the front, directly in front of the teacher's desk. All the students were in their places before class began. A gentle conversation was heard coming from the hall. A small man with a shy smile and an arm full of papers came into the room. He placed the papers on the desk, shuffled them, and looked up, quietly saying, "My name is Leslie White."

He looked more like a postmaster in a small Midwestern town than the dragon slayer I had pictured. He took out his note cards and began lecturing. His mind worked like [Albert] Spaulding's: sharp, sophisticated wit and a devastating sarcasm, all presented in a gentle voice. . . . He would offer an empirical generalization regarding some position or bias alleged to have characterized Boas and proceed to read fifteen quotes documenting the validity of his generalization. It was, however, a very different approach to data [from James B. Griffin's]. White gave you the generalization or meaning first and then proceeded to document its validity by an appeal to empirical data. His logic was made explicit, his interpretations were put out for criticism, and he supplied you with the criteria and rules for criticism.

Being a graduate student under Leslie White at Michigan in the early 1950s was exciting and exhilarating. We students had the feeling that we were being armed with powerful intellectual tools with which to go out and conquer the world for evolution and culturology. And in the early 1950s much of the world remained to be conquered. Most of it, in fact, was in enemy hands. At anthropology meetings it was Michigan against the field, and we would engage in prolonged and intense discussions with graduate students from other schools, especially Columbia, Chicago, and Northwestern. We never doubted for a moment that our views (White's views), then held by only a tiny minority, would ultimately triumph.

I must add that we did this entirely on our own. We were never sent out to fight for White's theories. On the contrary, White disliked discipleship and never encouraged it. He attracted students very readily, but never tried to found a "Whitean School." Indeed, under his tenure as chairman, the department at Michigan adopted a policy of not hiring its own Ph.D.s.

Let me turn now to some of Leslie White's personal characteristics. The one trait that struck me above all others was the quick incisiveness of his mind. No lapse of logic or imprecision of thought or expression was likely to get by him. A small incident will serve to illustrate this. As a young graduate student in 1950 I volunteered to do some research for White in connection with his manuscript "The Evolution of

Culture." My assignment was to find statistics on coal, iron, and steel production in Russia from the turn of the century to the present. I consulted the *Statistical Year-book of the League of Nations* and a book by an individual author with no institutional sponsorship as sources for production figures. For certain years the two sources differed, and in those cases I simply took the figures given in the League of Nations *Year-book*. Later, in explaining this to White, I blandly said that where the sources disagreed, I had used the more reliable one. "Or the more respectable one," he shot back. And of course he was right. I had no real basis for judging which figures were more reliable, and had unthinkingly equated respectability with reliability. But although the distinction had escaped me, it did not escape White for one moment. [13]

Another marked characteristic of Leslie White was his personal and professional integrity. His colleague Elman Service wrote in his obituary of White:

. . . of all the important things he taught, the most memorable remains . . . a morality of total, utter honesty, unblemished by even a hint of academic careerism or any other kind of self-seeking. And this was taught in the most effective way, by unwavering example. (Service 1976:616) [14]

One manifestation of White's integrity was his complete disdain of bandwagons. He never espoused a cause merely because it was popular. On the contrary, he was often on the unpopular side of an issue. A letter he wrote to the *Newsletter* of the American Anthropological Association in 1973 illustrates this. It was then fashionable for anthropologists, especially younger ones, to "confess" the "sins" they had committed while studying groups of American Indians. After a number of letters had appeared in the *Newsletter* in which the writers had abjectly told how they had "exploited" the Indians they had worked with, White could stand it no longer and replied:

I am rather weary of the mea culpa attitude with regard to the American Indian that has had considerable vogue lately. . . . Exponents of this attitude acknowledge their guilt and indict other anthropologists for exploiting Indians and profiting from this exploitation. I resent this accusation. I occupied myself with ethnological fieldwork among the Pueblos intermittently from 1926 to 1957. I do not believe that my researches ever injured Indians, deprived them of anything of value or harmed them in any way. I have known many anthropologists during the past 50 years and I do not know of any who have exploited Indians for personal gain. I certainly did not profit financially. . . . I never sold a "story" about Indians—or a set of kinship terms. None of my monographs was copyrighted. I never received a cent in royalties. I was out of pocket on every field trip I ever made. (1973b:2)

White went on to challenge the underlying assumption of the mea culpa writers:

Since when has the culture of a people become their private property that can be bought and sold—or stolen—like commodities? The universal process of diffusion makes anyone's culture everyone's culture. Boas published *Keresan Texts*, Benedict distinguished psychological types, Bunzel helped us to understand and appreciate the great aboriginal drama, the Shalako of Zuni. . . . In what way are Indians deprived of anything in all this? How does the dissemination of facts about, and communication of understanding of, Indian culture injure or exploit the Indians? On the contrary, does not the work of the ethnographer give Indian culture a new dimension by placing it securely in its proper niche in the annals of mankind?

And he ended by stating:

The members of the mea culpa chorus miss one big point and that a vital one: many Indians want to have a record made of their rapidly disappearing culture, a description and interpretation of their cultural identity—as communicated by the Indians themselves to the ethnographer. Many have told me, with deep feeling, of this desire and their earnest hope that they will not disappear without trace. I have produced a few comprehensive studies of some of the Pueblos; they stand (with all their faults and shortcomings) as enduring memorials to what was once their world. Devoted Indians helped me to make these studies and others treasure them as reminiscences of the lives of their mothers and fathers. I do not see how I could have rendered these Indians a greater service.

The obverse of the coin of strict integrity is sometimes a certain inflexibility and lack of receptivity toward ideas different from one's own. Of this allegation, sometimes made against Leslie White, I do not think he can be entirely absolved. My first experience with this aspect of his character was in 1947 when I was a sophomore taking White's introductory course in anthropology. *Time* magazine had just appeared with a cover story on the recently published one-volume abridgment of Arnold Toynbee's *A Study of History*. I had neatly clipped the article and brought it to White after class, thinking it would interest him. When he realized what it was, he remarked, without looking at it any further, "Oh, that must be a terrible book!" Even though I held no brief for Toynbee's philosophy of history, this summary rejection of my offering jarred me and left me feeling deflated and chagrined.

It is important, though, to understand the source of White's seeming intolerance and defensiveness. For years he had been an embattled figure in anthropology, with the leading names in the profession ranged against him. He had proclaimed views unpalatable to them, and as a result he had been scorned and branded a maverick or worse. How many scholars, faced with decades of this kind of hostility, would continue to meet opposing views with benign receptivity?

In speaking of White's supposed dogmatism, though, it is important to make a distinction. While White had a sure feeling for what was sham or shallow and was quick to reject it, he was by no means so certain when it came to expressing what he believed. He often stressed that many questions in anthropology remained unanswered. In his introductory course he once said, "Why, we can't even account for monogamy!" Later in his life he told his classes how important it was "to not know," and regretted that the English language did not have a single verb for it. In the last lecture he ever gave, less than a year before he died, he remarked with evident pride, "I probably 'not know' more than most of my acquaintances."

Though there was an intellectual toughness in White's attitudes toward those of his professional colleagues with whom he disagreed, in his personal dealings with them he was unfailingly considerate. I have heard several of them attest to kindnesses and courtesies that White had extended to them over the years.

I turn now to the contributions of Leslie White to the science of anthropology. Chief among these was the resuscitation of cultural evolutionism. It must be difficult for younger students today to imagine that there was a time in American anthropology when cultural evolutionism was rejected and denounced. But such a rejection there was, and the results of it were crippling to anthropology. As White wrote, "It is particularly unfortunate that [Boas] and his disciplines have rejected the theory of cultural evolution so vigorously and so thoroughly, for it has tended to deprive ethnology of one of science's most fundamental and vitalizing conceptions" (1947a:192). However, he did not believe that this rejection could continue indefinitely, and he wrote, "The time will come, we may confidently expect, when the theory of evolution will again prevail in the science of culture as it has in the biological and the physical sciences" (White 1943:356). And it was White who was largely instrumental in making this prediction come true. Single-handedly at first, he led the struggle to restore evolutionism to ethnology.

The opening salvo in this battle, scarcely heard at the time, was fired in the early 1930s. Bernhard J. Stern's *Lewis Henry Morgan, Social Evolutionist* had just been published, and in it Stern had written that "cultures, no matter how primitive, are too complex and the forms of combinations of social institutions too variable to fit into any definite social evolutionary scheme" (Stern 1931:135). In reviewing the book, White took exception to this statement, saying, "Mr. Stern, like many preceding critics, points out errors of Morgan's procedure, and then throws overboard the concept of evolutionary development of culture. This is quite unwarranted, in the reviewer's opinion. Mr. Morgan's shortcomings in the seventies do not invalidate a concept of cultural evolution in 1931" (White 1931:483).[15]

The ensuing struggle to rehabilitate cultural evolutionism which White undertook was long and difficult. In one of the last passages he ever wrote, White gave us a glimpse of what it was like:

The ethnologist who held to the theory of evolution found neither friend nor refuge on the anthropological landscape. For years I was virtually alone in my advocacy of cultural evolutionism. To make matters worse, I came to the defense of Lewis H. Morgan; I felt that he had been treated very unfairly by Boas and his disciples . . . and labored to restore him to the place of dignity, honor, and great scientific achievement that he had enjoyed during his lifetime. . . . I was ridiculed and scoffed at. Everyone knew that evolutionism was dead; my non-conformist behavior was regarded as an aberration. (White, in press) [16]

In his attempt to reestablish evolutionism, White met not merely intellectual opposition but personal derision. Rarely did he talk about it, but he did leave us a brief but poignant account of one such instance:

In 1939 I presented a paper at the annual meeting of the American Anthropological Association held at the University of Chicago in which I spoke out in a forthright manner in support of evolutionist theory in ethnology. When I had finished, Ralph Linton, the chairman of the session, remarked that I ought to be given the courtesy extended to suspected horse thieves and shady gamblers in the days of the Wild West, namely, to allow them to get out of town before sundown. (White, in press) [17]

In time, of course, Julian H. Steward and V. Gordon Childe came to be regarded as allies of White in this struggle, and their prestige and influence no doubt helped evolutionism appear less the personal crotchet of one man. But the roles played by Steward and Childe in the fight for evolutionism remained limited and qualified. [18] Steward himself wrote: "For many years Leslie White stood virtually alone in his uncompromising support of the 19th century cultural evolutionists and in opposition to the followers of Franz Boas" (1960:144). [19]

In rehabilitating the concept of evolution White had to refute the various arguments raised against it by members of the Boas school. Lowie had argued, for example, that the facts of diffusion negated evolution, and White replied that one had to distinguish between the culture history of a people and the evolution of culture as a whole. Among the Boasians the feeling prevailed, born out of an exaggerated cultural relativism, that cultures are incommensurable, as Ruth Benedict put it. Thus they could not be rated objectively, let alone rank-ordered numerically. To this White answered that Boas and his students failed to distinguish between "arbitrary" and "subjective." All standards of measurement are arbitrary, he said, but not necessarily subjective. There were indeed objective ways in which cultures could be compared, such as the amount of energy harnessed per capita per year, and on this basis they could not only be compared, but also ranked in numerical order. And to the argument, "How can one speak of evolutionary regularities when, among the Australian aborigines, a simple technology is coupled with a complex social organization?" White replied that one must not confuse a certain intricacy in kinship systems with overall complexity of social structure. [20]

White's first major affirmation in print of the validity of cultural evolutionism appeared in "Science is *Sciencing*" in 1938. He reaffirmed it the following year in his article "A Problem in Kinship Terminology." [21] However, the first article that he devoted entirely to evolution and its causes was "Energy and the Evolution of Culture," published in the *American Anthropologist* in 1943. If one were to choose the first milestone in the revival of cultural evolutionism, it would have to be this article, in which White for the first time proposed what has since been called "White's Law," namely, that culture evolves as the amount of energy harnessed per capita per year increases.

In 1947 White was afforded an opportunity to expound this thesis to a much wider audience. The United States Rubber Company was then sponsoring the nationwide Sunday afternoon broadcasts of the New York Philharmonic Orchestra and decided that the intermission feature that year would be a series of lectures called "The Scientists Speak." Each Sunday, a distinguished scientist was invited to talk on a major topic in his field. On Sunday, February 16, 1947 Leslie White gave a brief lecture, heard by millions of people, on "Energy and the Development of Civilization." [22]

The campaign to rehabilitate cultural evolutionism within anthropology was hard and slow. White published a succession of articles (1945a, 1945b, 1947a, 1947b, 1947c) in which he pressed the issue vigorously. These articles, he later wrote, "attracted considerable interest, but won very few converts—except, possibly, among graduate students" (White, in press). It took fifteen years or so following the publication of "Energy and the Evolution of Culture" before it could be said that evolutionism in ethnology had fought its way back to respectability. We can take 1959, the year of the Darwin Centennial, as marking the final triumph. The hundredth anniversary of the publication of *The Origin of Species* was celebrated by a major symposium at the University of Chicago in which a galaxy of internationally known scientists participated, as well as by a series of lectures by distinguished anthropologists at the Anthropological Society of Washington. White read papers at both meetings, and both were later published (White 1959b, 1960b).

The great reaffirmation of evolution that swept the sciences in 1959 certainly made the final return of cultural evolutionism considerably easier. But without the steady pressure that White had been applying for years through his incisive articles, I doubt that cultural evolution would even then have been welcomed back into the fold of anthropology quite so readily.

The same year, 1959, saw the publication of White's volume *The Evolution of Culture*. And the following year, writing in the foreword to Sahlins and Service's *Evolution and Culture*, White felt able to proclaim that "antievolutionism has run its course and once more the theory of evolution is on the march" (1960a:vii).

Naturally, White was pleased to see cultural evolutionism

restored to a place of honor in anthropology. But he once observed to me that now that evolutionism had become not only respectable but fashionable, evolutionists seemed to be coming out of the woodwork. And he went on to say that anthropologists he had once regarded as adversaries on this issue were now talking as if they had been evolutionists all along. As usual, White was leery of bandwagons. Noting the common tendency for Johnny-come-latelies to try to take over a movement, he once commented, "Now that cultural evolutionism has become orthodox, I hope I won't be excommunicated."

In discussing modern evolutionism, especially as expounded by Leslie White, a number of anthropologists have referred to it as "neo-evolutionism." White bridled at this term. In the preface to *The Evolution of Culture* he wrote:

. . . let it be said, and with emphasis, that the theory set forth here cannot properly be called "neo-evolutionism." . . . Neo-evolutionism is a misleading term: it has been used to imply that the theory of evolution today is somehow different from the theory of eighty years ago. We reject any such notion. The *theory* of evolution set forth in this work does not differ one whit in principle from that expressed in Tylor's *Anthropology* in 1881. (1959a:ix)

In class, White often poked fun at "neo-evolutionism," saying there was no such thing, any more than there was "neo-whiskey." Like many of White's colorful expressions, this one made the rounds of the department at Michigan. On his sixtieth birthday a party was held for him at the house of Marshall Sahlins, and while Sahlins was taking his guests' orders for drinks he turned to White and said, "Leslie, how about some neo-whiskey?"[23]

Apart from rehabilitating evolutionism, White's most important contribution to anthropology was his clarification of the concept of culture. His article "The Concept of Culture," published in the *American Anthropologist* in 1959, is probably the most acute analysis of the concept that has ever appeared.[24] It far excels in this respect Kroeber and Kluckhohn's monograph *Culture* (1952), which is essentially a catalog of definitions of the term, with only a tentative attempt to arrive at a consensus definition. And it is questionable that a consensus of definitions then prevailing would have proved satisfactory. The definition of culture that was probably most common at the time was that culture is learned behavior. But since animals as far down the phylogentic scale as cockroaches can learn, cockroaches would then have culture. Confronted with this conclusion, I think that even the most broad-minded of anthropologists would demand a more restrictive definition.

Into this miasma of conflicting and inadequate definitions, White introduced his own classic one: "Culture is a class of phenomena, comprising objects, acts, ideas, and attitudes that are dependent upon the use of symbols." White held that there was a qualitative difference between the mind of man and that of all other animals, including the higher primates, and he believed that this difference was based on the uniquely human capacity to invent symbols by bestowing meaning on things in which meaning did not inhere.[25]

A milestone in the discussion of the basis of culture was White's article "The Symbol: The Origin and Basis of Human Behavior," first published in 1940. In view of the enormous impact the article has had, its publication history may be of some interest. White first submitted it to the *American Sociological Review*, but the editor, Read Bain, rejected it. He then submitted it to *The American Journal of Sociology*, but its editor, Ernest Burgess, also rejected it. Finally the article was accepted by the journal *Philosophy of Science*. Since its original publication, it has been reprinted no fewer than nineteen times.[26] The proposition set forth by this article was simple:

All culture . . . depends upon the symbol. It was the exercise of the symbolic faculty that brought culture into existence and it is the use of symbols that makes the perpetuation of culture possible. Without the symbol there would be no culture, and man would be merely an animal, not a human being. (White 1940:460)

In addition to characterizing the concept of culture, White proposed that the science that studied culture as a distinct and autonomous class of phenomena should have a special name, and he called it "culturology."[27] The word, as well as the concept, met great resistance (White 1969:xxxv). Objections were raised that "culturology" was a barbarism, that it grated on the ear, that it combined Greek and Latin roots, and so on. C.W.M. Hart (1950:88), for example, found it "a label . . . horrible to look at and as horrible to hear." (The same objections greeted the introduction of the term "sociology" into the English language [Carneiro 1974a:549].) Nevertheless, White had the satisfaction of seeing the term included in the second edition of *Webster's New International Dictionary* (unabridged) in 1959, where it was defined as "The science of culture; specif., that branch of cultural anthropology that treats human technologies, philosophies, etc., as autonomous phenomena, independent of biological, psychological, or sociological laws."

White expounded culturology most fully in his book *The Science of Culture*, which appeared in 1949.[28] While the volume was in press, he discovered that in coining the term "culturology" he had been anticipated by the German chemist and philosopher Wilhelm Ostwald, who had used it (in the form *Kulturologie*) in his *Energetische Grundlagen der Kulturwissenschaft* in 1909 (White 1969:xxxv). This discovery had an exhilarating effect on White. He once told me that he was so excited the day he made it that he was unable to sleep, and had to take a long walk through the streets of Ann Arbor that night to calm himself down.

The idea underlying culturology has been resisted and decried fully as much as the term itself. For example, Laughlin and d'Aquili (1974:199) have said that "'culturology' has had an insidious . . . influence on anthropology in particular, and . . . on the social sciences in general." Indeed, culturology is by far the least accepted part of White's philosophy. It was opposed by the same sorts of persons who had opposed Kroeber's "The Superorganic" in 1917, namely, those whose professional endeavors focused on the thoughts and feelings and actions of individuals *as such*. For them, leaving the human being out of the equation explaining culture seemed unwarranted and even perverse. White dealt with these objections repeatedly, especially in "Culturological *vs.* Psychological Determinants of Human Behavior" and "Cultural Determinants of Mind," both chapters in *The Science of Culture*.

Opposition to culturology comes from new sources nowadays. Chief among them are those ecologically oriented anthropologists who are closely associated with the field of animal ecology. Culture, for them, is simply the behavior of a particular animal species, *Homo sapiens*. And they tend to regard human behavior as no different in kind from the behavior of other animals. Or at least they propose to study it *as if* it were no different. [29] To those who see no qualitative difference in, say, the mode of hunting of a band of Pygmies and a troop of baboons, White might have asked: How would a baboon proceed to give the left hindquarter of every animal he killed to his mother-in-law while at the same time embarrassedly avoiding her glance?

However, there is a more fundamental question to be raised about White's view of the study of culture, one not so easily dispelled. Is there an inconsistency or contradiction between White's culturology and his cultural materialism? Can he hold that cultural phenomena are to be explained solely in terms of other cultural phenomena and at the same time argue that raw materials and energy sources, things whose existence is external to culture, are the prime movers of cultural development?

A slightly different aspect of the same general question was raised by Elvin Hatch in his book *Theories of Man and Culture* (1973). Hatch quotes several statements by White, such as, "the function and purpose of culture are to make life secure and enduring for the human species" (White 1959a:8; see also White 1947a:182, 183, and 1949b: 360, 370, 373, 375), and labels this view "utilitarian" (Hatch 1973:145). He argues that for White "it is by reference to the function or utility of an institution that it is made intelligible," and that in White's view, "traits not only condition . . . one another, but they are also joined together in the pursuit of certain ends" (Hatch 1973:145).

We can say that for White, traits often come into existence as a response to problems of adaptation and survival. Thus, in accounting for the origin of the incest taboo, White accepts Tylor's argument that it arose by human societies reacting adaptively to the choice between "marrying out or being killed out." But if culture traits arise in response to the exigencies of life, how can we say that they are explainable solely in terms of themselves? If the availability of raw materials and energy sources, and their incorporation into a culture, play a determining role in the way that culture develops, must we not say that external environmental factors, no less than the interplay of existing culture traits, have shaped that culture? And if so, what happens to the autonomy of culture?

That White himself had become aware of this dilemma and felt that he had to resolve it is evident from certain passages in his last published work, *The Concept of Cultural Systems* (1975). Here White remarks that thinking about cultural systems while writing this volume made him realize that the idea that "the function of culture is to serve the needs of man" now seemed as invalid as it had been "obvious" to him before. On the other hand, he says, the statement, "'culture is a thing, or process, *sui generis*' means just what it says; and 'culture is to be explained in terms of culture' still holds" (White 1975:xi). He adds that he was led "to see culture in a new light. No longer was it viewed as a handmaiden of Homo sapiens, to preserve and comfort him, but as a sector of reality in its own right whose behavior was governed by laws of its own" (White 1975:xi). And finally, in the concluding chapter of the book he repeats: "We no longer think of culture as designed to serve the needs of man; culture goes on its own way in accordance with laws of its own" (White 1975:159).[30]

White thus felt the weight of the inconsistency and tried to resolve it. But was his resolution satisfactory? Is not culture, first and foremost, something which man interposes between himself and the external world in an effort to secure his survival? And does it not have to fill that role before it can fill any other? Before it can take on "a life of its own" does it not have to ensure the life of its carriers? Is not culture, then, irresistably concerned with the practical necessity of adapting man to his environment? And if this is so, can culturology dispense with ecology? Must it not in fact embrace it as an indispensable ally? And finally, cannot culturology grant a major causal role to those aspects of the environment affecting subsistence, security, and survival and still retain a large measure of validity?

White was well aware of the importance of the environment, but he kept it at bay theoretically while propounding culturology. This he did by saying that the environment, although significant in forming particular societies, could be averaged out when dealing with "culture as a whole," and therefore canceled from the equation used to account for evolutionary developments at large.

This way of dealing with the issue never satisfied Julian Steward, who was always very much concerned with the environmental side of cultural ecology. As early as 1949, in his review of *The Science of Culture*, Steward wrote:

Cultural differences are in part a function of the environmental variable, which White will not admit into the formula of causality. He disposes of environment in one short paragraph (p. 339), which declares it to be a constant, and in a brief footnote (p. 368) which admits its local importance but states that culturological "laws" are concerned with culture as a whole, *all* environments being averaged to form a constant factor! ... Evidently shunning the stigma of "environmental determinism," he refuses to see that any given cultural heritage would have to be adapted to local habitats and that the processes of adaptation, the cultural ecology, would be creative ones. (Steward 1950:209)

This latter criticism seems to me somewhat overstated. White would surely agree with Steward that environment partly determines individual cultures: the Plains shaped the

Sioux and the Arctic shaped the Eskimo. No one can doubt
that. The real issue is: Can White legitimately rule out the
environment in laying out the evolution of culture as a whole?

Before we can answer this question we first need to ask,
just what *is* "culture as a whole"? Is it the sum total of all
particular cultures, or at least of most of them? If so, since the
environment is always operative on particular cultures, and
operative in widely different ways, doesn't it necessarily affect
"culture as a whole"? In that case, can we really hold it
constant and cancel it out of the equation? The answer would
seem to depend on the problem at hand. If we are trying to
account for the existence of such traits as the couvade or
teknonymy or the mother-in-law taboo, the effect of environment would appear to be negligible. Thus, in such instances,
we could probably cancel it out. But what about other problems? What if our problem were, let us say, to account for the
origin of the state?

Elsewhere (Carneiro 1970) I have argued that the state
first arose in heavily populated areas sharply circumscribed by
mountains, seas, or deserts. For reasons unnecessary to pursue
here, this type of environment gave an impetus to state formation. To be sure, the state could and did arise elsewhere, in
areas where the encircling and impinging element was not
environment but people. But where the state arose as a result
of social rather than environmental circumscription it did so
more slowly and thus substantially later. So we must conclude
that environment was not neutral with regard to state formation. One type of environment favored it, another type hin-
dered it. Can we then say that in attacking the problem of
state formation the environment is really cancelable? Not
without vitiating our best explanation of the process.

A good deal more must be said on this subject before it is
finally resolved. In the meantime, I would simply ask if culturology should not consider entering into a treaty of peace and
mutual assistance with ecology.

Let me return to the matter of Leslie White's relationship
to cultural ecology and try to show that it is erroneous to think
of him as lying outside this field. In my opinion, when every-

thing is considered, he can be found to be very much in the ecological camp.

In an article entitled "The Ecological Approach in Anthropology," June Helm (1962:638n.–639n.) has written that "the Whitean school . . . is antipathetic, in its sweeping universalism, to the empirical tradition that has fostered the ecological approach in anthropology." But Helm is wrong. The "empirical tradition" did not start cultural ecology; the theoretical tradition did. So long as the "empirical tradition" ruled the roost, the concern of anthropologists was with facts rather than with their interpretation. It was only when theoretically minded scholars like Steward and White began to ask, "How do we account for cultures?" that the ecological approach was launched and began to yield significant results.

Julian Steward is generally credited with being the father of cultural ecology, and there is no intent here to minimize his contributions to this field.[31] However, if judged by the number of students actually stimulated to pursue work along cultural-ecological lines, and the positive accomplishment of these students, White need not take second place to anyone. As Willey and Sabloff (1974:219n.) noted after quoting the passage from Helm cited above, "the 1960s have shown [that] White's students have been in the forefront of the development of a systematic, ecological approach to archaeology." And the same can be said of their role in advancing the ecological approach in ethnology as well.

In White's days as a teacher, before he ever thought there might be a contradiction between culturology and cultural materialism, he taught them both, and his students absorbed them both. He constantly stressed the importance of the material conditions of existence, including the environment, and emphasized the function of culture as an adaptive mechanism in coping with these conditions. "Culture is a system that grows by increasing its control over the forces of nature," he wrote (1949a:379), and "The science of culture . . . includes considerations of historical, ecological, and topological factors" (1969:xxv).

His students saw in this a clear invitation to try to

account for particular social systems by the interplay of particular environmental, technological, and economic factors. And a number of us tried to do just that. Marshall Sahlins' Ph.D. thesis, "Social Stratification in Polynesia" (which though written at Columbia was really a Michigan dissertation) was an attempt to do so for Polynesia (Sahlins 1958). My own dissertation, "Subsistence and Social Structure: An Ecological Study of the Kuikuru Indians," undertook to do the same for a tribal village in central Brazil. And there were others as well.

Among these, one can hardly fail to cite Lewis Binford, who in the introduction to his book *An Archaeological Perspective* (1972:6–9) makes clear his great intellectual debt to Leslie White. Binford has, in turn, been enormously influential in bringing White's evolutionism and cultural materialism to bear on archeology. Under the pressure of his trenchant writing, he has force-fed Leslie White to a reluctant discipline and helped create the "new archeology" thereby. (See also Trigger 1978:12.)[32]

Closely related to White's advocacy of the autonomy of culture was his espousal of cultural determinism. According to this view, what one believes and how one behaves—no matter how much it may seem to come from the most intimate recesses of one's personality—is actually the product or reflection of one's culture. "Human behavior," wrote White, "is but the response of a primate who can symbol to this extrasomatic continuum called culture" (1949b:379).

White was a strict determinist. He denied there was such a thing as free will, maintaining it was merely an illusion. And he not only asserted that human behavior was determined by culture, he stressed that among these cultural determinants the material ones were paramount. Thus he minimized the role of ideas, values, and purpose, regarding them simply as epiphenomena of the former. For White, the culture process was *impelled* by forces rather than being *drawn* by ideas.[33]

This point of view was unpalatable, even anathema, to many. As White himself attested, a number of persons found the philosophy of cultural determinism "exceedingly repugnant" (1969:xxi). Today, thirty years after the publication of *The Science of Culture*, the issue is by no means dead. Even among anthropologists there are those who still deny cultural determinism outright, or at least seek to restrict its application.

If cultural determinism was opposed within the ranks of anthropology, whose members had been thoroughly exposed to the concept of culture, one can well imagine that this philosophy would have been resisted all the more outside of the profession. And this was true not only among literary, humanistic, and lay audiences, but among practitioners of other sciences as well. Thus, biologists who read White tended to reject his cultural determinism. The distinguished neurologist C. Judson Herrick (1956:196), for example, held that White's "reification of culture as an autonomous and self-sufficient entity leads to a dismal fatalism and is a confession of defeat." And George Gaylord Simpson (1949:291n.), the most catholic and sophisticated of biologists, while finding White's article "Man's Control Over Civilization: An Anthropocentric Illusion" (1948) "an able . . . exposition" of cultural determinism, concluded that the argument was nonetheless "essentially fallacious."

Some who reject cultural determinism find solace and sustenance in the alternative philosophy that assures them that their fate is in their own hands. This is, of course, an ancient philosophy, and as White wrote, "primitive philosophies had other functions than explanatory [ones]; they sustained man with illusions, they provided him with courage, comfort, consolation, and confidence." However, the scientific status of a philosophy is not to be gauged by how much it inspires, consoles, or assuages, but by how well it explains events. And on this score White's culturological and deterministic treatment of such problems as the rise of monotheism or the invention of the steam engine is much more discerning and convincing than an explanation based on the "iconoclasm" of Ikhnaton or the "genius" of James Watt (see White 1949a:190–281). Indeed, in its clarity of exposition and persuasiveness of argument, White's discussion of the Great Man *vs.*

the culture process excels even the celebrated treatments of the subject by Herbert Spencer (1873), William F. Ogburn (1922), and A. L. Kroeber (1944).[34]

As noted above, critics of White sometimes assailed him as a fatalist (generally failing, however, to distinguish between fatalism and determinism). White, however, took pains to contrast what was determined and expectable in culture with what was, from a culturological point of view, adventitious. That is to say, he distinguished between the *culture process* and *history*. The culture process was a stream of interacting cultural elements whose general direction was clear, and whose course could not be deflected by the intervention of even the most forceful or gifted individual. History, on the other hand, was a fabric in which the idiosyncratic and the fortuitous could leave their mark.

White's most pointed expression of the role of historical accident occurred at the meeting of the American Anthropological Association in Chicago at which he gave his controversial paper on religion. The paper was highly deterministic, emphasizing how the economic and social system of a society determined its religious system. After the formal presentation, someone in the audience asked White if he didn't believe in contingency in history. Without hesitating, White replied: "Yes, I believe in contingency in history. If a certain Corsican girl had not left her scarf on the beach one night two hundred years ago and gone back to retrieve it, the whole course of European history could have been different."

The ideas of Leslie White are today well known and widely accepted in anthropology, and one reason for this is the manner in which they were expressed. I know of no other anthropologist who can match Leslie White as a prose stylist. His writing is lucid, vivid, forceful, and precise. It is full of evocative phrases, and yet is completely free of pretense or affectation. In this era of proliferating jargon, when every factor has become a "parameter," when things are not explained but "explicated," and when a statement is no longer true but "isomorphic with reality," it is refreshing to read the crisp and pungent prose of Leslie White.[35]

Another characteristic of White's writing style which struck me even as an undergraduate was the pains he took in quoting the views he criticized, and always with complete citations. Over the years he had amassed an enormous file of quotations, and this provided him with ready ammunition both for teaching his courses and for preparing his many controversial articles.

His forceful writing and his arsenal of quotes made Leslie White a formidable polemicist. Through the years he fought a number of battles in print, most notably with Robert H. Lowie over cultural evolution (White 1943, 1944, 1945b, 1947b, 1947c; Lowie 1946a, 1946b). Much as we students enjoyed reading his spirited refutations of his opponents, some of us came to feel that White devoted too much of his time to them. He had been too long and unrelenting in his destruction of Franz Boas (e.g., White 1963, 1966). The old antievolutionist had been killed and his corpse interred. There seemed no need to dig up the body and pummel it again.[36] We would much rather have seen Leslie pursuing his own researches. We dearly wanted him to complete his history of ethnological theory, his biography of Lewis H. Morgan, and his manual of culturology—works that he had conceived and talked of more than twenty years before he died, but which he never came close to executing.[37]

On rare occasions, White seems to have recognized and regretted the trammels that his crusade against antievolutionism had placed on him. At least that is how I interpret a passage in his foreword to Sahlins and Service's *Evolution and Culture*. After summarizing in some detail the original contributions made in this volume by his former students, White remarked, a bit ruefully and perhaps with a touch of envy:

The opponent of these theories [of antievolutionism] had to adapt himself to the propositions advanced by the Boasian antievolutionists and was therefore restricted in his scope and perspective. He had to develop a type of theory in opposition to specific criticisms and attacks. But these younger anthropologists have been free from such handicaps. They were not reared in the atmosphere of antievolutionism; they accepted cultural evolutionism from the very start and have therefore been relatively free from the restrictions of polemics; they have been free to explore the implications of the theory of evolution as it applied to culture and to develop its many and fruitful possibilities. (White 1960a:xi)

Of White's other contributions there is room to list only a few. He contributed, for example, to a solution of the vexing problem of the Crow and Omaha systems of kinship terminology (White 1939; Murdock 1949:125, 168, 240–41, 246, 309). He resurrected Tylor's solution to the problem of the origin of the incest taboo, buttressed it with further argument and evidence, and gave it much wider currency (White 1948b). His treatments of invention, of the culture process, of the individual and culture, and of the Great Man theory, to which I have already alluded, are all noteworthy elucidations of these problems. His article "The Expansion of the Scope of Science" (White 1947d) presents the first major theory of the filiation of the sciences since the classic treatments of this problem by Comte and Spencer in the nineteenth century.

Some persons, familiar only with White's contributions to theory, have tended to regard him as an "armchair theorist" unacquainted with the chastening realities of fieldwork. Yet this was anything but true. Not only did White do fieldwork; he published separate monographs on five Keresan Indian Pueblos—Acoma, San Felipe, Santo Domingo, Santa Ana, and Sia (White 1932a, 1932b, 1935, 1942a, 1962). It is true, though, that he rarely cited his Pueblo data in his theoretical writings, maintaining that fieldwork and theorizing were separate and distinct activities. Indeed, his field monographs are descriptive treatises with no theoretical slant.[38]

White's intellectual interests and influence carried well beyond the boundaries of anthropology. Through the years he corresponded with a wide range of thinkers, including H. L. Mencken, Charles Beard, Leon Trotsky, Max Planck, Stuart Chase, Robert Millikan, Thomas Mann, Lin Yutang, Lewis Mumford, Warren Weaver, Harold Ickes, Ralph W. Gerard, George Gaylord Simpson, Edmund Wilson, and S. I. Hayakawa.[39]

It is not easy to summarize Leslie White's contribution to anthropology since it was so extensive and profound. But to my mind the essence of it was this: White entered anthropology at a time when the prevailing current of opinion stressed the diversity, idiosyncrasy, and incommensurability of cultures. Accordingly, cultures were dealt with descriptively, historically, and even artistically. Generalizing and theorizing were frowned upon and avoided; anthropology was idiographic rather than nomothetic. White reacted against this tradition. He knew what science was in its fullest sense, and he saw the need for something more than collecting and classifying facts. He felt the necessity to develop concepts and theories, to see culture as a unified process displaying regularities and revealing general trends. Thus, he began to try to reconstruct the evolution of culture, and in so doing concerned himself not only with sequences and stages but with the dynamics of the process as well. Gradually, he hammered out and riveted together a coherent and powerful philosophy that could bring order and intelligibility to the multiplicity of cultures. And he was eloquent, forceful, and untiring in his attempts to show the profession that this was where the future of anthropology lay.

White never felt he had to conquer the world single-handedly, though. He saw his task as that of laying out a ground plan for others to follow and fill in the details. Once, when I asked him why he had never actually calculated the amount of energy harnessed per capita per year by any society, he replied, "That's for you to do." He saw himself, I think, as one who had forged the tools, and was content to have his successors accomplish with them what he had left undone. And those of us who studied under White felt not only that we had been technically equipped for the task, but also that we had had instilled in us all the incentive needed to pursue it.

How will history treat Leslie White? It is the fate of many germinal thinkers to suffer a temporary eclipse in the years immediately following their death. As they cease to be "contemporary," an increasing portion of their work remains unread. At the same time, their contributions may be absorbed into the intellectual bloodstream of their science and no longer be remembered as their own. Or they may even be assigned to someone else, as occurred to Herbert Spencer in relation to Charles Darwin.

This fate may yet overtake Leslie White. Already there is some evidence of it. I would offer as an example the treatment White receives at the hands of Marvin Harris in *The Rise of Anthropological Theory* (1968), the book from which most students today derive their history of the science. In my opinion, Harris consistently belittles or ignores White's contributions. In the rare instances where he finds something positive to say about White, he quickly moves on to something else or dilutes the appraisal with some qualification (Harris 1968:291–93, 635–51). Yet the curious fact remains that the three *leitmotifs* of Harris' book—evolutionism, cultural materialism, and the importance of energy—all were either introduced into anthropology by Leslie White, or at least were most strongly championed by him.[40]

But White influenced too many people too profoundly for a distorted view of his work to remain unchallenged for long. There are enough anthropologists whose ideas were molded under White's tutelage to bring the pendulum of professional opinion back where it belongs if it is pushed too far the other way.

Ultimately, as with other thinkers, White will survive through his effect on those he taught, directly or indirectly. The magnitude of the influence on those who studied under him is perhaps difficult for others to comprehend. This influence was intellectual and professional rather than personal, but it was also more than that. Without being paternal, as was the case with Franz Boas, it was nevertheless encompassing. It affected not only careers but lives as well. I can vouch for this from personal experience.

Early in May of 1975 I was with Napoleon Chagnon in a small mission station on the Upper Orinoco in the middle of Yanomamö territory. We had just left the Yanomamö villages we had been studying and had come to the mission on our way back to civilization. Some mail had accumulated for Chagnon and the first letter he opened was from Leslie White. Despite his ill health, he had written to express interest in the progress of the field trip. After finishing this letter, Chagnon opened one from his wife, and learned that Leslie White had died. Chagnon told me the news. After a moment I said, "If it hadn't been for Leslie White, I wouldn't be here right now." And Chagnon replied, "Neither would I."

Discussion

SPENCER TERKEL: I think it's clear from White's writings and also from his predecessors'—Spencer, Morgan, Tylor, and the Russian evolutionists—that this is a Lamarckian evolutionism. Could you talk about the relationship of White's evolutionism to the Darwinian concept of evolution?

CARNEIRO: I think White's evolutionism was first and foremost Spencerian. Spencer was convinced that Lamarck was right only in the sense that he saw that evolution explained things better than creation did. I don't see White's evolutionism in terms of Lamarck at all. I don't know that he ever read Lamarck; he certainly wasn't influenced by him. I also think you have to distinguish two aspects of evolution: one is the process itself, the nature of the process; and the other is the kind of dynamic that you introduce to account for the process. The nature of the process, as White sees it, is essentially one of increasing complexity, which is straightforwardly Spencerian. The motive force that pushes evolution ahead he sees, of course, as energy.

Darwin's evolutionism sees really any kind of change in the organism as being evolutionary; this is the basis of specific evolution. The Spencerian view—White's view—is to accept as evolutionary only those changes that give rise to greater differentiation of structure and specialization of function.

ALEXANDER LESSER: I was impressed with your description of Leslie White's gentle personality and his pleasant relations with other people. One point you made brought back a question that has been in my mind. You remarked that many of you had come to feel that he should stop the belaboring attacks on Boas, and, nevertheless, he really didn't. There was a great deal in his attacks on Boas that was bitter and personal. I have been asked why many times, and I have never been able to answer. I have heard one theory, that Leslie White wanted to take a Ph.D. at Columbia and that Boas refused to entertain him as a student; I know this is false. There are all sorts of reasons why White's personal links with Columbia should have been friendly. For instance, White did most of his field research under the patronage of Elsie Clews Parsons, who was very close to Boas and did a great deal of financing for students at Columbia as well.

CARNEIRO: White never talked about this with me, but it's pretty evident that for ten or fifteen years White was a virtual outcast. He was espousing theories that Boas' students, and most American anthropologists, thought erroneous and wrongheaded; they belittled him and scorned him. The defensiveness and the ire aroused by being in a minority position and having abuse heaped on him for years took its toll on him. All I can say about the extended attack on Boas is: I don't condone it; and I can't explain it.

ERIC WOLF: You identified Leslie White as one of the ancestors of the ecological interest. It's true that a lot of the people who were influenced by White have been interested, in their work, in the relationship of technology, environment, and energy; it's also true that Leslie White wrote the preface to the Sahlins and Service book, in which general and specific evolution are discussed and in which a strong ecological influence appears. But in earlier statements White said that environment is a constant in the evolution of culture; that when we look at the evolution of culture in general, at the cultural process in general, the environment can be regarded as a constant. I have wondered whether there was a shift in his position at some point. At one time White and Steward locked horns; although they both talked evolution, they really talked past each other.

But there may have been some accommodation between them, perhaps in the late 1950s.

CARNEIRO: I'm not aware that White ever changed his position on the effect of the environment. He did say, in speaking of the evolution of culture as a whole, that one could hold environment constant; I don't know that he ever modified this view. I also don't know of any evidence that Steward influenced him. What he's written about Steward has generally been critical, although in his courses we were encouraged to read Steward. We were made to feel that his ecological approach was a positive way of attacking problems. I don't see any interstimulation between the two that led to a modification of views.

I don't believe that one can hold environment constant in explaining culture process as a whole. For example, in looking at the rise of civilization, there are certain key environmental variables. But White used to put an equation on the board in which he used symbols for environment, for technology, for energy, and so on. The environment was one such factor which you had to take account of in explaining a specific situation. Certainly we students came away with the feeling that it was perfectly legitimate and valid and promising to apply the ecological approach and to introduce environmental factors. White rarely used the word "ecology," but we absorbed this point of view; it was implicit in the way he talked that this line of approach would be a rewarding one to follow.

SYDEL SILVERMAN: In Murphy's discussion of Steward he said he believed that an anthropologist's real teachers were the people he or she worked with, and not his academic professors. Yet for all the ethnographic work that White pursued in the Southwest, there seems to be no link between his ethnography and his theory. Do you see any such link?

CARNEIRO: Not really, and White himself was aware of it. Barnes takes this point up in his Festschrift foreword. One would have to say that in expounding his theory White simply found better examples elsewhere than in the Southwest. He thought of this work in the Southwest as straightforward ethnography, not essentially different from that carried out by members of the Boas school—just recording what the native culture had been. When it came to theorizing, the entire panoply of the world's cultures was available to him, and he selected whatever suited his purposes.

MAY EBIHARA: In view of White's antipathy to Boas, it is rather curious that his undergradate course was called "The Mind of Primitive Man."

CARNEIRO: I think I know where the name comes from. White had established a course by that title at the University of Buffalo, and then brought it with him when he started to teach at Michigan. The name does not surprise me at all; remember, that until the early 1930s he was still a Boasian. He had absorbed Boas' ideas from Goldenweiser and Sapir, and had no reason not to borrow the title of the famous book by Boas for his course. It was a very varied course, and he changed the content quite considerably from one year to another.

ROBERT BETTEREL: I can remember him saying at the beginning of "The Mind of Primitive Man" that the content did not have anything to do with the title, that he had inherited the title a long time ago and it had become associated with him; so he just kept the title and shifted the content.

STANLEY NADEL: He also used to say that he gave true/false questions for exams; he didn't bother changing the questions from year to year, he merely changed the answers.

On the point about ecology, White always made a break very sharply between evolution and history; ecology fell under the rubric of history as being something specific. This was not the idea of specific evolution, which I don't think he subscribed to. His conception of evolution always began with technology, and never considered environment or ecology.

BETTEREL: Yes, he made a very definite distinction between history and evolution, and there was never much of a connection between the two. History was specific, adaptation was specific, ecology was specific. Evolution had to do with changes of a global sort, that had nothing to do with specific societies.

CARNEIRO: I think that explains why in his book *The Evolution of Culture* he doesn't try to cast, say, Andean civilization or Mesopotamian civilization into his framework, or bring into his discussion details of the actual history of these areas. That was uncongenial to what he wanted to do.

GERTRUDE DOLE: Even though White didn't stress ecology, or even focus on it, he did stress another distinction—that between culture in general and *a* culture or society. With respect to the latter, in *a* culture he saw the environment as being effective; that had to do with his concept of contingencies in the history of mankind. The evolution of culture referred to cultures in general, and in that context, environment could be held constant.

SILVERMAN: Was White's position on the qualitative difference between man and other animals ever modified as a result of the development of primate studies and the newer views of human evolution, which led many people to reject his rather dogmatic stance?

CARNEIRO: I don't know whether, in the last ten years or so of his life, he really kept up to date with the new studies. I have no indication that he ever did modify his views. I personally think that the evidence isn't all in.

Biographical Note

Robert L. Carneiro was born in New York City in 1927 and grew up in the Riverdale section of the Bronx. His interest in the quantitative expression of facts goes back to this childhood; he "practically teethed on the *World Almanac*." After graduating from the Horace Mann School, Carneiro went to the University of Michigan. The experience of working for a Congressional candidate led to a major in political science, but he grew disenchanted with it as he found it was not a science at all. Enrolling by chance in an anthropology course with Leslie White, he discovered a discipline that had the theoretical and factual arsenal he sought.

A graduation present from his father took Carneiro on a trip around the world, after which he entered the family's newspaper-machinery export business. After five months he decided to return to Michigan for graduate work. There Carneiro "became a dedicated culturologist and evolutionist, and enjoyed arguing these approaches with anyone who would listen."

Wanting to do fieldwork with primitives as untouched as possible, Carneiro went to the Amazon Basin in 1953–54. His dissertation, "Subsistence and Social Structure, An Ecological Study of the Kuikuru Indians," earned him the Ph.D. in 1957. Subsequently, he worked with two other Amazonian groups, the Amahuaca of eastern Peru (1960–61) and the Yanomamö of southern Venezuela (1975).

Carneiro taught at the University of Wisconsin in 1956–57. The following year he joined the American Museum of Natural History as an assistant curator of South American ethnology; he has been a curator since 1969. He has held visiting appointments at the University of California at Los Angeles, Pennsylvania State University, and the University of Victoria.

Carneiro's major theoretical interest is cultural evolution; the most important intellectual influence on him, after White, has been Herbert Spencer. Carneiro's evolutionism is joined to an ecological approach, which he has applied to such problems as the origin of the state and the social implications of slash-and-burn cultivation. He has a passion for facts—for quantified information, for formulas that express distilled facts in their logical relationship, and for the field-work experience of putting down on paper cultural data that no one else has ever recorded before. Carneiro's work has been guided by the belief that "the function of theory was to explain fact, and that the more one immersed himself in facts, the better theory he could do."

Robert Redfield at the University of Chicago

Robert Redfield ⁸
Nathaniel Tarn

A fellow student of Leslie White's at the University of Chicago was Robert Redfield. The joint department of sociology and anthropology, which at its founding in 1892 was the first sociology department in the United States, was then the center for the urban-ecological studies of the Chicago school of sociology, led by Redfield's father-in-law, Robert E. Park. Anthropology was still in the Boasian tradition, but the functionalist anthropology developing at the time was also influential—an influence that became pronounced after anthropology became a separate department and A. R. Radcliffe-Brown joined it (remaining from 1931 to 1937). Redfield spent his entire professional life in that department.

Robert Redfield was born in 1897 in Chicago, Illinois. His father was a prominent corporation attorney, his mother the daughter of the Danish consul. He was educated in the University of Chicago system, from elementary school through postgraduate studies. After interrupting his schooling during World War I to serve in France as an ambulance driver with the

American Field Service, he received his B.A. in 1920 and went on to the Law School, taking his degree in 1921. Redfield practised law briefly with his father's firm, but a trip to Mexico shortly after the revolution aroused his interest in anthropology, and he returned to the University of Chicago to undertake graduate work.

Redfield went back to Mexico in 1926 to conduct fieldwork in the village of Tepoztlán. In part a holistic study in the spirit of the new functionalism, in part an application of Chicago urban sociology to the hinterlands beyond Mexico City, this research was the beginning of Redfield's enduring interest in folk (later called "peasant") communities and in the influence of urban society upon them. In 1927 Redfield began teaching at the University of Chicago, receiving his Ph.D. the following year. He became a professor of anthropology in 1934. From 1934 to 1946 he served as dean of the social sciences division of the university.

During the 1930s Redfield and his associates carried out an ambitious comparative study of four communities in the Yucatán peninsula of Mexico, which led to his formulation of the folk-urban continuum—a theory of polar types and of the processes of change from tribal to urban life. In the 1950s Redfield became increasingly interested in the comparative study of civilization, and he initiated a series of conferences in which anthropologists and humanist scholars collaborated on problems of the great civilizations. Redfield was still an active teacher and scholar at the time of his death in 1958.

Redfield, the first American anthropologist to do fieldwork in a peasant village, was one of the originators of the anthropology of complex societies. Beginning with Tepoztlán he was a pioneer of community studies, and in the 1930s he inspired a number of landmark studies of communities in modern nations. His folk-urban concept was enormously influential in both anthropology and sociology during the 1940s and 1950s. As the predominant theoretical framework for dealing with complex societies at the time that anthropology expanded its interests in that direction after World War II, it was not only applied to many areas of the world, but it also stimulated a critical literature that led to the development of alternative approaches. Redfield's later general works on the little community and on peasant society and culture became the first texts in the anthropological study of peasantry.

Redfield's interests focused on culture understood as meanings and values, and he saw social relations primarily as vehicles for the communication of ideas. This view was developed most explicitly in his concept of great and little traditions within civilizations. Like Benedict on national character, he applied to complex societies the culture concept in its ideational and integrative sense—as conferring and organizing meaning—but his view of civilization was more differentiated and processual than Benedict's. His approach contrasts diametrically with Steward's application of the culture concept to complex societies, which gave priority to "basic socio-economic institutions" and emphasized the differences among subcultures rooted in different productive processes. Redfield's work became the foundation for important symbolic studies of civilizations.

The following paper differs in style and purpose from the others in this book. It was written by a student of Redfield's who, after completing major research in Mesoamerica and in Southeast Asia, left anthropology. He writes as poet and anthropologist both, considering Redfield from a distance of twenty years, and considering the relationship between anthropologist and poet.

THIS PERFORMANCE has been, and will be until it ends, a sundance for me, with the sun dark. Because there is no language in which it can be written, which will satisfy both you and me. For weeks I fantasized reentry into the anthropologosphere (ten blank years, let me remind you, and twenty since the Redfieldian sector) as a novel code, breaking open a field between us, whose existence I suspect but which I cannot yet find. The anthropologist's discourse moves towards knowledge, the poet's moves outward from knowledge. The anthropologist records but knows no meaning until the part recorded fits into a whole. The poet starts from whole, spend-

The author's title for this paper is "The Literate and the Literary: Notes on the Anthropological Discourse of Robert Redfield."

ing the rest of his life, or his poem, mining whole for parts. The anthropologist predicts, the poet prophesies. The poet knows what he wants from the beginnings, he knows *before*; he has precognition, and he takes the rest of the poem to find it out. The anthropologist does or should not know what he wants until the end but by that time he knows it. How shall you and I, and the you in I, talk together? How *dialogue* in Don Roberto's favorite sense of communication?

And the thing has not come out well for a second reason which is that we are here to praise in this ritual and that my text, alas, is no great praise. It is as if it were the first expressions of dismay, prior to praise. But you will see, I hope, that it is not Don Roberto I dispraise: rather it is a discourse which I suffer at through him. Bueno pues, Don Roberto, vamos a clear the air a little, así es que Usted tiene que perdonarme si vengo a molestar a Usted, Don Roberto, *rilaj acha*, pero the fact is, as they would say in Newyorican these days, that I have to talk to these gente here about you and us because, when all is said and done, *Dios rajawal kaj, Dios rajawal ulew*, we are all, above all, gente . . .

The virginity of anthropological discourse is almost inviolable. Yet, on this reentry, I am tempted to see whether any area of it can still yield to any form of deconstruction. Anthropology prides herself, from time to time, on her stylists—though I for one have sought her Muse in vain. Perhaps, whoever she was, she has now given way to the Clio in herself—for a pack of hungrier self-historians than anthropologists I have hardly ever seen. But, my God, how recently, how pre-Socratic and morninglike it always was in Don Roberto's writing! The books there, still advancing like the waves of a tide, exploring now one beach, now another of some favorite island, but always with the same lips of water, thicker, thinner, protean—but the same water. Like aviation, it seems, you have flashed from balloon to spacecraft, all technique of computerization now, with the Sopwith or the Supermarine barely fledged before scrapped. Let me then address myself to the text of one who had not sold himself completely out of a readable language and who might therefore pay the price of finding himself a scapegoat. Style, for us literary people, is that wound into the innocence a discourse still has in writing itself through a writer: by the time he is masked in jargon, a scalpel no longer cuts but glances merely off the text, unable to diagnose or cure. As for myself, *larvatus prodeo:* I advance masked, for only in language can I avoid being used or consumed, though the ultimate aim be to free language everywhere and in every discourse.

*

Your indulgence begged for my not being informed of current writing and thus putting you in danger of a lot of reruns, let me add that I am not going to rehearse all those details of the life and thought which Charles Leslie—the person who should have given this lecture—has been documenting for some long while now. In putting much of Redfield in brackets, I shall be failing a major purpose of these seminars. The Redfield I *can* deal with today sets sail from *The Primitive World and its Transformations* (PWT,1953) and the tide runs at its highest perhaps under what, if he had lived in this metaphor, he might have called his "little" *Little Community* (LC,1955). In this last book, after examining his debts to Maine, de Coulanges, Morgan, Tönnies and Durkheim and after his acknowledgement that "no very great claims to originality may be made by those of us who have made use of and developed these ideas in the twentieth" century, Redfield defines his own progress as follows. It will stand here for a resumé of his career:

My own efforts went to develop an imagined or ideal-typical folk-society in considerable detail of characterization and to make use of the conception in describing, in more general and abstract terms than is usual in studies of changing primitive society, some comparisons among tribal, peasant, and urban communities in Yucatan. More recently [he is talking of the late forties and early fifties] I have become interested in the characterization of the over-all transformations of human living from precivilized to modern times, as guided by the conception of the folk society and in the examination of the types of urban societies as they affect the folk societies and give rise to new forms of society. (1955:143)

A few dates will stand for this progress: *Tepoztlán, a Mexican Village: A Study of Folk Life* (1930); *Chan Kom: A Maya Village* (with Alfonso Villa Rojas) (1934); *The Folk Culture of Yucatán* (1941); *A Village That Chose Progress: Chan Kom Revisited* (1950). A few flashes to go with these titles: Redfield, out of W. I. Thomas and his father-in-law Robert Park, is interested almost immediately not in tribes but in peasant villages; not in the ethnographic present but in the tenses of change; not in the social isolate but in the part-society turned like a sunflower towards a large whole; not in society itself all that much but in the structure of culture, sensed as a spider's web with a spider at the center.

PWT (1953) is his first "cogitational" work; LC follows it in short order in 1955. In this latter work, Redfield is at his most secure in the uses of models. He writes, "The intellectual forms for describing communities hover over the writer of many an ethnographic account" (1955:164), but it is he that is the windhover or falcon here and we have a strong and exhilarating sense of a mind in movement. It is in this work that his abiding interest in ideal-type constructs and his holistic approach to culture come together most convincingly. Here the text dances so, and Redfield hovers so above it, that he can play off one model against another according to the greater or lesser precision of focus, the wider or narrower width of frame that he desires. The sense of discourse is everywhere present, as it had been in PWT; anthropology is made of words that are *said* or *heard* in dialogue before they are thought about:

If we try to *say* something about the important qualities of a people, we have not many choices as to the manner in which we *say* it. We can attempt to *say* something that includes all aspects of that mode of life; we can *mention* all the principal customs and institutions of that society. Then we find ourselves describing at length. (1953:84; italics mine)

or, in what is for us so often the equivalent of *hearing:*

in the accounts of these I *read* how the associations fulfill personal needs or societal functions that help to integrate society. Or, if we

read . . . [X, Y, and Z] have shown us how the Plains Indian soldier
societies . . . . (1953:122; italics mine)

He will speak of the "major principle of composition" which
governs the presentation of this or that model (1955:56); he
makes frequent reference to anthropological uses of "metaphor" or "suggestive analogy" (1955:74–75); he has a fascinat-
ing aside on the role that "portraiture" plays both in works of
literature and in ethnographies (1955:161); he is constantly
using dramatic metaphors, such as the "every world-view is a
stage set" of PWT (1953:86, 91, 93; see also 1955:28, 102). This
reaches something like apotheosis in his comparison of a "written account of a community" with the community itself in LC
(1955:150); a passage I hope to return to. All of this, in my
readings, imparts a curious innocence to the text; it is as if it
were rolling up its sleeves like a conjurer and showing exactly
what is or is not there: "Trust me" the text says, "it is morning here, we are just beginning." And indeed, the analyses are
extraordinarily broad and generous. As many have said, Redfield did not write polemically: he preferred to bring in as
many views as he could and find out what one could learn from
them. If he sometimes seems to slip into the wings, leaving the
conflicting views in dialogue one with another, without really
having told us what he thinks about the issue, or if he will
often invoke a model modesty ("a sketchy review" [1953:27];
"the vagueness of all universal characterizations" [1953:93]; "a
background of even off hand characterization" [1953:96]; "a
study far beyond my competence" [1953:58]; "it is only the
first paragraphs . . . with which I dare concern myself"
[1953:113]; not to mention the sometimes overfamiliar use of
the word "little" in LC at large), the result can only charm you
the more as you feel style, indeed, becoming—in Whitehead's
phrase quoted by Leslie concerning Redfield—"the ultimate
morality of the mind" (Leslie 1976:160). And it does not
concern you overmuch if he often seems to retreat from a difficult position into the details of ethnography; after all, isn't
that where one always feels safest in any book?

In LC, the little community is seen in the first and last
chapter as "a whole" and "whole and parts" (I am now quot-

ing the titles). In between, it is examined as "an ecological system"; a "social structure"; a "typical biography"; a "kind of person"; an "outlook on life" (or world view); a "history"; a "community within communities"; and a "combination of opposites." Note, in passing, that if we conflate (as a detailed thematic study would lead us to do) the "kind of person" model and the "typical biography" model, the "world-view" model stands exactly in the center of the book, Alas, I do not have time for a detailed thematic study here even if I were to wish for it, but instead must move on to something else. What I would like to trace, if possible, has to do with another aspect of Redfieldian innocence, a negative aspect to my eyes. I stress again before doing so the paradox that Redfield was exceedingly far from being the worst offender in his time; it is merely the positive innocence of his style that allows us to see the fault in him more clearly than in most of his fellow anthropologists.

At this point, I want to stay with the models or "forms of thought" Redfield uses, rather than their content which I shall get to later. Early in LC, he envisages that, of the various models set up, some are going to have to become parts of other models which are more holistic. He never makes it completely clear how this is to happen and there is considerable play between the proffered hope of this integration and his own denial of its possibility:

The systems, so far as here suggested, do not connect themselves one to another by any rule or principle that I can see . . . [and] . . . I do not pursue further the problem of relating these systems to one another and the very difficult problem of representing the whole community by an ordering of part-systems. (1955:24)

Indeed, we discover soon enough that certain models are going to inhibit others as well as enhance each other. A general movement away from the social towards the cultural, however, is clear: again and again, basically Radcliffe-Brownian ecological and social structure models, as reported by Evans-Pritchard, Firth, or Fortes, prove themselves too narrow and leave no place for the mind: ecology is not made of fields and plants alone as such: "the human environment is in large part mental" (1955:30). "'Market' means both a state of mind and a place to trade" (1956:30); social structure only becomes interesting as a set of norms and expectations or a "set of ethical paradigms, an exemplary; an ideal system of demands that men can follow" (1955:47). A number of suggestions concerning his shift of interest here interweave with each other. One is that the narrow frame is scientific whereas the wider frame is going to have to belong to the humanities, indeed, specifically to the arts (1955:16, 70). Another is that this shift is one from anthropology to what we might have to call a meta-anthropology: first we think about the facts, "And then we turn to the form of thought we have used in thinking about [them] so, and we think about this thought" (1955:16). *Pace* certain suggestions that have been put forward, incidentally, I very much doubt that this makes Redfield a structuralist (cf. Singer 1976:222). If there were time, I would like to go into the whole question of Redfield's relations with France; his reception there in the early fifties and my sense—not unknown to Redfield as I now discover (1963a:33–34)—that his kind of anthropology can only come about in an educational system without a solid base of philosophical training.

But I return to my main track by noticing, now, a curious paradox in Redfield which has to do with the stress he places on all that is *individual* at the heart of every discussion of the *collective*. Of course, behind this stand Benedict, and Mead, and even, perhaps, Radin, but the stress permeates the work. At the very moment when he first asks what it means to consider a little community as a *whole*, he gives the answer: "It means that a band of hunters or a long-established village is unified, as is a personality, and has its own character, as does a personality" (1955:9). In another image, he states: "The face of a living person is such an immediately apprehended whole" (1955:17). Even when he is comparing the views of various anthropologists he feels that "we shall go forward more safely if we follow, for a time, the guidance of some one of these men" (1955:33). Matter of substance or of rhetoric? I have never stopped feeling that this was a deep-seated inhibitor of the comparativist he sought to be in social science.

The connection of this stress with what I take to be the basic axis of Redfieldian concern cannot be missed. The axis of the shift from narrow to wide focus, science to humanities, anthropology to meta-anthropology, is the concept of world view; world view, in turn, is the paramount locus of a yet more important shift, perhaps, from the "outside view" to the "inside view." This first appears in LC where Redfield calls for "concepts to describe the little community which are not so exterior to [the] villager's mind as is the concept of ecological system" (1955:32). This must separate initially two facets of the inner/outer binary, one ethnographic, one anthropological. The first is connected to the central fact about his fieldwork based on the bridge between the little community he knows and the wider world, external to it, which culminates in the urban metropolis. The second facet appears around LC page 64, where Redfield discusses the problem of entering the human mind and the tools we have had for doing so since Freud.

I hinted earlier at Redfield's apparent difficulties in his two chapters on "Typical Biography" and "Kind of Person" in sorting out (i) the biographical from the modal personality approaches and (ii) both of these, but especially the second, from "ethos" and "values." He tries to follow Kroeber—as so often—on the flying trapeze of "getting into metaphors that personify culture as if it has a will and purpose of its own" (1955:69). After worrying at the scientific validity of all this, he ends, nonetheless, with the individual:

World-view, temperament or group personality, and ethos are (remarked Milton Singer) all on the self axis. All represent the shift of description from products of culture to psychological characterization. (1955:79)

The concern with ethos, unresolved in these chapters, continues in chapter 6 on "The Little Community as an Outlook on Life" though we have in the meantime established that "value system" is "more of an inside view" than an outside one (1955:75). Discussing world view as the overall outlook on the universe around them held by a little community looking out at it, Redfield, already aware of the possible centripetal collapse of his discipline as exemplified by the silence of Frank Cushing, declares:

This tension between the inside view and the outside view, this obligation to manage correctly the relationship between them, is the *central problem* in studies of culture and personality. (1955:82;italics mine)

We are now close to a statement on Redfield's part of the full complexity of the situation:

It is because we have moved from conceptions developed from a consideration of institutions and institutionalized relationships between kinds of persons to conceptions that lie on the axis of the self, that the management of the relationship between inside and outside views has become so difficult and subtle. There is the inside view of what a person is. There is that view of what he ought to be, his own inside view. There is our outside view of what the person there is. (What we think he ought to be is, by the declared rules of science, excluded from our subject matter.) And there are our formulations made in terms admissible to science, of these three things. All this without adding the relations among what people think they are or should be and what the outsider finds them to be or the development and explanation of these things! (1955:85)

In the following pages, Redfield manages to sort out the relative positions of group personality, ethos, and world view; to ask what would happen if one "attempted to maintain the inside view over the whole range of the native's life without a preliminary commitment to value" (1955:86); to see a danger in this question and bring us very quickly back to the recognition that the normative and the cognitive cannot be separated from one another *anywhere* outside *our* minds, although this is bought at the price of a category slippage in which cognitive, affective and normative collapse into and become aspects of world view. Meantime, after stressing that "it is *their* order, *their* categories, *their* emphasis [i.e. the natives'] upon this part rather than that which the student listens for" 1955:88), Redfield returns to the "horns of the ethnographical dilemma" (1955:92). What the outsider, i.e. the anthropologist, is doing, since any attempt to present the inner view directly *in its own terms* would be unsuccessful, is *translating* the inside view to his fellows on the outside:

If we use only his terms [the native's] and forms of thought we merely become natives like those we study, speaking and thinking as he does—imagining for a moment this possibility could be achieved— and no communication to outsider would result. . . . and that way lies a permanent solipsism of the cultures." (1955:92)

The solution for Redfield seems to lie in an "alternation of talking and listening," that is to say, in a dialogue about "the common human" (1955:93–94), and it is with this reassurance that the world-view chapter ends.

The person standing outside the little community and the outside mind looking into it are one and the same. For what the reader cannot fail to notice twenty years later—with astonishment at how few could notice it then—is that there is someone missing in this dialogue and that is the informant himself. Redfield's stress on the inside view should have brought him, as much as any anthropologist, to the realization that this could one day mean the informant himself becoming the anthropologist, insisting that translation be a two-way process and that he should be in on the dialogue. Further, it might have dawned on him, not merely that there was a danger of solipsism if the outsider ceased to anthropologize, but that the insider could call an end to anthropology by refusing to entertain this purely imaginary peripheral status of his periphery. As Eric Wolf, among many others, has pointed out in the interval, what is left out is the question of power (Wolf 1972:257). Is this the reason why Redfield might feel uncomfortable with the concept of ethos in this book and that we find ethos has no separate chapter in this key methodology by one of anthropology's greatest ethicists? It would be good to think so despite his open acceptance of double standards in the matter of cultural relativism at the end of PWT. Could this also be some sort of reason for the constant, nervous return to the "axis of the self"? The scientist-judge, with his impeccable moral stance, corresponding to the impeccable informant mediating, albeit "slowly" (1963a:34), on his world view and his ethos within his little community: these two individuals who are, when all is said, Redfield's two favorite objects of study, are they not masks for the collectives on both sides which can then be relegated to the abstractions of social structure and the like? Or collapsed upon themselves in the true solipsism which is going on here: when the culture in "culture and personality" collapses into personality alone? Is it not difficult to trust today a view in which history itself becomes merely one more of the forms of thought with which to look at any community, little or big? Might it not be, if the outsider to the little community happens also to be its only translator, that the very folk-urban continuum itself becomes questionable as one of the tools with which the center may have blinded us to the rights of the peripheries? The ultimate confusion may well be, at a late point in LC, the goodhearted equation of the discourse and its subject:

A written account of a community is something like the community itself: to understand it one needs to take the inside view of it. Of the published study, the inside view is the author's view. With what ends in mind did he make the study? (1955:150)

For, of course, it is still the outsider who is the author here, and shall we then spend too much time on the inside of the outside? Perhaps not. Perhaps it is more important to look at the outside of the inside. Redfield, at least, had the courage to trot out the monster which revealed him for what he himself was, for without discussing the outside, we could not have had the outsider, or even the beginnings of the suggestion that the insider could complain. It is not so much, I repeat, Don Roberto who is in question here, but rather the profession and the culture his book is embedded in. I deliberately oscillate here between a view of style that implies the individual track a text's author makes, when he steers the writing working through him, upon that writing—and another view of style in which the world, social or cultural, surrounding the author impresses that track in a variety of codes as the writing comes into being, through the author indeed, but independently of authorial intention. "Anthropological discourse" as I use it here is such a sociocultural style. Redfield's innocence arises out of his sense as a writer of the gap between personal style and sociocultural style and his refusal to allow the first to be devoured by the second. He remains innocent by refusing the mask which the second style implies, that is to say, he is "sincere." What I previously referred to as a wound in this case is complex, involving not style per se but a discrepancy between two styles. Here "sincerity" (sometimes a literary device) is "wound" in the sense that it involves a price. The price is an uneasy conscience of what is speaking through one nevertheless, in that other, second, style: the classical liberal discomfort to which Redfield has given a more elegant expression than anyone else. A more complete analysis, including an overview of all the social, educational, and ethical writing, would doubtless reveal this more clearly. It would be hard to do the same with the jargon-ridden pages of many of his contemporaries, or immediate followers, for they wear the iron mask and it is elsewhere than in the style that one must hunt for dragons.

*

But since you have, at this time, the rare, almost unheard-of, luxury of hosting a poet among you, let me shift for a moment to the view from my world. It is perhaps not a matter of chance that the only interview with another poet I have ever published—one entitled, significantly enough, "From Anthropologist to Informant"—was with one of the foremost defenders in contemporary literature of localism and regionalism against centralized control (Tarn 1972). I refer to Gary Snyder. Myself, you understand: I was born in too many places simultaneously to afford the luxury of roots. But even if this had not been so, I would have been most doubtful of Don Roberto's division of civilizational components into those that are "universal, reflective, and indoctrinating" and those that are "local, unreflective, and accepting" (1962:395). I am prepared at everyone's leisure to generalize a great deal more about power and control in the literary world and, in so doing, imply that there might be some questions worth raising in a fertile field—whose existence I suspect without being able to delimit it as yet—which, heaven help us, would go under such names as Aesthetic Anthropology or, even, Comparative Aesthetics. I am not talking here of Ethnopoetics alone (whose much narrower band of definition has been, in *Alcheringa*, amply available to anthropology for some time, although I do not know to what extent anthropology has availed itself of it). Nor am I talking of the politics internal to the literary life, such as a Richard Kostelanetz may have exposed them in this country. No, the excuse for bringing in this matter of the poet is that it might help me to voice some further comments on Redfield's concepts in cultural anthropology.

Stanley Diamond has shown how and why, in his view, Plato sent the poet home (Diamond 1974). Given his sense of the word "primitive," his identification of "sending the poet home" and "sending the primitive home" (a theme we have just looked at in Redfield) cannot but be highly gratifying to poets. It is certainly more acceptable than the Kroeberian monstrosity cited by Redfield with approval (1953:160) to the effect that "The bestowal of social rewards for the inability to distinguish subjective experiences from objective phenomena, or for the deliberate inversion of the two, is a presumable mark of a lack of progress." I wish that Diamond had said more about everything that has happened since Plato: if he has done so, of course, I beg his pardon and will read him pronto. For sending the poet home has been a favorite occupation of all and sundry in our society since Plato's rather distant time. To jump to our own miraculous years, let me quote you a few lines from a work of criticism. There are about half a dozen works of literary criticism worth reading in any half century, and I think this may be one of them in ours. Nevertheless perpend and see if this is not familiar:

There is another reason why criticism has to exist. Criticism can talk, and all the arts are dumb. In painting, sculpture, or music it is easy enough to see that the art shows forth, but cannot *say* anything. And, whatever it sounds like to call the poet inarticulate or speechless, there is a most important sense in which poems are silent as statues. Poetry is a *disinterested* use of words: it does not address a reader directly. . . . The axiom of criticism must be, not that the poet does not know what he is talking about, but that he cannot talk about what he knows. . . . The poet may of course have some critical ability of his own, and so be able to talk about his own work. But the Dante who writes a commentary on the first Canto of the Paradiso is merely one more of Dante's critics. What he says has a peculiar interest, but not a peculiar authority. It is generally accepted that a critic is a better judge of the *value* of a poem than its creator, but there is still a lingering notion that it is somehow ridiculous to regard the critic as the final judge of its meaning, even though in practice it is clear that he must be. The reason for this is an inability to distinguish literature from the descriptive or assertive writing which derives from the active will and the conscious mind, and which is primarily concerned to "say" something. (Frye 1957:4–5)

It is hardly necessary to stress, it seems to me, the parallels between a literary critic, writing in 1957 about poets, and an anthropologist, writing at roughly the same time, about primitives and folk. Our culture had reached the stage in which we could assure the public that poet and primitive both knew what they were doing but needed the critic, on the one hand, and the anthropologist, on the other, to represent them, translate them, allow them to talk and be heard. Mr. Northrop Frye, mind you, was reacting (or so his rhetoric goes) to "the conception of the critic as a parasite or artiste manqué . . . still very popular [oh boy is it popular!], especially among artists" (1957:1), whereas the anthropologist had probably not yet heard the anthropologized tell him "gringo go home." "The community," Redfield tells us, "stands there always ready to serve the student of the mechanisms of learning, of the work-

ings of simple economics, of the natural history of social movements" (1955:156). Is that still so today?

Let me be this wall here, for a moment, between Pyramus
and Thisbe and stand for informant. I am a poet. I am also a
university professor. As a university professor, I am paid a
reasonable sum to teach the poets who died before me. Except
in very rare, privileged cases, I cannot teach *myself*. And I am
paid virtually nothing, ever, anywhere, to *be* myself. There is
at least a possibility that, after my death, another poet will
come along in order to teach me. He will not be paid a penny
to teach himself, or be himself. This is the situation I am in,
being *interested* enough, *pace* Mr. Frye, in or out of my writing, to fill at least *this* belly. The price I pay for the money,
leaving dignity aside, is the time I lose for poetry, but, of
course, we have all known for years, have we not, that poetry is
a spare-time hobby. Here, in any event, are the professors:
making careers, buying houses, having children, breeding pets,
growing roses, taking vacations abroad and all because there
was once a John Keats, a Walt Whitman, a William Carlos
Williams. And shall we add: an X tribe, a Y folk society, a Z
urban barrio as well, not to mention names since we are all
involved?

In short, the writer says to the critic "You people teach
literature, but I AM literature" while the critic answers "You
are not literature until we say you are and we are not likely to
open our mouths until you are dead or have won the Nobel
Prize which is probably the same thing." So much for the love
and amity between poets and critics: I offer it up on the altars
of any future discussion of Redfield's *literati* and *intelligentsia*.
But the social scientist might raise his voice and ask whether
the very fact that so many poets have had to seek their belly-
fuls from the academy is not, itself, evidence of a consensus. Is
there not, someone might ask, some sort of conspiracy between
University and Avant-Garde in a progressive tradition—and
here we would be dealing with much more than poets—with
each artist or thinker followed, one generation down, by his
exegete, who in turn will be followed by his own? Is it
unthinkable that some such artists or thinkers might allow

themselves to become too "complex," "obscure," or "elitist" *partly* because of their *expectation* of such exegesis? There is certainly an extraordinary development in some discourses at this time (I am thinking of philosophy and criticism primarily) of what might be characterized as "the text at large" or, as some would call it, "intertextuality." It is a situation in which, briefly, the exegete claims as much autonomy in what he is writing, as much contextuality with what he comments upon, as the object of his exegesis claims. The artistic fiat, it may be said, reigns supreme. The implications for what scientists are bound to see as the triumph of irresponsibility, while the poets and their kin might hope that it will lead to a new definition of responsibility, are certain, from any perspective, to be profoundly unsettling. My hope is that it will finish off the academy in its present form within the next 100 years: I only wish I could see the future more clearly for what will take its place.

Something too much of this. But Redfield might not have been all that much surprised. His meditations on Griaule's Ogontemmeli and Paul Radin's primitive philosopher (see Redfield 1960) might have made him say something like "ah yes, first the bound text, with its Talmudic variant; then the restrained text, with its academic respect for the footnote, still honoring the tradition of exegesis; and now the text at large. Let's do another 'Characterization and Comparison of Cultures' number in Chicago!" Forgive me, I do but follow Thucydides in putting into the mouth of each speaker whatever he would probably have said in the course of the war.

*

"Where that superhighway runs, there used to be a cornfield. In June the unfolding leaves made a neat, fresh carpet there—nine acres of it. In August one walked slowly between the rows of stalks, taller than one's head. When we went into the corn on very hot nights and stood still and listened, we used to tell ourselves that we heard the corn growing. And over there farther, there was a piece of aboriginal prairie that had never been broken by the plow. Only native plants grew there, prairie dock and tickseed, downy phlox and bluegrass. And up there where there are so many houses, the oak stood very old and tall, and I used to find yellow adder's tongue growing beneath some of them.

"Do you know what I miss? I am thinking just now, although the season of the year is not appropriate, that I miss very much the sound of whetstone on the scythes—a good, clean sound. Oh, and many other things I miss—the voice of the bobwhite, the flight of the red-headed woodpecker as he flashed along the dirt road to fling himself like a painted dart against a telephone pole. And I miss the fields filled with shooting stars. And the clang and rattle of the windmill when the vanes swung around in a shift of breeze and the puddles of water at the well where the wasps came in summer." (Redfield 1963b:276)

That passage was published in 1958, the year of Redfield's death. It is embedded in a rather bad paper, rather poorly written, called "Talk with a Stranger," in which Redfield imagined a conversation with a man from space, perhaps a Martian anthropologist.

Among the many liberation movements today, there is one which belongs to the oldest race of all, further back than race itself, sex, color and all such divisions. It is called Poets' Liberation and everyone is free to join.

*

At the very opening of LC, Redfield refers to massive cultural units which are of interest to me:

Each person, each stable human settlement with an organized way of life, each historical people, *even each art or body of literature* associated with such people, has a sort of integrity which is recognized both by common sense and by much scholarship, human-istic or anthropological. . . . But the discussion here will be with reference to small communities only. The generalization of the prob-lems to other kinds of human wholes is a further and much more dif-ficult problem. (1955:2; italics mine)

Redfield constantly referred to art and aesthetics (he told a certain student of his that, because of his aesthetic bent, he was sending him to a place—Lake Atitlán, Guatemala—where he would bless his mentor every morning on opening the wooden shutters), but it is not my impression that he ever did much more than salute them from afar. It is possible (there is a hint of this in LC, p. 111) that his "aesthetic expectations" were satisfied entirely by his own holistic approach. It is also my impression that Redifeld is interested in *Literate* Man rather than in *Literary* Man: the text he reads is ultimately a political, not an aesthetic text. Yet Literary Man goes back a long way in civilization, does he not . . . not to mention them little oral-tradition poems?

More on this later. I have just tried to hint at one of the ways in which we could look at our whole literature today: as both a conflict and a conspiracy between producer, consumer and self-styled quality control manager, and I dare say there are studies that could take this back some way in time. I want to end this assay with a quick, glancing take on Redfield's use of the terms *literati* and *intelligentsia* as a means of extending this concern.

In a rich, long article on "Robert Redfield's Development of a Social Anthropology of Civilizations," Milton Singer (1976) sees his subject moving around 1949, out of the study of cultures seen from "the bottom up" and into that of civilizations seen from "the top down." Let it be said here, incidentally, what a great debt Redfield owed Singer in this enterprise. In this move, Redfield asked for the cooperation of Orientalists and other students of major civilizations. Many of us now have doubts as to whether the primitive isolate wasn't a convenient figment of anthropological imagination, as well as doubts on whether it is not *state* rather than *city* that matters in elite control of peasantries. However this may be, Redfield's ever-growing insistence on peasants for his view of people as no longer isolated from the world around them but embedded in situations great segments of which were determined by urban leaders, led him to study acculturation as something more like what one author (I forget whom) called Transculturation. That is: he wished to find out what aspects of town culture were at work in the lives and, especially, in the minds of peasant villagers and also what part of the latter's folk culture was at work in the lives and minds of the urban elite. An attempt to deal with such major civilizations as Islam, Hinduism, and Confucianism (rather, I think than China, India, Arabia, etc. per se), required the addition to his conceptual apparatus of a concept which would come to grips with the aeons over which he saw civilizations enduring.

I am not at all sure of being happy with Redfield's concept of "historic structure" as Singer depicts it, but, in fairness, Redfield had little time in which to develop it. I also feel Redfield continued to underestimate the work of humanists (especially European members of such bodies as the École des Hautes Études, the École Française d'Extrème Orient or the London School of Oriental and African Studies). It is not that he was unaware of this work: sometimes Redfield seemed to know of models more complex than he was using but declined to change his middle-level approach (I was about to say middlebrow) for reasons best known to himself. However this may be, it is part of Redfield's positive achievement that he was prepared, against much criticism, and for what he saw as the universal good, to make this effort. The guiding "form of thought" was that of "Great and Little Traditions." Here, Redfield and Singer looked at how ideas at large in the folk society might be systematized so as to grow into what they came to call indigenous primary civilizations, reacting back upon the folk as a set of intellectual and moral standards ideologically corresponding to the politicoeconomic rule of the elite over the peasants. In contrast stand secondary civilizations involving cases in which "a folk society, precivilized, peasant or partly urbanized, is further urbanized by contact with peoples of widely different cultures from that of its own members" (Redfield and Singer 1954:61). At the level of cities, we have a basic distinction

between the *carrying forward into systematic and reflective dimensions an old culture* and *the creating of original modes of thought that have authority beyond or in conflict with old cultures and civilizations.* We might speak of the orthogenetic cultural role of cities as contrasted with the heterogenetic cultural role. (Redfield and Singer 1954:58; italics in original)

This latter stage might also include feedback to the periphery, whose moral orders, disturbed by heterogeneity, would be reorganized. Redfield, as some have suggested, may have been over-optimistic about the degree of trauma involved for the periphery. Others saw the trauma as deep and enduring. At the level of personnel, finally, the primary-orthogenetic complex seems to involve mainly V. Gordon Childe's *literati* who use literacy to evolve or continue the local sacred tradition, while the secondary-heterogenetic type seems to involve mainly Toynbee's *intelligentsia* who use literacy to mediate between the external urban world and the inner folk world (see as far back as Redfield 1953:44).

Note that we are back once more to the *in* and the *out*. A long analysis of the matter (unperformable here) would, I believe, bring out yet more of the ambivalences I have discussed before. Such a study would involve a close look at the relation of *cosmology* to *world view* in the development of Redfield's thought from PWT onwards (involving somewhat unrelated contentions that cosmology can be both an inner elaboration of a world view by an indigenous philosopher *and* the elaboration of such a world view by an outside observer, i.e., an anthropologist). It would then involve the same kind of study of the terms *literati* and *intelligentsia*, revolving, for me, around the fact that the *literati* are not only insiders but *also* mediators between rulers and ruled, when they move out of the little community to elaborate the orthogenetic city (see Redfield and Singer 1954). In later writings, these terms begin to carry too much weight and are clearly very vulnerable. By 1957, Redfield seems to be supplanting them by the term *intellectual* which—it is not too clear—may be inclusive of them both (1960:358). In any event, the confusions between these binaries again involve political issues revolving around the question of ruler and ruled. Of greater concern to me here is his associating "originally creative artists" and philosophers with civilization, while mere "proto-artists and proto-intellectuals" are linked with the periphery (1960:359). It would not be too difficult to trace in Redfield a condescension towards primitives perhaps greater than he would have wished to reveal, given his "double standard" of cultural relativism.

I am somewhat dismayed, in glancing back at Redfield's later work, with the distance which had grown up between his social and cultural anthropology. It worries me that I cannot find the exact link Redfield intends to make between peasant and Toynbee's internal and external proletariats: I pencil in a note there (at PWT, p. 50) which reads "but what is the relation? Is a proletarian merely an angry peasant or what?" It worries me, thinking about the relation of all this to our culture, that, in all the later work, I find only one reference to "suburbanites" (1953:52). I find only two references to mass culture (1955:147; Redfield and Singer 1954:70). It is clear that Redfield sees himself as never getting near our own situation. When he does, he finds his concepts stalling on him: "It may be that for a rapidly changing and heterogenous civilized people the notion of world view is quite unmanageable" (1962:398). Most worrisome of all is that I can find only one, elusive, reference to class (1953:42), just before the first discussion of *literati* and *intelligentsia* as it happens. So what do we have finally? The folk on the one hand, the elite on the other, and nothing in the middle? But is any equivalent to the middle classes really that late in civilization? Not only do we get very little attempt to distinguish between political, economic, religious, aesthetic leadership and the like but in addition we have a conceptual desert between folk and elite. It may be that once social anthropology has got you it will never let you go, but I find it hard to buy a cultural anthropology at such a price!

And it is a pity because I am so sure that it is not only the sociology of literacy that has not yet been written (1953:36), but also the sociology of the literary. "The precivilized hunter or villager is preliterate;" he had said a few lines before, "the peasant is illiterate". What exactly is modern consumer man? I am concerned, in our own culture—and for me and my like it is a question of *bare* survival—with the fate of the arts. What I see, briefly, is a rapidly dwindling folk anywhere in the world and also here in these States; an elite that is far more concerned with power and money than with culture, and an immense, constantly growing, stupefied and consumerized middle range whose concern with culture is almost purely oriented in terms of status acquisition. The war between poet and critic pales into insignificance beside the role of the media in defining what culture it is that this middle range is going to acquire next. I need concepts today to raise the almost forgotten issue of "taste" and to deal with a host of problems involving "taste" in the production and consumption of art objects. These might range, without sticking to literature, from, say, the study of the passage from function to decoration (so called) in such a humble "folk-art" object as the North Atlantic, Great Lakes, and West Coast duck-hunting decoy; via the study (say again) of how "gift-shop," "kitsch," or "airport art" arises and is dealt with by places such as the one I live in (New Hope, Pa.) all the way across to Laguna Beach, California and Skagway, Alaska; to (say yet once more) a full sociology of readership, t-visionship or other forms of art consumption that we suffer through in our time. You will doubtless gather from this that I am an unreformed normativist in aesthetics; in this perhaps I would have gained some degree of approval from Don Roberto.

We are used to thinking of exploitation and alienation in very material terms. It occurs to us very rarely that we might be exploiting and alienating both others and ourselves in producing or consuming tasteless and unworthy culture. Even the radicals in our bourgeois society see this less clearly than they see what hits the pocket, the bank account, the standard of living. Of course, a major political problem is raised immediately by the word "taste" since, the question immediately follows: "whose taste do you mean?" Nevertheless, we can make a beginning perhaps by asking exactly what, or more precisely who, is doing what to whom when Seattle floods the Alaskan market with its own or Japanese totem poles and ivory carvings; or when San Francisco and Los Angeles import Guatemalan textiles by the thousands of yards; or when laboriously execrable furniture is specifically designed for peripheral consumption and the like. Or we can ask ourselves why it is that our culture can make such a fetish of "natural pollution" while almost totally ignoring "cultural pollution," there being no linkup whatsoever between the institutions that deal with the one and those that deal with the other.

It may turn out to be one of the greatest ironies of our time that it was the fascist poet Ezra Pound who has yet said most clearly that bad language equals bad morality and bad government. Consumer man is not postliterate, but he may well be postliterary. When I first left England for this country (their poetry and their anthropology having become somewhat terroristic as well as obsolescent) what first struck me was the tremendous vitality of poetic language here, especially in the post-Poundian school: with Zukofsky, Williams, Oppen, Olson, Duncan, Rexroth, Creeley, Dorn, Kelly, Eshelman, Rothenberg, Enslin, and the like. What strikes me now is the abysmal decay of language in almost all public sectors: the media, government, the market, even the university. I am *not* an academician fearful of the evolution of language, I am a poet, terror-struck in a tremendous solitude. The requirement upon the poet today continues to be that he should fight his way out of all possible human discourse into a language as yet unknown, and it lies heavier and heavier upon him as *attention* to language wanes. For, we must face it: the whole poetic enterprise today, whatever the talent around and whatever lip service is paid to it, is fast becoming a vanity operation and almost totally incestuous. Read only by other poets, published only by other poets, reading and publishing only other poets, the poet is in danger of being a disappearing species. Perhaps a Woody Guthrie or a Bob Dylan (I am not directly comparing them) are where it should really be at, but I do not think so: they too are compromised every moment by the consumer octopus. Perhaps that is what will have to go before the trend is reversed, if it ever is, and it is for this that both poet and primitive must survive on their peripheries (Tarn 1979).

I fear I am getting lost and may be disappearing over the horizon into an unheard-of form of the primitive isolate. I doubt this has made you into poets yet or has turned me back

into an anthropologist. But we have made the trip now and
have made it in Robert Redfield's company. It is a tribute to
him, I think, that this could be. There are not many of his
profession with whom we could have made it. Perhaps it is
because while respecting the handmaiden science far more
than we sometimes think he did, he knew that the "true gods
within the temple" are "understanding and her apotheosis,
wisdom" (1955:168; see Tarn 1976).

*

To end on a less ponderous note, maybe, as they say in
show business, I have time for just one more quick little
number. A few weeks ago, I had a letter from the *Chicago
Review*. They had just found my name and address in the
alumni directory. Big mystery to me. I had been a noted
Chicago professor. Big mystery to me. All this being so, would
I send them a poem for the special issue of the magazine about
writers associated with Chicago. I wrote back: sure, but I have
no new poems; all my poems are sold, I'll have to do you a special. Be sure, I added, to write back and tell me if you like my
special. Well they haven't written back: you know how the
mail is. But here is the poem and it isn't one of my heavy ones:

lines for the c. issue of c.r.

> for charles, zelda, manning, claude, bob, walter, ed, clark, victor,
> margaret and some whose names only i have forgotten.

it was a place for
       and remembering most
grey stone, red door,
       and remembering most
my hand on a black bed by the el.
all year, i cd. stretch out to that
       couple in love, my
own scarce satisfactions.
it was a place for
       and remembering most
rides on the el at two a.m.
       the spooky papers

like scarecrows over vacant lots.
no trees in that part of the land
where most distant jazz clubs were
and churches whose women went up in smoke.
     they asked you at the door
(your girls) to wear their stockings.
     it was a time for growing
professional on the vine
     in days they still believed
in the professional.
     a fellow-student held us
week after week with the same songs—
he knew enough never to weary—
in the middle of each program i sang my song
which was a medieval song and known as
     tarn's song, the one he did
every time in the middle of the program.
     it was a scoring song
and it even undid
the daughter of the man of god
who worked in the library
and wanted to be caught by her father
love-making at home.
     there was our cooking:
my room-mate's and mine
which had the reputation for being european
so that many traveled whole blocks
for salad with a little vinegar and oil.
it was a place for
     growing so professional
that i never saw the city
until i bought equipment for my trip south
and then i took many pictures of it
with my room-mate in the foreground.
we were invited everywhere as a couple
     although heterosexual
because everyone was married except us.
     when we did get married,
     to women i mean,
we were concerned until our wedding days
with messages from on high about our doctorates;

all my wedding photos in a distant country
(europe) show a corner of a u. of c. envelope
sticking out of my inside pocket.
the chairman was wishing me a good wedding
and telling me the doctorate was delayed
         for this or that reason.
it was a place for
         and remembering most
visits to evanston and to wisconsin
to see a real american campus
where it was impossible to believe
         the yachts and swimming suits.
         it was all too easy to believe
that grey gothic of ours
         was a university
         but sometimes the women
would look human on the long wide green
between grey and grey.
         we had explained to eggan
that the europeans had not formed us
nearly as well as he thought
and, almost every week,
we threw ourselves on our knees in front of redfield
         and, like falstaff, repented.
they never seemed to believe us
so we worked like dogs the whole year
and i was the first to lecture there
on the elementary structures of kinship.
redfield drove me home once. i asked him how
he wove his car in and out those sixty lane
highways and he said it was the only thing in the world
         that relaxed him.
it was a place for
         and remembering most
the cut of the wind at 9 a.m.
when washburn was discovering walking
and tax his foxes, and singer *gopi*-girls
         i gather the department
has been backwards and forwards from california
         at least twice since

but it is still the greatest, etc.
       i did not do crazy things there
like i had done in paris and london and even new york
and would do again in many places.
       it was perhaps the purest time of work
in all my life: neither manic as before,
nor sour as afterwards.
i loved the library and nearly wept when i left.
it would be natural for an awful lot of me
to finish off in that mid-country:
i who have been a man of coasts
with no land in between.
       a poem in "the house of leaves"
will inform anyone who cares to enquire
that this is not the only poem of mine about c.
       before going there,
i remember an epic lunch with kroeber, steward and shapiro
in the faculty lounge at columbia,
kroeber being quiet almost all of the time
and saying in the end
       "young man you go to c./ you
will need a thick scarf."
       at about this time,
had i known about it,
       i cd. probably have gone
to black mountain in the south
instead of going even further south than that
and getting so near lost in all the beauty
redfield had told me i would have every morning
       because i was "aesthetically inclined"
i damn near never came out of it
       to begin the life you know so well.

p.s. i . . .
it was a place for
       for i remember radin with his dinner
(regarding our cooking)
in a small paper parcel under his arm
coming for it to be cooked now and then,
cooked european.

i discovered he and my grandfather were landsmen
and that my people were bookbinders
          in a village of horse thieves.
(regarding p.s.ii)
a journalist in pennsylvania sd. this morning:
"t. in order to understand those poems
          i will have to have that life."

Biographical Note

Nathaniel Tarn was born in Paris in 1928. He was taken to Belgium at the age of seven and then, at the outbreak of war, to England. He studied at Cambridge, taking a B.A. in English and history in 1948. That year he went back to Paris, where he happened to see a movie in which the young hero visits the Musée de l'Homme. Tarn went there the next day, was overwhelmed, and three days later enrolled in university studies in anthropology. His work was done primarily under Marcel Griaule and Claude Lévi-Strauss.

In the early 1950s Tarn went to the University of Chicago under a Fulbright grant, studying with Fred Eggan, Robert Redfield, and others. Redfield included him in a project on "Comparison of Total Cultures" and in 1952 sent him to Guatemala to do a study of world view. The following year Tarn returned to England and became a graduate student at the London School of Economics under Raymond Firth and Isaac Schapera. There he wrote a thesis on his Mesoamerican research, obtaining the Ph.D. from Chicago in 1957. In 1958 he went to Burma to study the social organization of Buddhist institutions and became interested in what he referred to as "Messianic Buddhism." Following this fieldwork, he returned to London to take up a lectureship in South East Asian Anthropology at the School of Oriental and African Studies, a post he held until 1967.

Tarn's first book of poetry was published in 1964. Three years later, he decided "he could no longer conciliate the mental sets expected of him as an anthropologist and those he wished to achieve as a poet." He resigned from his post at S.O.A.S. and joined the publishing house of Jonathan Cape Ltd., where he founded and edited a multidisciplinary series of texts and a poetry press. Subsequently, Tarn published over a dozen books of his own poetry, as well as translations of Latin American and French poetry and numerous other works. In 1969–70 he held visiting professorships at the State University of New York at Buffalo and at Princeton. Deciding at this time to move to the United States, he joined the Rutgers faculty, where he is a professor of comparative literature.

Tarn's anthropological interests reemerged in 1975 as a result of work as a consultant to Native Arts groups in Alaska. He has since returned to Guatemala to do further fieldwork.

Tarn's interests within anthropology have centered on religion, above all on the effort to elucidate complex symbolic systems. In recent years, he has been exploring the relationships between anthropology and literature. "Torn all his life between a recording angel and a creative angel . . . he has begun to look now for the possibility of a new genre lying between anthropology and literature."

Notes, References Cited,

and Index

Notes

1. Franz Boas

1. This paper, with some variations in content, has been presented at the University of Pennsylvania (1973), Yale University (1973), Calgary University (1974), Cornell University (1974), Barnard College (1975), Hofstra University (1975), and McMaster University (1975). The author acknowledges the kindness of the American Philosophical Society for use of materials from the Boas collection.

2. Boas' comments on this occasion are reported in the *American Anthropologist* (1907), 9:646–47.

3. Dr. Marian W. Smith was trained at Columbia and was an active anthropologist for years in the United States before she went abroad, where later she became Secretary of the Royal Anthropological Institute of Great Britain and Ireland. She was well experienced in both American anthropology and British social anthropology.

4. All quotations in this paragraph are from Boas' Diary from Baffinland (APS, 2).

5. This quotation·is from "Proceedings of the American Ethnological Society" in the *American Anthropologist* (1921), 23:514.

2. Alfred L. Kroeber

1. I've always thought this was something of a blessing, since it enabled him to write in the middle of a pandemonium of children and grandchildren without ever hearing them. It also served him in conversation. He would locate certain people on his deaf side, and smile reassuringly as they would explain their position and make them feel they had their day in court. Then Kroeber would emerge with his ideas quite unchanged.

2. The social historian Carl Schorske has written a sensitive and illuminating piece (1962) on similar responses among Viennese intellectuals before World War I.

3. This article also invited a response from Radcliffe-Brown, who was at one with Kroeber in chastising Malinowski for making reference to "human needs" as having something to do with culture. Radcliffe-Brown and Kroeber both detested the idea that such utilitarianism should ever have raised its head in anthropology.

4. The same can be said of Leslie White.

3. Paul Radin

1. This paper is based, in part, on material included in my essay on Radin in the *International Encyclopedia of the Social Sciences* (1968, 13:300–3).

I was neither a student nor a disciple of Paul Radin, merely a colleague and friend who came to respect and tried to understand him and his work. The first time I met him was at Columbia in 1948. He had come to give one of the famous and, quite literally, seminal Wednesday seminars, having been particularly invited in order to respond to Leslie White's crusade against Boas, which had then reached its height. I had been assigned as White's graduate assistant that summer, and I was rather interested in what Radin had to say. He attacked White for his undiscriminating attacks on Boas, which were, and continued to be, intemperate, if not fanatical. At the same time, Radin analyzed White as a mechanical materialist, while subtly situating himself in the Marxist tradition; although this was never declaimed, it was strongly implied in his own work. The result was delightful, humorous, and devastating.

I saw him over the years from time to time, and then established a closer collegial and personal relationship with him when he accepted our invitation to come to Brandeis in 1957, two years before his death.

2. His lack of careerist continuity and bureaucratic responsibility was held against him by many anthropologists. One even managed to strike a pejorative tone in the obituary he prepared.

3. Perhaps appropriately, he recorded Winnebago medicine rites in a hotel room in a midwestern city, since his informant, who had developed into an aboriginal anthropologist of sorts, was risking his life and possibly Radin's in imparting sacred information.

4. Bronislaw Malinowski

1. This essay covers some of the same ground as my introductions to the symposium *Man and Culture* (Firth 1957) and to the translation of his field diaries, but focuses more specifically on Malinowski's theories. I am indebted to Phyllis Kaberry, Audrey Richards, and other colleagues for help at various times in preparing this memoir. I have also been encouraged by audiences at the New York Academy of Sciences (1971), and Departments of Anthropology at Chicago (1971), Cambridge (1973), Berkeley and Davis (1974) to rewrite what was originally a lecture not intended for publication. I have given few biographical details of Malinowski here. These will be found in my article on Malinowski in the *Encyclopaedia Britannica* (15th ed., 1974) and that by Rhoda Metraux in the *International Encyclopedia of the Social Sciences* (1968). A full biographical study, using family correspondence and much other unpublished material, is being prepared by his daughter, Mrs. Helena Wayne.

2. Significant reviews of *A Diary in the Strict Sense of the Term* (1967), as by Anthony Forge (*New Society*, August 17, 1967), Clifford Geertz (*The New York Review*, September 14, 1967), Audrey Richards (*Cambridge Review*, January 19, 1968), and George Stocking (*Journal of History of Behavioral Sciences*, April 1968, Vol. 4, no. 2), have brought out the relevance of Malinowski's reactions to the field situation.

3. I am indebted for information and an example of this stamp to Matthew Ciolek. Malinowski's portrait, flanked by a Trobriand yam house, also appears on a ten-cent stamp of the Territory of Papua and New Guinea, issued on August 19, 1970 as part of a celebration of the forty-second congress of the Australian and New Zealand Association for the Advancement of Science, held in Port Moresby. (These are probably the only portrayals of an anthropologist on postage stamps so far.)

4. See *Sex and Repression in Savage Society* (1927a:113, 143, etc.). H. A. Powell, in a detailed review of Trobriand evidence and Malinowski's interpretation of it, supports the orthodox Freudian position, using the telling argument that in Kiriwina such formal authority as is wielded over a small boy is exercised by his father, who is also his sexual rival with the mother. But the matter is complex and much depends on the weight placed on the personal affective as against jural components in the relationships (Powell 1969:184–86). Michel Panoff, on the other hand, is impressed by Malinowski's model of the dynamics of a matrilineal family, in which he showed how the Melanesian facts corresponded to a logical transformation of the Freudian model in the different setting (Panoff 1972:80–81; cf. Lombard 1972:74–79).

5. These passages come from "A Glimpse of Malinowski in Retrospect," *Journal of the Anthropological Society of Oxford* (1974), 5(2):104–8. I am indebted to Phyllis Kaberry for permission to reproduce them.

6. President Kenyatta has placed his acknowledgement on record in the preface to his book *Facing Mt. Kenya* (London: Martin Secker & Warburg, 1938), p. xvii. Malinowski wrote an introduction to this work.

7. Reprinted as chapter 9 of Gluckman (1963:235–43). The review was published in slightly different form at two earlier dates.

8. Richard Thurnwald (1921:16), quoted in Malinowski (1926b:24n). The page reference indicated by Malinowski is incorrect.

9. See foreword to J. P. Singh Uberoi (1962). The foreword is by Max Gluckman and I. G. Cunnison, but I have attributed the most characteristic expressions to

Gluckman alone. Cunnison and Gluckman later published a comment on their foreword (*American Anthropologist* (1963), 65:1135) emphasizing the accuracy of Malinowski's rich material and its "honest comprehensiveness." A brief account of a visit to the Trobriands in 1947 by the government anthropologist to the territory of Papua and New Guinea gives vivid confirmation of Malinowski's description of the ritual respect paid to the Tabalu chief of Omarakana. See Charles Julius, "Malinowski's Trobriand Islands," *Journal of the Public Service of the Territory of Papua and New Guinea* (1960), 2:5-13, 57-64. This report does not appear in Uberoi's bibliography, nor does the analysis of ownership rights by Rudiger Schott, "Die Eigentumsrechte der Trobriand-Insulaner in Nordwest-Melanesien," *Anthropos* (1958), 53:88-132.

10. An interesting sidelight on the influence of Malinowski in a literary field is given by René Étiemblé, who cites Malinowski on the definition and function of myth, noting with approval Malinowski's "excellent critique" of nature mythology and of the constructions of the historical school (Étiemblé 1961:43, 407).

5. Ruth Benedict

1. This paper grew out of a lecture I was invited to deliver at the Graduate Center of the City University of New York, in 1976. I am indebted to Jacqueline Mintz and Sydel Silverman for very useful suggestions and editorial comments on earlier drafts.

2. Modell (1975, 1978) has attempted to develop her interpretation of Benedict's work along parallel lines. We discovered our similar views when I sent her the transcript of the original lecture from which this paper has been adapted. In a recent letter (October 16, 1979), Modell reports that she is preparing a revised version of her dissertation for publication.

3. I confess that my memory of the matter is somewhat different. While the pamphlet was, indeed, denounced in Congress, one of the objections voiced by Congressman Andrew May of Kentucky was that Ad Reinhardt's cartoon showing Adam and Eve on page four depicted Adam with a navel. The real reasons why the pamphlet was denounced, of course, had to do with the position taken by the authors on the concept of race itself, and on the equality of the races.

4. In retrospect, it strikes me that, whatever their attacks on anthropology, very few of our critics of the 1940s were offering alternative models for the study of humankind. Anthropology might have been considered romantic, irrelevant, unscientific, egalitarian—but hardly anyone thought at the time that humans were only complex computers, smart apes, genetic print-outs, turf-conscious hippopotamuses, or terrestrial dolphins. The cries of outrage that once greeted the heresy that humankind was not unique apparently now greet the assertion that, in other regards, it is.

5. The Office of War Information, according to Margaret Mead (1959:352).

6. Julian Steward

1. This essay grew out of a lecture delivered at the Graduate Center of the City University of New York. Although the present paper departs from the original talk, it owes much to questions and comments from members of the audience. I am also indebted to Morton Fried, Sydel Silverman, and Eric Wolf for their reviews of the manuscript, and to Brian Ferguson for his continuing support and motivation.

2. Kroeber was a visiting professor at Columbia from 1948 to 1952.

3. A fuller coverage of Steward's career is given in my introduction to the volume *Evolution and Ecology* (Steward 1977:1–39). This essay also presents a systematic overview of the totality of Steward's work.

7. Leslie White

1. For reading an earlier draft of this paper and giving me the benefit of their perceptive and incisive criticisms, I am indebted to Barbara Bode, Sydel Silverman, Mary Ann Harrell, Gertrude E. Dole, Elman R. Service, Christian E. Guksch, and Beth Dillingham. To Dr. Dillingham, co-literary executor with me of Leslie White's unpublished papers, I am especially grateful. She has spent many hours going through Dr. White's letters and papers, and has generously and unstintingly made available to me, for use in writing this paper, the fruits of her extensive gleanings.

2. As much as he came to resemble Veblen in thought and manner—iconoclastic, tough-minded, controversial—White seems to have left no indication of what influence, if any, Veblen had on him.

3. The manuscript of this book review is on deposit in the Bentley Historical Library, Michigan Historical Collections, University of Michigan, Ann Arbor. A copy of this manuscript was made available to me by Beth Dillingham.

4. Thus, in the outline of chapter 1 of White's original thesis proposal, we read: ". . . in this additional category, the superorganic, we may find that by which we may explain or interpret man *qua* man." And on page 9 of this chapter White wrote: "5. Personality and Culture. A. Mind is a formation, not a datum. B. It is the cultural milieu which gives form and content to the individual mind. (Where else could it be acquired?)."

5. White had long intended to write a biography of Morgan, but Beth Dillingham informs me that the appearance of Carl Resek's *Lewis Henry Morgan: American Scholar* in 1960 took away some of his incentive to do so. White reviewed Resek's book favorably in the *American Anthropologist* (1960c), calling it "vastly superior" to the only other biography of Morgan, Bernhard J. Stern's *Lewis Henry Morgan, Social Evolutionist* (1925).

6. It is apparent from reading White's book review of John Dewey's *Human Nature and Conduct*, which he wrote while he was a student at Columbia in 1922, that by this date White already had some notion of historical materialism and a positive attitude toward it.

7. Morris Opler, in a disingenuous attempt to discredit White by exposing the Marxist roots of his historical materialism, wrote in 1961: "It is curious that our neo-

evolutionists constantly acknowledge their debt to Darwin, Tylor, and Morgan and never have a word too say about the relation of their ideas to those of Marx, Engels, Bukharin, Plekhanov, Labriola, Suvorov, Lenin, Stalin, et al. Yet it is patent that their formulations are a great deal closer to those of Bukharin and, indeed, to those of any thoroughgoing materialist than they can ever be to those of Tylor or Morgan" (Opler 1961:18). The irony of Opler's paper is that it purports to be a critique, not of White at all, but of Betty Meggers. Indeed, the masquerade is carried to such lengths that in the eighteen pages of the article there is not a single mention of White's name. Opler returned to the same theme the following year (Opler 1962), but at least this time found it possible to mention White by name a few times. (For a similarly oblique ascription of Marxist roots to White's philosophy see Melville Jacobs [1964:29].)

8. For example: ". . . the type of social organization, art, and philosophy of a given cultural system will be determined in form and content by the underlying technology" (White 1949b:378). In class he sometimes made this point by saying: "The locomotive always precedes the Brotherhood of Railway Trainmen."

9. This point has been made by others. Morton Fried (1976:600), for example, remarked of White that "throughout his life, if anything characterized his work, it was the absence of the dialectic." (See also Harris 1968:637.) At least one Soviet anthropologist, S. N. Artanovskii, has pointed out the ways in which White falls short of being a true Marxist, and has described him as "a prisoner of various anti-Marxist evolutionary theories" (Artanovskii 1964–65:26).

10. However, he appears to have been introduced to it by his older contemporaries A. L. Kroeber and Robert H. Lowie: "I discovered the science [of culture] retrospectively, so to speak, from Kroeber's 'The Superorganic' (1917); Lowie's *Culture and Ethnology* (1917); then Tylor's first chapter of *Primitive Culture* (1871): 'The Science of Culture'" (White, in press).

11. It has always seemed to me that the real contribution of this book is its brilliant and lucid presentation of functionalism, rather than its portrayal of cultural evolution (Carneiro 1960:6–7). Others share this view. Thus, Elman Service (1976:613) found its evolutionism disappointing, and said "it contained more of a functionalist message . . .".

12. Mary White, who was a generous and understanding helpmate, died in 1959, a loss which deeply affected Leslie and from the effects of which he never really recovered.

13. This brief stint as a research assistant for White acquainted me with another aspect of his character. I had eagerly volunteered to work for him, happy to contribute in some small way to a distinguished scholar's major work. I never thought of being paid for it, and indeed would have declined pay. But White, who could not afford to pay me, worried that he might be "exploiting" me.

14. And to this passage Service added the following note: ". . . (although the oldest and by far the most eminent of the Michigan department's faculty, he was not the highest paid, having never 'played an offer')" (1976:616n.).

15. For leading me to this passage I am indebted to Elvin Hatch (1973:148).

16. Robert F. Murphy (1977:28) has written that "the efforts of Leslie White . . . to revive the work of Morgan must rate as one of the most courageous intellectual stands ever taken by an anthropologist." As for White's "non-conformist behavior," White once told me that on one occasion Ruth Benedict had psychoanalyzed him to his face, as if his deviation from the established views of the profession must reflect some underlying personality disorder.

17. According to Esther Goldfrank, a number of Boas' friends and former students who were at the meeting "quickly rose to his defense." Boas himself was also in attendance, but: "The eighty-year-old dean of American anthropology alone seemed unmoved. When the session ended, he left the room surrounded by those closest to him, his silence louder than any biting retort" (Goldfrank 1978:153). However, White salvaged some satisfaction from the occasion: ". . . later A. V. Kidder congratulated me upon my paper and said, in effect, that the Boas school 'had a good licking coming to them—and I hope you'll give it to them!'" (White, in press).

18. Thus, in the first chapter of his little book *Social Evolution* (1951), Childe repeats nearly every antievolutionist cliché. And Steward, after reaching the high-water mark of his evolutionism with the publication of his famous article "Cultural Causality and Law" (1949), retreated from this bold formulation and spent the rest of his life defending a very limited "multilinear evolution" which he never actually practiced. (See Carneiro 1974b:93–96.)

19. Over the years, additional expressions of this recognition have appeared in print. Thus, Willey and Sabloff have written: "For a long time Leslie White had been [cultural evolutionism's] only protagonist" (1974:178). And Bohannan and Glazer observed: "Leslie White for years stood alone in his conviction that evolutionary theory as expounded by Herbert Spencer, Lewis H. Morgan, and Edward Tylor was the beginning of the right track for a science of culture. He can now look about him in full awareness that the whole field knows he was right" (1973:333; see also Oswalt 1976:9).

20. These and other aspects of the controversy between White and the antievolutionists are discussed in great detail, with extensive quotations of the Boasian side of the argument, in White (1947a).

21. Here he wrote "The fundamental process in cultural (superorganic) phenomena as well as in organic and even inorganic, phenomena is, in the judgment of the present wirter, evolutionary. The application of the viewpoint and principles of the philosophy of evolution is as essential to the solution of many problems in culturology as it is in biology or physics" (White 1939:571).

22. Since he was being sponsored (and presumably well paid) by a large corporation, White seems to have had certain qualms about making the broadcast. He evidently expressed them to his old friend Harry Elmer Barnes, but Barnes wrote back allaying his doubts, remarking, "after all, how often does one get a chance to rape a queen?"

23. I do not know of a single student of Leslie White who calls what he is doing "neo-evolutionism." Thus Melville Jacobs (1964:29) is quite mistaken when he writes that followers of White "speak of themselves proudly as neo-evolutionists."

24. In the introduction to his reprinting of this article, Ashley Montagu writes: "In this essay [White] provides one of the most cogent clarifications of the meaning of the anthropological concept of culture to be found in any language. . . . it will always remain one of the most readable and helpful elucidations of the most fundamental of all anthropological concepts" (Montagu 1974:539).

25. Even if one accepts the results of recent experiments with chimpanzees such as Washoe, Sarah, and Lucy (Linden 1974) as showing that at least one other primate is able to grasp the meaning of symbols, arrange them in intelligible sequences, and even create new symbols by bestowing meaning on things that previously lacked it, the fact remains that they do so only under the guidance of a human experimenter and not as part of their natural behavior. In my view, therefore, the exercise of the symbolic

faculty remains the sine qua non of culture, and since no other animal but man normally exercises this faculty, no other animal has culture.

26. If the reprinting of his articles is a measure of the stature of a scientist, then surely Leslie White towers in his profession, for a number of his articles have been reprinted half a dozen times or more. In this regard, I believe he far outstrips any other anthropologist, living or dead.

27. The word was first used in print by White in 1939 in his article "A Problem in Kinship Terminology" (1939:571), but he had previously used it in class.

28. *The Science of Culture*, in addition to going through three editions in the United States, has been translated into Spanish, Italian, and Serbo-Croatian.

29. The most explicit statement of this point of view is probably to be found in Vayda (1965:4). See also Vayda and Rappaport (1968:492–94).

30. Why did Leslie White recant his earlier view? Apparently because he became increasingly impressed with the cruelties that cultural systems, especially modern ones, have inflicted on the human species. As he expressed it, "Although they have provided man with food and the fire with which to cook it, huts and houses to protect him from the elements, games and dances to entertain him, gods and myths to beguile him, they have also slaughtered millions of men, women, and children in warfare, tortured and killed them in inquisitions, or burned them to death as witches. They have initiated or aggravated great plagues by urban congestion and unsanitary practices. The cultural systems brought into being and perpetuated by the Agricultural Revolution reduced the majority of mankind to slavery and serfdom, condemning them to a life of labor, privation, and piety" (White 1975:10). There is a certain disenchantment in these lines that brings to mind the growing pessimism with which Herbert Spencer came to view the course of world events during his declining years.

31. While he disliked Steward's brand of evolutionism, White, I think, respected him. One day in 1950 I happened to walk into White's office shortly after he had read the critical review by Steward of *The Science of Culture*. This review had followed on the heels of another critical one by C.W.M. Hart. White remarked that it didn't really bother him when a "Lilliputian" like Hart failed to understand the book, but he couldn't help being disappointed when someone of Steward's stature failed to do so.

32. The initial reluctance of archeology to accept White stemmed from an ingrained antievolutionism, which characterized archeology no less than ethnology. Thus, Willey and Sabloff have written, "In the mid 1950s, when Willey and Phillips published their scheme for New World prehistory [in which they were careful to avoid speaking of evolutionary stages], cultural evolutionism was still largely proscribed in American anthropological circles" (1974:178).

33. Of course, men are not zombies, behaving mechanically and purposelessly. Ideas, desires, and ambitions must be in their minds for them to act. But the question is, how do these motives enter people's minds; White's response was, by being absorbed from the surrounding cultural milieu.

34. It also surpasses, in my opinion, the treatment of this question by Robert K. Merton, who, among sociologists, is the person whose name is most closely associated with the study of the process of invention. The reader is invited to compare White's chapter, "Genius: Its Cause and Incidence," in *The Science of Culture* (1949a:190–232), with Merton's "Singletons and Multiples in Scientific Discovery" (1961).

35. In a letter to White, Thomas Mann complimented him on his "elegant style of writing" (Beardsley 1976:619).

36. Moreover, there were new foes of White's philosophy abroad in the land against whom he might better have directed his arguments. But White, who later in life told me he hardly ever had time to read anymore, was unable to keep up with the latest developments in anthropology.

37. Among the things he did live to bring to publishable form were "The Fuel Revolution" and "Modern Capitalist Culture." Originally, these were to be the second and third parts of a single volume to be called "The Evolution of Culture." However, when he presented a manuscript of more than 1,000 pages to his publishers, they balked at its length. White then removed the second and third parts and had the first part published alone as *The Evolution of Culture* (1959). In the ensuing years, "The Fuel Revolution" and "Modern Capitalist Culture" remained in manuscript. White did little or nothing to the former, which was essentially complete as it stood, but the latter he revised and enlarged extensively. Indeed, he was still doing so when he died. Beth Dillingham and I, whom Dr. White appointed his literary executors, have the responsibility of arranging for the publication of these manuscripts, and they will appear in due time. Preceding them, though, will be a volume of White's later essays, which he selected for publication some time before his death. These essays are mostly ones that appeared in print since his first collection of essays, *The Science of Culture* (1949a). The anthology will be published by Columbia University Press.

38. Elvin Hatch (1973:130) has even gone so far as to state, "White's Pueblo studies, even the latest, give little evidence of the theoretical side of his thought; they could have been written by any one of a number of Boasians who were dogmatic anti-evolutionists."

39. I am grateful to Beth Dillingham, who has gone through much of Leslie White's correspondence in the Bentley Library of the University of Michigan, for providing me with a comprehensive list of persons to whom we wrote, from which I have selected the few named above.

40. Harris' unwillingness to give White any of the credit due him is seen again in his most recent work, *Cultural Materialism* (1979). One wonders why it is that, in a book devoted entirely to cultural materialism, the only mention Harris can bring himself to make of Leslie White is to relegate him to the camp of the idealists for his "insistence that culture is a realm of symbols" (Harris 1979:236).

References Cited

Aberle, David F. 1960. "The Influence of Linguistics on Early Culture and Personality Theory." In Gertrude E. Dole and Robert L. Carneiro, eds., *Essays in the Science of Culture in Honor of Leslie A. White*, pp. 1–29. New York: Crowell.

APS (American Philosophical Society), Boas Archives. Philadelphia.
   1. Vita. Ms. post-Gymnasium.
   2. Diary from Baffinland.
   3. Letter from Franz Boas to Ernst Boas, August 6, 1914.
   4. Letter from Max Yergan to Helene Boas Yampolsky.

Artanovskii, S. N. 1964–65. "The Marxist Doctrine of Social Progress and the 'Cultural Evolution' of Leslie White." *Soviet Anthropology and Archaeology*, 3:21–30.

Barnes, Harry E. 1960. Foreword. In Gertrude E. Dole and Robert L. Carneiro, eds., *Essays in the Science of Culture in Honor of Leslie A. White*, pp. xi–xlvi. New York: Crowell.

Beals, Ralph. 1968. "Alfred L. Kroeber." In *International Encyclopedia of the Social Sciences*, 8:454–64.

Beardsley, Richard K. 1976. "An Appraisal of Leslie White's Scholarly Influence." *American Anthropologist*, 78:617–20.

Benedict, Ruth. 1934. *Patterns of Culture*. Boston and New York: Houghton Mifflin.

—— 1936. "Marital Property Rights in Bilateral Society." *American Anthropologist*, 38:368–73.

—— 1940. *Race, Science, and Politics*. New York: Modern Age.

—— 1941. "Race Problems in America." *Annals of the American Academy of Political and Social Sciences*, 216:73–78.

—— 1942. "Victory over Discrimination and Hate: Differences vs. Superiorities." *Frontiers of Democracy*, 9:81–82.

—— 1946a. *The Chrysanthemum and the Sword*. Boston and New York: Houghton Mifflin.

—— 1946b. "The Study of Cultural Patterns in European Nations." *Transactions of the New York Academy of Science*, 8(8):274–79.

—— 1947. (manuscript) "Postwar Race Prejudice." (In Margaret Mead, *An Anthropologist at Work: Writings of Ruth Benedict*, pp. 361–68.)

—— 1948. "Anthropology and the Humanities." *American Anthropologist*, 50:585–93.

Benedict, Ruth and Gene Weltfish. 1943. *The Races of Mankind*. New York: Public Affairs Pamphlet 85.

Binford, Lewis R. 1972. *An Archaeological Perspective*. New York: Seminar Press.

Boas, Franz. 1897. "The Social Organization and the Secret Societies of the Kwakiutl Indians. Based on Personal Observations and on Notes Made by Mr. George Hunt." *Report of the U.S. National Museum for 1895*, pp. 311–738.

—— 1899. "The Cephalic Index." *American Anthropologist*, 1:448–61.

—— 1901. *Kathlamet Texts*. Smithsonian Institution, Bureau of American Ethnology Bulletin No. 26. Washington, D.C.: Government Printing Office.

—— 1910. "The Real Race Problem." *The Crisis*, 1:22–25. New York, National Association for the Advancement of Colored People.

—— 1911a. *Changes in Bodily Form of Descendants of Immigrants*. Senate Document 208, 61st Congress, Second Session. Washington, D.C.: Government Printing Office. (Reprinted 1912; New York: Columbia University Press.)

—— 1911b. *The Mind of Primitive Man*. New York: Macmillan.

—— 1927. *Primitive Art*. Oslo: H. Aschehoug.

—— 1928. *Anthropology and Modern Life*. New York: Norton.

—— 1930b. *The Religion of the Kwakiutl Indians*. Columbia University 2:73–110.

—— 1930b. *The Religion of the Kwakiutl Indians*. Columbia University Contributions to Anthropology, vol. 10. New York: Columbia University Press.

—— 1938a. "An Anthropologist's Credo." *The Nation*, 147:201–4.

—— 1938b. Introduction. In Franz Boas, ed., *General Anthropology*, pp. 1–6. Boston: Heath.

—— 1940. *Race, Language, and Culture*. New York: Macmillan.

—— 1945. *Race and Democratic Society*. New York: Augustin.

Bohannan, Paul and Mark Glazer, eds. 1973. *High Points in Anthropology*. New York: Knopf.

Carneiro, Robert L. 1960. Review of *The Evolution of Culture* by Leslie A. White. *Natural History*, 69(2):4–7.

—— 1970. "A Theory of the Origin of the State." *Science*, 169:733–38.

—— 1974a. Herbert Spencer's *The Study of Sociology and the Rise of Social Science in America*. *Proceedings of the American Philosophical Society*, 118:540–54.

—— 1974b. "The Four Faces of Evolution." In John J. Honigmann, ed., *Handbook of Social and Cultural Anthropology*, pp. 89–110. Chicago: Rand McNally.

Childe, V. Gordon. 1951. *Social Evolution*. London: Watts.

Codere, Helen. 1966. Introduction. In Franz Boas, *Kwakiutl Ethnography*, pp. xi–xxxii. Helen Codere, ed. Chicago: University of Chicago Press.

Dewey, John. 1932. "Human Nature." In *Encyclopedia of the Social Sciences*, 7:531–36.

Diamond, Stanley, ed. 1960. *Culture in History: Essays in Honor of Paul Radin*. New York: Columbia University Press.

—— 1974. *In Search of the Primitive*. New Brunswick, N.J.: Transaction Books.

Dole, Gertrude E. and Robert L. Carneiro, eds. 1960. *Essays in the Science of Culture in Honor of Leslie A. White*. New York: Crowell.

Elmendorf, W. W. and Alfred L. Kroeber. 1960. *The Structure of Twana Culture, with Comparative Notes on the Structure of Yurok Culture. Research Studies*, A Quarterly Publication of Washington State University, vol. 28, no. 3. Monograph supp. no. 2. Pullman: Washington State University Press.

Étiemblé, René. 1961. *Le Mythe de Rimbaud: Structure du mythe*. Paris: Gallimard.

Evans-Pritchard, E. E. 1965. *Theories of Primitive Religion*. Oxford: Clarendon Press.

Firth, Raymond. 1936. *We, The Tikopia: A Sociological Study of Kinship in Primitive Polynesia*. London: Allen & Unwin.

—— 1946. *Malay Fishermen: Their Peasant Economy*. London: Kegan Paul, Trench, Trubner.

—— 1951. *Elements of Social Organization*. London: Watts.

—— 1964. *Essays on Social Organization and Values*. London: Athlone Press.

—— 1975. "An Appraisal of Modern Social Anthropology." *Annual Review of Anthropology*, 4:1–25.

Firth, Raymond, ed. 1957. *Man and Culture: An Evaluation of the Work of Bronislaw Malinowski*. London: Routledge & Kegan Paul.

Flugel, J. C. 1921. *The Psycho-Analytic Study of the Family*. London: International Psycho-Analytic Library, no. 3.

Fried, Morton H. 1976. "Energy and the Evolution of Leslie A. White." *Reviews in Anthropology*, 3:592–600.

Frye, Northrop. 1957. *Anatomy of Criticism*. Princeton, N.J.: Princeton University Press.

Geertz, Clifford. 1962. "Studies in Peasant Life: Community and Society." In B. J. Siegel, ed., *Biennial Review of Anthropology, 1961*, pp. 1–41.

Gluckman, Max. 1955. *Custom and Conflict in Africa*. Oxford: Blackwell.

—— 1963. *Order and Rebellion in Tribal Africa*. London: Cohen & West.

Goldfrank, Esther S. 1978. *Notes on an Undirected Life: As One Anthropologist Tells It*. Queens College Publications in Anthropology, no. 3. Flushing, N.Y.: Queens College Press.

Gregg, Dorothy and Elgin Williams. 1948. "The Dismal Science of Functionalism." *American Anthropologist*, 50:594–611.

Harris, Marvin. 1968. *The Rise of Anthropological Theory*. New York: Crowell.

—— 1979. *Cultural Materialism: The Struggle for a Science of Culture*. New York: Random House.

Hart, C. W. M. 1950. Review of *The Science of Culture* by Leslie A. White. *American Journal of Sociology*, 56:88.

Hatch, Elvin. 1973. *Theories of Man and Culture*. New York: Columbia University Press.

Helm, June. 1962. "The Ecological Approach in Anthropology." *American Journal of Sociology*, 67:630–39.

Herrick, C. Judson. 1956. *The Evolution of Human Nature*. Austin, Tex.: University of Texas Press.

Hymes, Dell. 1961. "Alfred Louis Kroeber." *Language*, 37:1–28.

—— 1965. "Some North Pacific Coast Poems: A Problem in Anthropological Philology." *American Anthropologist*, 67:316–41.

Jacobs, Melville. 1964. *Pattern in Cultural Anthropology*. Homewood, Ill.: Dorsey Press.

Kluckhohn, Clyde and Olaf Prufer. 1959. "Influences During the Formative Years." In Walter Goldschmidt, ed., *The Anthropology of Franz Boas*, pp. 4–28. American Anthropological Association, Memoir 89, vol. 61, part 2.

Kroeber, Alfred L. 1923. *Anthropology*. New York: Harcourt Brace. (Rev. ed. 1948, under title *Anthropology: Race, Language, Culture, Psychology, Prehistory*.)

—— 1925. *Handbook of the Indians of California*. Smithsonian Institution, Bureau of American Ethnology, Bulletin No. 78. Washington, D.C.: Government Printing Office.

—— 1935. "History and Science in Anthropology." *American Anthropologist*, 37:539–69.

—— 1939. *Cultural and Natural Areas of Native North America*. University of California Publications in American Archaeology and Ethnology, vol. 38. Berkeley, Calif.: University of California Press.

—— 1943. "Franz Boas: The Man." In A. L. Kroeber et al., *Franz Boas 1858–1942*, pp. 5–26. American Anthropological Association, Memoir 61, vol. 45, no. 3, part 2.

—— 1944. *Configurations of Culture Growth*. Berkeley, Calif.: University of California Press.

—— 1949. "An Authoritarian Panacea." *American Anthropologist*, 51: 318–20.

—— 1952. *The Nature of Culture*. Chicago: University of Chicago Press.

—— 1957. *Style and Civilizations*. Ithaca, N.Y.: Cornell University Press.

—— 1959. Preface. In Walter Goldschmidt, ed., *The Anthropology of Franz Boas*, pp. v–vii. American Anthropological Association, Memoir 89, vol. 61, no. 5, part 2.

—— 1960a. "Statistics, Indo-European and Taxonomy." *Language*, 36:1–21.

—— 1960b. "Evolution, History, and Culture." In Sol Tax, ed., *Evolution after Darwin*, 2:1–16. Chicago: University of Chicago Press.

—— 1962. *A Roster of Civilizations and Culture*. Chicago: Aldine.

—— 1963. *An Anthropologist Looks at History*. Berkeley and Los Angeles: University of California Press.

Kroeber, Alfred and Clyde Kluckhohn. 1952. *Culture: A Critical Review of Concepts and Definitions*. Papers of the Peabody Museum of American Archaeology and Ethnology, Harvard University, vol. 47, no. 1.

Kroeber, Theodora. 1970. *Alfred Kroeber: A Personal Configuration*. Berkeley, Calif.: University of California Press.

Kuper, Adam. 1973. *Anthropologists and Anthropology: The British School 1922–1972*. London: Allen Lane.

Langendoen, D. T. 1968. *The London School of Linguistics*. Cambridge, Mass.: MIT Press.

Laughlin, Charles D., Jr. and Eugene G. d'Aquili. 1974. *Biogenetic Structuralism*. New York: Columbia University Press.

Leach, E. R. 1957. "The Epistemological Background to Malinowski's Empiricism." In Raymond Firth, ed., *Man and Culture: An Evaluation of the Work of Bronislaw Malinowski*, pp. 119–37. London: Routledge & Kegan Paul.

Leslie, Charles. 1968. "Robert Redfield." In *International Encyclopedia of the Social Sciences*, 13:350–53.

—— 1976. "The Hedgehog and the Fox in Robert Redfield's Work and Career." In *American Anthropology, The Early Years*, pp. 146–66. 1974 Proceedings of the American Ethnological Society. St. Paul, Minn.: West.

Lesser, Alexander. 1968. "Franz Boas." In *International Encyclopedia of the Social Sciences*, 2:99–110.

—— 1978. *The Pawnee Ghost Dance Hand Game*. Madison, Wisc. and London: University of Wisconsin Press. (Orig. 1933, as vol. 16 in Columbia

304 References Cited

University Contributions to Anthropology, New York: Columbia University Press.)

Lévi-Strauss, Claude. 1950. "Introduction à l'oeuvre de Marcel Mauss." In Marcel Mauss, *Sociologie et anthropologie*. Paris: Presses Universitaires de France.

—— 1962. *Le Totémisme aujourd'hui*. Paris: Presses Universitaires de France.

—— 1973. *Anthropologie structurale deux*. Paris: Plon.

Linden, Eugene. 1974. *Apes, Men, and Language*. Harmondsworth: Penguin Books.

Linton, Adelin and Charles Wagley. 1971. *Ralph Linton*. New York and London: Columbia University Press.

Lombard, Jacques. 1972. *L'Anthropologie Britannique contemporaine*. Paris: Presses Universitaires de France.

Lowie, Robert H. 1920. *Primitive Society*. New York: Boni & Liveright.

—— 1944. "Franz Boas, 1858–1942." *Journal of American Folklore*, 57:59–64.

—— 1946a. "Evolution in Cultural Anthropology: A Reply to Leslie White." *American Anthropologist*, 48:223–33.

—— 1946b. "Professor White and 'Anti-Evolutionist' Schools." *Southwestern Journal of Anthropology*, 2:240–41.

Malinowski, Bronislaw. 1916. "Baloma: Spirits of the Dead in the Trobriand Islands." *Journal of the Royal Anthropological Institute*, 46:353–430.

—— 1922. *Argonauts of the Western Pacific*. London: Routledge.

—— 1923. "The Problem of Meaning in Primitive Languages." In C. K. Ogden and I. A. Richards, *The Meaning of Meaning*, pp. 451–510. London: K. Paul, Trench, Trubner.

—— 1926a. "Address on Anthropology and Social Hygiene." In *Foundations of Social Hygiene*, pp. 54–84. London: British Social Hygiene Council.

—— 1926b. *Crime and Custom in Savage Society*. London: Kegan Paul.

—— 1926c. *Myth in Primitive Psychology*. London: Kegan Paul.

—— 1927a. *Sex and Repression in Savage Society*. London: Kegan Paul.

—— 1927b. *The Father in Primitive Psychology*. London: Routledge.

—— 1929. *The Sexual Life of Savages in North-Western Melanesia*. London: Routledge.

—— 1935. *Coral Gardens and Their Magic*. 2 vols. London: Allen & Unwin.

—— 1939. "The Group and the Individual in Functional Analysis." *American Journal of Sociology*, 44:938–64.

—— 1944. *A Scientific Theory of Culture*. Chapel Hill: University of North Carolina Press.

—— 1945. *The Dynamics of Culture Change*. Phyllis M. Kaberry, ed. New Haven, Conn.: Yale University Press.

—— 1947. *Freedom and Civilization*. London: Allen & Unwin.

—— 1967. *A Diary in the Strict Sense of the Term*. New York: Harcourt, Brace & World.

Mauss, Marcel. 1923–24. *"Essai sur le don: forme archaique de l'échange."* *L'Année Sociologique*, 1 (n.s.):30–186.

Mead, Margaret. 1959. *An Anthropologist at Work: Writings of Ruth Benedict*. Boston: Houghton Mifflin.

—— 1974. *Ruth Benedict*. New York, and London: Columbia University Press.

Merton, Robert K. 1961. "Singletons and Multiples in Scientific Discovery: A Chapter in the Sociology of Science." *Proceedings of the American Philosophical Society*, 105:470–86.

Metraux, Rhoda. 1968. "Bronislaw Malinowski." In *International Encyclopedia of the Social Sciences*, 9:541–49.

Mintz, Sidney W. 1960. *Worker in the Cane: A Puerto Rican Life History*. Yale Caribbean Series, vol. 2. New Haven, Conn.: Yale University Press.

Modell, Judith. 1975. "Ruth Benedict, Anthropologist: The Reconciliation of Science and Humanism." In T. H. H. Thoreson, ed., *Toward a Science of Man*, pp. 183–203. The Hague: Mouton.

—— 1978. *"A Biographical Study of Ruth Fulton Benedict."* Ph.D. dissertation, University of Minnesota.

Montagu, Ashley, ed. 1974. *Frontiers of Anthropology*. New York: Putnam.

Murdock, George P. 1949. *Social Structure*. New York: Macmillan.

Murphy, Robert F. 1971. *The Dialectics of Social Life*. New York and London: Basic Books.

—— 1972. *Robert H. Lowie*. New York and London: Columbia University Press.

—— 1977. Introduction. In Julian Steward, *Evolution and Ecology*, pp. 1–39. Jane C. Steward and Robert F. Murphy, eds. Urbana, Ill.: University of Illinois Press.

Murphy, Robert F. and Julian H. Steward. 1956. "Tappers and Trappers: Parallel Processes of Acculturation." *Economic Development and Cultural Change*, 4:335–55.

Ogburn, William F. 1922. *Social Change*. New York: Huebsch.

Opler, Morris E. 1961. "Cultural Evolution, Southern Athapaskans, and Chronology in Theory." *Southwestern Journal of Anthropology*, 17:1–20.

—— 1962. "Two Converging Lines of Influence in Cultural Evolutionary Theory." *American Anthropologist*, 64:524–47.

Oswalt, Wendell H. 1976. *An Anthropological Analysis of Food-Getting Technology*. New York: Wiley.

Panoff, Michel. 1972. *Bronislaw Malinowski*. Paris: Payot.

Powell, H. A. 1960. "Competitive Leadership in Trobriand Political Organization." *Journal of the Royal Anthropological Institute*, 90:118–45.

—— 1969, "Genealogy, Residence, and Kinship in Kiriwina." *Man*. 4:177–202.

Radin, Paul. 1913. "On Ojibwa Work, 1913." *Summary Reports*, Canada, Geological Survey, p. 374.

—— 1919. *The Genetic Relationship of the North American Indian Languages*. University of California Publications in American Archaeology and Ethnology, vol. 14, no. 5. Berkeley: University of California Press.

——1920. *The Autobiography of an American Indian*. University of California Publications in American Archaeology and Ethnology, vol. 16, no. 7. Berkeley: University of California Press.

—— 1923. *The Winnebago Tribe*. Bureau of American Ethnology, Annual Report, No. 37, 1915–1916. Washington, D.C.: Government Printing Office.

—— 1924. *Wappo Texts*. University of California Publications in American Archaeology and Ethnology, vol. 19, no. 1. Berkeley: University of California Press.

——1927. *Primitive Man as Philosopher*. New York: Appleton.

—— 1929a. "Huave Texts." *International Journal of American Linguistics*, 5:1–56.

—— 1929b. *A Grammar of the Wappo Language*. University of California Publications in American Archaeology and Ethnology, vol. 27. Berkeley: University of California Press.

—— 1930. "A Preliminary Sketch of the Zapotec Language." *Language*, 6:64–85.

—— 1933a. *The Method and Theory of Ethnology: An Essay in Criticism*. New York: McGraw-Hill.

——1933b. "Mixe Texts." *Journal de la Société des Americanisties de Paris*, 25:41–64.

—— 1933c. "Notes on the Tlappanecan Language of Guerrero." *International Journal of American Linguistics*, 8:45–72.

——1934. *The Racial Myth*. New York: McGraw-Hill.

——1937. *Primitive Religion: Its Nature and Origin*. New York: Dover.

——1944. "The Classification of the Languages of Mexico." *Tlalocan*, 1:259–65.

—— 1945. *The Road of Life and Death: A Ritual Drama of the American Indians*. Bollingen Series, no. 5. New York: Pantheon.

——1953. *The World of Primitive Man*. New York: Schuman.

Redfield, Robert. 1930. *Tepoztlán, A Mexican Village: A Study of Folk Life*. Chicago: University of Chicago Press.

—— 1941. *The Folk Culture of Yucatán*. Chicago: University of Chicago Press.

—— 1950. *A Village That Chose Progress: Chan Kom Revisited*. Chicago: University of Chicago Press.

—— 1953. *The Primitive World and Its Transformations*. Ithaca, N.Y.: Cornell University Press.

—— 1955. *The Little Community: Viewpoints for the Study of a Human Whole*. Chicago: University of Chicago Press.

—— 1956. *Peasant Society and Culture: An Anthropological Approach to Civilizations*. Chicago: University of Chicago Press.

—— 1960. "Thinker and Intellectual in Primitive Society." In Stanley Diamond, ed., *Culture in History: Essays in Honor of Paul Radin*, pp. 3–18. New York: Columbia University Press.

—— 1962. "Civilizations as Cultural Structures?" In Margaret Park Redfield, ed., *Human Nature and the Study of Society: The Papers of Robert Redfield*, 1:392–401. Chicago: University of Chicago Press.

—— 1963a. "The Educational Experience: Exploration, Conversation, Creation." In Margaret Park Redfield, ed., *The Social Uses of Social Science: The Papers of Robert Redfield*, 2:30–73. Chicago: University of Chicago Press.

—— 1963b. "Talk with a Stranger." In Margaret Park Redfield, ed., *The Social Uses of Social Science: The Papers of Robert Redfield*, 2:270–83. Chicago: University of Chicago Press.

Redfield, Robert and Milton B. Singer. 1954. "The Cultural Role of Cities." *Economic Development and Cultural Change*, 3:53–73.

Redfield, Robert and Alfonso Villa Rojas. 1934. *Chan Kom: A Maya Village*. Carnegie Institution of Washington, Publication No. 448.

Resek, Carl. 1960. *Lewis Henry Morgan: American Scholar*. Chicago: University of Chicago Press.

Richards, Audrey. 1943. "Bronislaw Kasper Malinowski: Born 1884–Died 1942." *Man*, 43:1–4.

Sahlins, Marshall D. 1958. *Social Stratification in Polynesia*. Seattle: University of Washington Press.

Schorske, Carl E. 1962. "Schnitzler und Hofmannsthal." *Wort und Wahrheit*, 17:367–81.

Service, Elman R. 1976. "Leslie Alvin White, 1900–1975." *American Anthropologist*, 78:612–17.

Simpson, George Gaylord. 1950. *The Meaning of Evolution*. New Haven, Conn.: Yale University Press.

Singer, Milton B. 1976. "Robert Redfield's Development of a Social Anthropology of Civilizations." In *American Anthropology, the Early Years*, pp. 187–260. 1974 Proceedings of the American Ethnological Society. St. Paul, Minn.: West.

Smith, Marian W. 1959. "Boas' 'Natural History' Approach to Field Method." In Walter Goldschmidt, ed., *The Anthropology of Franz Boas*, pp. 46–60. American Anthropological Association, Memoir 89, vol. 61, no. 5, part 2.

Spencer, Herbert. 1873. *The Study of Sociology*. New York: Appleton.

Stern, Bernhard J. 1931. *Lewis Henry Morgan, Social Evolutionist*. Chicago: University of Chicago Press.

Steward, Julian H. 1936. "The Economic and Social Basis of Primitive Bands." In Robert H. Lowie, ed., *Essays on Anthropology in Honor of Alfred Louis Kroeber*, pp. 311–50. Berkeley: University of California Press.

—— 1937. "Ecological Aspects of Southwestern Society." *Anthropos*, 32:87–104.

—— 1938. *Basin-Plateau Aboriginal Sociopolitical Groups*. Smithsonian Institution, Bureau of American Ethnology Bulletin 120. Washington, D.C.: Government Printing Office.

—— 1941. "Determinism in Primitive Society?" *Scientific Monthly*, 53: 491–501.

—— 1949. "Cultural Causality and Law: A Trial Formulation of the Development of Early Civilizations." *American Anthropologist*, 51:1–27.

—— 1950. *Area Research: Theory and Practice*. Bulletin 63. New York: Social Science Research Council.

—— 1950. Review of *The Science of Culture* by Leslie A. White. *Scientific Monthly*, 70:208–9.

—— 1960. Review of *The Evolution of Culture* by Leslie A. White. *American Anthropologist*, 62:144–48.

—— 1973. *Alfred Kroeber*. New York: Columbia University Press.

—— 1977. *Evolution and Ecology: Essays on Social Transformation*, Jane C. Steward and Robert F. Murphy, eds. Urbana: University of Illinois Press.

Stocking, George W., Jr. 1969. *Race, Culture, and Evolution: Essays in the History of Anthropology*. New York: Free Press.

Symmons-Symonolewicz, Konstantin. 1958. "Bronislaw Malinowski: An Intellectual Profile." *Polish Review*, 3:1–22.

Tarn, Nathaniel. 1972. "From Anthropologist to Informant: A Field Record of Gary Snyder." *Alcheringa*, 4:104–13.

—— 1976. "The Heraldic Vision: Some Cognitive Models for Ethnopoetics." *Alcheringa: Ethnopoetics*, n.s. 2(2):23–41.

—— 1979. "Open Letter Regarding a Proposal for an Order of Silence." *Montemora*, no. 5, pp. 74–80, 115–16.

Thurnwald, Richard. 1921. *Die Gemeinde der Banaro*. Stuttgart: F. Enke. (English translation under title *Banaro Society*, published as American Anthropological Association iii, Memoir 4, 1916).

Trigger, Bruce G. 1978. *Time and Traditions*. New York: Columbia University Press.

Uberoi, J. P. Singh. 1962. *Politics of the Kula Ring: An Analysis of the Findings of Bronislaw Malinowski*. Manchester: Manchester University Press.

Van Doren, Mark. 1945. Foreword. In Paul Radin, *The Road of Life and Death*. New York: Pantheon.

Vayda, Andrew P. 1965. "Anthropologists and Ecological Problems." In Andrew P. Vayda, ed., *Man, Culture and Animals*, pp. 1–5. American Association for the Advancement of Science, Pub. no. 78.

Vayda, Andrew P. and Roy A. Rappaport. 1968. "Ecology: Cultural and Noncultural." In James A. Clifton, ed., *Introduction to Cultural Anthropology*, pp. 476–97. Boston: Houghton Mifflin.

Washburn, Sherwood L. 1963. "The Study of Race." *American Anthropologist*, 65:521–32.

Weiner, Lynn. 1969. "Leslie White, Ecclesiastical Brimstone Scientist." *The Michigan Daily* (Ann Arbor), March 23, p. 4.

White, Leslie A. 1925. "Personality and Culture." *The Open Court*, 39:145–49.

—— 1931. Review of *Lewis Henry Morgan, Social Evolutionist* by Bernhard J. Stern. *American Journal of Sociology*, 37:483.

—— 1932a. "The Acoma Indians." *Bureau of American Ethnology, 47th Annual Report*, pp. 17–192.

—— 1932b. *The Pueblo of San Felipe*. American Anthropological Association, Memoir 38.

—— 1935. *The Pueblo of Santo Domingo, New Mexico*. American Anthropological Association, Memoir 43.

—— 1938. "Science is *Sciencing*." *Philosophy of Science*, 5:369–89.

—— 1939. "A Problem in Kinship Terminology." *American Anthropologist*, 41:566–73.

—— 1940. "The Symbol: The Origin and Basis of Human Behavior." *Philosophy of Science*, 7:451–63.

—— 1942a. *The Pueblo of Santa Ana, New Mexico*. American Anthropological Association, Memoir 60.

—— 1942b. "Lewis H. Morgan's Journal of a Trip to Southwestern Colorado and New Mexico, June 21 to August 7, 1878." *American Antiquity*, 8:1–26.

—— 1943. "Energy and the Evolution of Culture." *American Anthropologist*, 45:335–56.

—— 1944. "Morgan's Attitude Toward Religion and Science." *American Anthropologist*, 46:218–30.

—— 1945a. "History, Evolutionism, and Functionalism: Three Types of Interpretation of Culture." *Southwestern Journal of Anthropology*, 1: 221–48.

—— 1945b. "Diffusion *vs.* Evolution: An Anti-Evolutionist Fallacy." *American Anthropologist*, 47:339–56.

—— 1946. "Kroeber's *Configurations of Culture Growth*." *American Anthropologist*, 50:78–93.

—— 1947a. "Evolutionary Stages, Progress, and the Evaluation of Cultures." *Southwestern Journal of Anthropology*, 3:165–92.

—— 1947b. "Evolutionism and Anti-Evolutionism in American Ethnological Theory." *Calcutta Review*, 104:147–59; 105:29–40, 161–74.

—— 1947c. "Evolutionism in Cultural Anthropology: A Rejoinder." *American Anthropologist*, 49:400–13.

—— 1947d. "The Expansion of the Scope of Science." *Journal of the Washington Academy of Sciences*, 37:181–210.

—— 1948a. "Man's Control over Civilization: An Anthropocentric Illusion." *Scientific Monthly*, 66:235–47.

—— 1948b. "The Definition and Prohibition of Incest." *American Anthropologist*, 50:416–35.

—— 1949a. *The Science of Culture*. New York: Farrar, Straus.

—— 1949b. "Ethnological Theory." In Roy Wood Sellars, V. J. McGill, and

Marvin Farber, eds., *Philosophy for the Future; The Quest of Modern Materialism*, pp. 357–84. New York: Macmillan.

—— 1951. "Lewis H. Morgan's Western Field Trips." *American Anthropologist*, 53:11–18.

—— 1957a. "How Morgan Came to Write *Systems of Consanguinity and Affinity*." *Papers of the Michigan Academy of Sciences, Arts, and Letters*, 42:257–68.

—— 1957b. "The Correspondence Between Lewis Henry Morgan and Joseph Henry." *University of Rochester Library Bulletin*, 12:17–22.

—— 1959a. *The Evolution of Culture*. New York: McGraw-Hill.

—— 1959b. "The Concept of Evolution in Cultural Anthropology." In Betty J. Meggers, ed., *Evolution and Anthropology: A Centennial Appraisal*, pp. 106–25. Washington D.C.: Anthropological Society of Washington.

—— 1959c. "The Concept of Culture." *American Anthropologist*, 61:227–51.

—— 1960a. Foreword. In Marshall D. Sahlins and Elman R. Service, *Evolution and Culture*, pp. v–xii. Ann Arbor: University of Michigan Press.

—— 1960b. "Four Stages in the Evolution of Minding." In Sol Tax, ed., *Evolution After Darwin*, vol 2: *The Evolution of Man*, pp. 239–53. Chicago: University of Chicago Press.

—— 1960c. Review of *Lewis Henry Morgan. American Scholar* by Carl Resek. *American Anthropologist*, 62:1073–74.

—— 1962. *The Pueblo of Sia, New Mexico*. Bureau of American Ethnology, Bulletin 184.

—— 1963. *The Ethnography and Ethnology of Franz Boas*. Texas Memorial Museum, Bulletin 6.

—— 1964. Introduction. In Lewis H. Morgan, *Ancient Society*, pp. xiii–xlii. Cambridge, Mass.: The Belknap Press of Harvard University Press.

—— 1966. *The Social Organization of Ethnological Theory*. Rice University Studies, vol. 52, no. 4.

—— 1969. *The Science of Culture*. 2d ed. New York: Farrar, Straus and Giroux.

—— 1973a. *The Acoma Indians*. Forty-Seventh Annual Report of the Bureau of American Ethnology, 1929–1930. Reprinted by the Rio Grande Press, Glorieta, New Mexico.

—— 1973b. "The Anthropologist and the American Indian." *Newsletter of the American Anthropological Association*, 14(6):2.

—— 1975. *The Concept of Cultural Systems*. New York: Columbia University Press.

—— n.d. Unpublished manuscript by Leslie White about his boyhood in Kansas. Dated Elkland, Pa., October 3, 1952. On deposit in the Michigan Historical Collection, Bentley Historical Library, University of Michigan, Ann Arbor.

—— In press. Introductory remarks to Beth Dillingham and Robert L. Carneiro, eds., *Anthropological Essays*. New York: Columbia University Press.

White, Leslie A., ed. 1937. "Extracts from the European Travel Journal of Lewis H. Morgan." *Rochester Historical Society Publications*, 16(2): 219–389.

—— 1940. *Pioneers in American Anthropology, The Bandelier-Morgan Letters 1873–1883*. 2 vols. Albuquerque: University of New Mexico Press.

—— 1959. *Lewis Henry Morgan: The Indian Journals, 1859–1862*. Ann Arbor: University of Michigan Press.

Willey, Gordon R. and Jeremy A. Sabloff. 1974. *A History of American Archaeology*. San Francisco: Freeman.

Wolf, Eric. 1969. "American Anthropologists and American Society." In Dell Hymes, ed., *Reinventing Anthropology*, pp. 251–63. New York: Random House.

Index